Women's Talk?

DATE DUE		
DEC 0 9 1998		
MAY 3 1 1999		
0 7 JUL 1999		
1 4 FEB 2002		
1 2 NOV 2004		

Women's Talk?

A Social History of 'Gossip' in Working-class Neighbourhoods, 1880–1960

MELANIE TEBBUTT

SCOLAR
PRESS

First published 1995 in hardback by Scolar Press

Paperback edition published 1997 by
SCOLAR PRESS   Ashgate Publishing Company
Gower House   Old Post Road
Croft Road   Brookfield
Aldershot   Vermont 05036
Hants GU11 3HR   USA
England

British Library Cataloguing-in-Publication data

Tebbutt, Melanie
    Women's Talk?: Social History of Gossip
    in Working-class Neighbourhoods,
    1880–1960
    I. Title
    302.224209

        ISBN 1-85928-026-9

Library of Congress Cataloging-in-Publication Data

Tebbutt, Melanie.
    Women's Talk?: a social history of "gossip" in working class
    neighbourhoods, 1880–1980 / Melanie Tebbutt
        p.   cm.
    Includes bibliographical references and index.
    1. Women—Social networks—Great Britain—History.   2. Working
    class women—Social networks—Great Britain—History.   3. Women
    —Great Britain—Communication—History.   4. Gossip—History.
    I. Title.
    HQ1593.T42 1995   94-27195
    302.2'24—dc20   CIP

ISBN 1 85928 026 9 (hbk)
ISBN 1 85928 435 3 (pbk)

Typeset in 10 point Sabon by Poole Typesetting (Wessex) Ltd, Bournemouth
Printed and bound in Great Britain by
Biddles Ltd, Guildford and King's Lynn

For Donald Rae and Alex Tebbutt,
with love

Contents

Acknowledgements

Writing this book has left me with many debts to friends, relatives and colleagues, and has been a source of both enjoyment and sadness. Mary Turner, a good friend who was never averse to a healthy gossip, died some time before it approached completion but shared much of my growing interest in the subject, and I hope would have been pleased with the outcome. The Leverhulme Trust, which generously provided a grant towards childcare and academic expenses has my particular thanks since without its help I doubt if this book would ever have become more than an article.

The book's gestation has, like any, been uncomfortable at times, and has both fed off and suffered from my job in community education, which like the public services generally has experienced many demoralizing changes in the last few years. Friends and colleagues have been an important support, and I am especially grateful to those in what was the Manchester Education Advice Service for Adults. I should also thank Tameside College of Technology which granted me a short period of unpaid leave to draw the book to a conclusion.

Dermot Healy provided his usual invaluable criticism at various stages of the manuscript's emergence and several others have taken time from their own busy lives to comment on it, including Elizabeth Roberts, Mike Rose and John Widdowson. Anna Davin has been a source of considerable advice and encouragement which I greatly appreciate. Audrey Linkman made useful suggestions about photographs. Staff in Tameside College Library have shared in and helped my search for local references, as have others at many other libraries, including those in Stockport, Bolton, Manchester, Northampton and Salford. Staff at the Centre for English Cultural Tradition and Language, Sheffield University were unfailingly helpful, as were Alice Lock and her colleagues at Tameside Local Studies Library. John Tomlinson of Chapter and Verse in Cardiff helped track down several elusive books, while Alec McAulay, my editor at Scolar Press, has kept faith despite postponements.

Finally, and most important, my family. To my parents, Marjorie and Les Tebbutt who have shared their experience and understanding – I owe them much. And to Donald and Alex who have put up with the book for so long and whose most sincere thanks are no doubt directed at its completion. All helped me keep the midnight oil burning. Any unevenness or errors are, of course, due to the midnight oil.

Abbreviations

BOHP   Bolton Oral History Project
MSTC   Manchester Studies Tape Collection
OLHG   Ordsall Local History Group
ORALU   Oral History Archive, Lancaster University

Introduction

The term 'romantic fiction is used in much the same way to designate the printed word of women as 'gossip' is used to designate the spoken word of women. It is an all-encompassing (and derogatory) term that places women's words beyond serious consideration. Neither 'romantic fiction' nor 'gossip' warrant analysis. Their inferior status is based not on an analysis but quite the reverse; such labels *preclude* analysis.[1]

Women's voices are hard to hear in history. Their so-called 'loose tongues' and sharp talk were often criticized, but remain largely silent in the written record. The voices we hear are, on the whole, only faint echoes of reality, and straining to understand the thoughts and feelings which gave them meaning can be rather like eavesdropping on whispers and half-heard conversations. Where women's voices are documented they tend to be patronized as a second class version of 'real' language. Whenever men's talk performs the same function as women's gossip it is simply called something else, a sleight of hand which Dale Spender illustrated in describing the frequent discrediting of women's talk through intimidation and various belittling techniques.

It is not surprising to find that there are no terms for man talk that are equivalent to chatter, natter, prattle, nag, bitch, whine, and, of course, *gossip*, and I am not so naive as to assume that this is because men do not engage in these activities. It is because when they do it is called something different, something more flattering and more appropriate to their place in the world. This double standard is of great value in the maintenance of patriarchal order.[2]

Talk about other people – gossip – is a significant feature of human language, its observations about behaviour performing an important integrative and socializing function. Social science literature presents a useful working definition of the subject as being information exchanged with acquaintances about other people who are known mutually. It is essentially talk about other people's activities and behaviour. An essential ingredient is the current activities of friends, relatives and acquaintances, this preoccupation playing an important part in the monitoring of behaviour and development of social relationships. Discussing the personal details of other people establishes an important arena for moral and political debate which means that gossip plays a formative part in the shaping of social values. An analysis of the gossip of a specific time and place can consequently tell us much about the rules governing a particular group's behaviour.[3] Indeed, gossip's measurement of newcomers against these values performs an important bonding function, since group identity is ensured by confirming a sense of shared history and tradition. 'The right to gossip about certain people is only extended to a person when he or she is accepted as a member of a group or set. It is a hallmark of membership. There is no easier way of putting a stranger in his place than by beginning to gossip: this shows him conclusively that he does not belong.'[4]

Contemporary research has established that practically everyone gossips, and that people only tend to be blamed for it when they break the rules in some way, as in passing on untrue stories, or in speaking maliciously. It is in this scandalmongering context that women are frequently portrayed as gossips, although behavioural psychologists have failed to identify any discernible gender differences in terms of malicious content.

Why gossip and working-class women?

Gossip has attracted increasing academic interest in recent years, and is a broad and rich subject with many fascinating avenues to explore. My own concern with it has been as a tool with which to highlight aspects of women's lives in working-class communities which would otherwise remain shadowy and indistinct. This book, in touching on larger issues, consequently restricts itself to the complex function which gossip histori-cally performed in working-class neighbourhoods, assessing its significance against the sharing and support networks which underpinned life in many such districts. In particular, it explores the strengths and limitations of gossip in bonding together disparate groups of working-class women between the late nineteenth century and the immediate post-war period.

Gossip seems an appropriate analytical form to apply given the self-enclosed, introspective nature of the working-class neighbourhoods which developed between the 1880s and 1950s, and which were characterized by distinct cultural forms and significant degrees of gender segregation. Many working-class women belonged to intimate social networks with strong ties to relatives and neighbours. Such 'closed' systems whose members socialized largely with each other rather than with outsiders were not surprisingly typified as 'urban villages' by Robert Roberts, since their char-acteristics were also common to many rural communities. The excessive degree of familiarity within such networks allowed a great deal of social pressure to be exerted over individual behaviour, unlike the case with more 'open' systems whose members were less well known to each other. These 'closed' networks, which were strongest among the poorer (although not poorest) members of the working class, were distinguished by the particu-lar visibility of gossip.

Recent research into gender differences in language helps define why gossip played such a critical part in the lives of many working-class women. The social networks upon which they depended were significantly affected by such variables as age, neighbourhood and employment opportunities. Closed networks, which are characterized by a high degree of familiarity among members, not only help preserve vernacular forms of language, but also provide a relatively sealed environment in which gossip and conformity with group norms of behaviour thrive. These were precisely the conditions which characterized many working-class communities in the period between the late nineteenth century and the Second World War. Although not invariably segregated, working-class women's limited access to recreation was often set apart from men, and their day-to-day conversation was more likely to be characterized by single sex rather than mixed sex interaction. In this sense, many supportive aspects of women's language which have been observed in socio-linguistic studies were apparent in the gossip of working-class women, reflecting, in part, the reciprocity which was such an important aspect of life in poor communities.

Gossip's role in the urban village

The idea of urban villages perhaps gives a misleadingly cohesive view of working-class life. Working-class experience was, in fact, a mosaic of different identities shaped by the street, corner shop, family and relatives, pub or club, and by paid work outside the home.[5] The talk of each venue had a slightly different dynamic. The corner shop, for example, comprised a small, intimate and tightly controlled world. Every working-class street had such a shop within short walking distance, and the tendency to stay largely loyal to the one nearest gave regular frequenters considerable power based on the exclusivity of their patronage. Oral 'tradition' was the bedrock upon which these communities were formed, and the daily gossip of street life provided an important dynamic through which the judgments and values of community life were transmuted and refined. Robert Roberts well-understood the 'detailed gossip of a closed society', which was traded with 'goodwill, candour or cattishness' by the 'matriarchs' who trailed in and out of his parents' corner shop examining 'the health, honesty, conduct, history and connections of everyone in the neighbourhood'.

> Misdeeds of mean, cruel or dissolute neighbours were mulled over and penalties unconsciously fixed. These could range from the matronly snub to the smashing of the guilty party's windows, or even a public beating. The plight of the aged, those without shelter or reaching near-starvation would be considered and their travail eased at least temporarily by some individual or combined act of charity.[6]

Gossip's myth-making qualities

It is a characteristic of gossip that 'The more exclusive a group is, the more will its members indulge in gossip and scandal about one another. And the more persistently will they repeat the same gossip again and again without getting bored.'[7] While not suggesting that the gossip of working-class communities was excessively seasoned with scandal, part of its interest for much of the period discussed in this book lay in its manifesting the views of a largely oral culture. Oral society was a culture largely concerned with the present, grounded in a form of communication which was 'communal and externalised and less introspective' than that of literate society. Even with the growth of working-class literacy between 1880 and the Second World War, the forms of pre-literate society still exerted considerable influence, particularly among the poorer sectors of the working class. Around one in ten adults was unable to write on the eve of the First World War, while many others, particularly among the middle aged, elderly, unskilled and women had only an uncertain grasp of the written word.[8] Female literacy rates had risen considerably by the end of the nineteenth century, yet women were still more likely than men to be locked within a largely oral world, since the domestic pressures to which girls and working-class women were subject limited the time available for literary pursuits even among those who were competent at and liked reading. The emergence of a print culture in the eighteenth and nineteenth centuries largely excluded women and implicitly downgraded their words by increasingly associating oral discourse with superstition and ignorance, women's 'lost status' reflecting their greater dependence on conversation and verbal communication.[9]

Focusing on women's speech helps draw them out of the shadows where this concentration on literacy and the role played by literary forms tends to place them. Women's lives were grounded in sensitivity to others' needs and behaviour, not only within the family but outside it. This sensitivity was honed by the expectation of service and awareness of the part which communication with kin and neighbours played in ensuring survival. Working-class women, for example, had to be finely tuned to the shifts which took place in local relationships since a casual remark could set off a complex sequence of recrimination. Knowing who was 'in' or 'out' with whom was vital in avoiding unwitting involvement in local quarrels, and a frequently sophisticated use of gossip was the means by which women kept up to date with these changes and 'ceaselessly analysed' their own lives and those of others.[10] The value placed on this exchange of views, observations and experience possibly helped reinforce the emphasis which working-class women in the period before the First World War tended to place on character rather than learning.[11]

A feature of largely oral societies is the tendency for endless repetition which so infuriated Robert Roberts's mother.

> Not only within the family, she said, but in shops, pubs and factories, life was so limited that people recounted the same stories, incidents and witticisms time and again until one became 'word perfect and weary'. 'Some folk,' she said irritably, 'were like drunken parrots!'[12]

Her reaction was typical of more literate observers of working-class society, who viewed formulaic epithets and cliché ridden sayings as symptomatic of a tired and stagnant culture. Yet such repetition was the inevitable dynamic of 'orality', a vital means of ensuring that accumulated knowledge and wisdom was not lost to succeeding generations, while producing a 'highly traditionalist or conservative set of mind' – precisely those qualities which so frequently featured in criticisms of working-class women.[13]

Repetition was also a characteristic of gossip, which reflected a speculative tendency whereby added detail and interpretations of behaviour gave some subjects a larger than life quality. Most working streets had their 'characters', those who stepped outside the usual social norms and became markers against which 'normal' behaviour was judged. Andy Davies has described how 'women who flouted the established moral codes in working class neighbourhoods were soon categorised'.[14] This was particularly true of women notorious for public displays of drunkenness or fighting; failure at household management, which could have an equally disastrous effect upon working-class family life, seems to have featured less in such mythologizing. Such 'inadequacies' lacked the dramatic qualities of drunkenness and fighting and were more frequently the subject of the daily exchange of gossip between neighbours. There was a hierarchy of judgment, ranging from such casual comments to the talk which inflated the larger figures of local community myth.[15]

To be termed a 'real character' did not necessarily imply disapproval. It could represent amusement, affection, even a certain admiration for the audacity displayed by someone whose reputation was exaggerated by continual re-telling. For 'colorless personalities' could not survive 'oral mnemonics', which concentrated on the dramatic and unusual as a means of expressing and perpetuating important collective lessons.

Mythic qualities also developed in the exaggeration of small experiences which could become 'representations of large meaning', as in the 'hoary folk tale' which Roberts recalled in Northern towns 'concerning the man who returned home helplessly drunk, only to be tied up by his wife and beaten into unconsciousness and future sobriety. This may well have taken place, but not, surely, with the frequency that legend has it.'[16] Nevertheless, the veracity acquired in its telling as gossip spoke of its symbolic value in the lives of local women.

Gossip in self-enclosed, stable communities such as these followed established patterns, expressing collective assumptions which absorbed and
transmuted new experience into recognizable forms. It was interpretative
in the sense that talk about other people helped define group identity by
recycling fragments of the past and relating the present to earlier experience. It provided the reassurance of continuity.

> Relatives or very close friends who have gone to live away are likely
> to be communicated with only by Christmas card, unless there is a
> special family event. But if they come back to live in the area the rela-
> tionship will be taken up as though it had never been interrupted. And
> if one-time near neighbours meet by chance in town there will be a
> good gossip, one which seems just a continuation of its predecessors.[17]

Origins of study

My own interest in the role which gossip played in such communities is in
many respects a natural progression from earlier work which examined the
role of the pawnbroker and other credit mechanisms among working-class
people. Research I began in order to write the history of a trade, gradually
acquired a greater fascination because of the powerful impact such strategies had upon the lives of many working-class women. Under the weight
of descriptive and legislative material which demonstrated the mechanics
and profitability of an overwhelmingly male business lurked the experiences of women who were the mainstay of the 'industrial' pawnbroker's
daily trade. The two could not be separated; the business had to be
refracted through the lives of the women who were the pawnbroker's main
customers, and interpreted against the various survival strategies which
women of the urban poor employed in their daily lives. Challenging the
stereotypes which surrounded their behaviour naturally led me to an examination of the 'idle, gossiping housewife' and curiosity about the role
which gossip really performed in tightly knit working-class communities.
A writer in the *Manchester City News* in 1893, for example, typically
described a pawnbroker's regular customers, 'None of the women, all
notable gossips, seemed any way shamefaced as to their errand, or made
any attempts at concealment.'[18] Such comments suggest the extent to
which gossip and lack of shame at pawning were seen as synonymous, yet
as Jane Lewis has written, 'When social investigators and philanthropists
condemned women for gossiping and deplored the excitement of street life,
striving to bring order and respect for quiet to the lives of the poor, they
were in fact often attacking the sources of neighbourly communication and
mutual aid.'[19] Reconstituting women's history from frequently fragile
sources inevitably demands much lateral thinking; nowhere is this

approach more essential than in defining how working-class women used and were abused by the gossip networks which frequently underpinned their communities.

Difficulties of sources and popular stereotypes of women's language

Before looking at the advantages of using gossip as an analytical tool in examining the lives of working-class women, it is worth making some general comments about women's language, for the links which Dale Spender makes between women's words and women's writing in the quotation at the beginning of this chapter pinpoint a significant tendency, until recently, to treat neither as serious subjects for study. They are a useful reminder that women's talk has traditionally been disparaged as an inferior form of conversation, lacking the significance of men's words, although their use of language has often been one of the few ways in which women could assert themselves, and for this reason has been a constant source of comment and prohibition. Western European culture is imbued with hostile representations of women, who appear as 'nagging, scolding and generally talking too much'. The ideal mode of discourse for women was judged for many centuries to be silence.[20] There is a lack of historical evidence that women talked more than men, although the frequency with which admonishments to be silent are found in folklore perhaps illustrate the very difficulty of getting women to adhere to the acquiescent behaviour which was expected of them.[21] Urged to be silent, and rarely recorded except in a derogatory sense, even the clichés of popular perception are worth exploring as much for their omissions and distortions as for apparent meaning.

In addition to the distortions of expression which have frequently marred views of women's language, an examination of gossip among working-class women presents particular difficulties in terms of sources. For if the voices of middle-class women are muffled in the historical record, those of their working-class sisters are often not even connected into the mainstream of written testimony about the past, particularly as studies of vernacular culture have typically been given a male definition which ignores or underestimates female forms and the fact that women, like men, are defined by their class experience.[22] Thankfully, the echoes of their lives are not entirely lost to the diligent searcher, although one problem of examining this fascinating subject from an historical standpoint is the lack of a single, substantial body of research material. Part of the challenge has inevitably been to identify and extract information from a diverse range of sources and indirect evidence, including autobiographies, oral testimony, the press and popular literature. This book is primarily an historical analysis, and does not purport to be a sociological study of contemporary gossip, although the nature of such research means it inevitably crosses disciplinary boundaries, drawing, for example, on anthropological and sociological works.

Folk linguistic belief or proverbs are perhaps one approach which can give us entry into the popular attitudes surrounding ordinary women. Thiselton-Dyer observed in his *Folklore of Women* in 1905, for example, that 'The persistency of a woman's tongue has been made the subject of frequent comment in our proverbial lore', and it was typically said to be as restless as a lamb's tail.[23] Proverbs larded popular speech, covering all manner of behaviour and practice while being typically dismissive in their treatment of women's language. Deeds were said to be 'males', but words were 'females'. Indeed, there were said to be three unreliable things in life – a horse's health, a woman's word, and a boy's love. Many women, many words; many geese, many turds. Such proverbs were an integral part of the oral culture although they also had a literary manifestation, first appearing in printed collections in the sixteenth century, which were notable for their many 'misogynist sayings'.[24] Their moral and practical admonitions encapsulated many popular attitudes, particularly pre-industrial attitudes, although their expression was very partial as far as women are concerned. The evidence of gender difference in usage is slim, although it has been suggested that in 'traditional rural society men tend to use proverbs more than women', which 'is consistent with the anti-female bias in the sayings themselves'. The fact that men compiled the written collections means, of course, they may never even have been told of women's sayings which were in common currency.[25] Nevertheless, although the adjectives used to describe such talk were usually negative and derogatory, the image conjured is a positive one of perpetual activity. It testified to an energy and vigour which was incessantly seeking a more fulfilling and positive outlet than the one mockingly defined by a local saying from Salisbury that:

> Nature, regardless of the babbling race,
> Planted no beard upon a woman's face;
> Not Freddy Keen's razors, though the very best,
> Could shave a chin that never is at rest.[26]

Flora Thompson described how the farm labourers from her Oxfordshire childhood had 'hundreds of proverbs and sayings', and many of these survived, albeit in diminished form, in the urban neighbourhoods of late nineteenth and early twentieth-century Britain, where interestingly, in contrast to the rural experience, women seem to have been their main users.[27] Robert Roberts, echoing the 'more intelligent' members of the Edwardian working class he described, faintly derided 'the many stale saws and clichés that peppered working class talk', expressions which 'brilliant at birth, had been worn to vacuity through over-use'.[28] Richard Hoggart's view of conversation in inter-war Hunslet, Leeds, was more positive, as he endeavoured to penetrate the meaning behind apparently hackneyed applications.[29] Proverbs certainly did provide 'stock responses to certain recurring conversational openings', yet in so doing they helped smooth the pattern of 'the most common verbal encounters exchanged with a chance-met acquaintance at a street corner; in shops or on buses; in the doctor's waiting room or across the backyard wall'. 'Among older working-class women a ritualised exchange of proverbs' could 'fill the greater part of a conversation', each piece of news being greeted with 'a standard consolatory response'.[30] (Elderly people seem to have been the main users of proverbs.) Recent linguistic research has talked of 'women's style' and 'men's style' of speaking, and it is worth considering that perhaps proverbs played a useful role in an urban context where support and reciprocity were so important for survival, particularly as one of their functions has been described as establishing or restoring social relationships and reinforcing peer group solidarity.[31]

Dangers of gossip

It is gossip's ability to make and break reputations which makes it so often feared, and it is this aspect which frequently forms the basis of popular perceptions of such talk. Gossip's dangerous tendencies were well recognized. It was, by its very nature, a collective activity, which in excluding men tended to threaten them, so that moral injunctions against it tended to isolate and separate women by urging them to keep their own counsel.[32] It is scarcely surprising, therefore, that the emphasis in popular culture tends to be upon the malicious, derogatory and scandalous aspects of talking about other people, since it is in this context that women are most frequently portrayed as gossips.[33] Indeed, the popular judgment that women maliciously gossip more than men is a widespread perception which is not confined to a British or Anglo-Saxon setting. Edwin Almirol's research on gossip in the Filipino community of central California, for example, describes the Filipino word *tsimosa*, which is

> a demeaning term for one who makes it his or her business to mind the business of others and broadcasts information he or she gathers with malicious intentions. As in the Andalusian community, a gossip in the Filipino community is always assumed to be a woman. If a man is found to be a gossip, insinuations are made that he has effeminate qualities. No one admits to being a gossip, but many admit that they have indulged in gossip 'once in a while'. All of those who have admitted to gossiping are women, and the men even seem offended

when asked whether they have participated in gossip or not. But indeed, the men often talk about other Filipinos' judgement.[34]

Almirol's observations on Filipino attitudes towards gossip incidentally underline an important distinction between the individual perpetrator of such talk and more general participation in the process of gossip which has much broader acceptance. There was an understandable wariness of the individual gossip in small communities, expressed in such local sayings as 'Them as brings'll carry', which reflected an implicit understanding that known gossips have a number of motivations, not least being the power and status to be found in passing comment on other people's activities.[35] This encourages a selective and embellishing approach which reinforces gossip's reputation for victimizing and undermining other people. It is this capacity for malice in talk about other people which has produced injunctions against gossip throughout history and across cultures. These proscriptions recognize the power which lies at the heart of discussion about other people's behaviour, particularly as there is a sense in which such 'stories' take on a life of their own, becoming a substitute for, even taking possession of the individual identity under discussion. This almost supernatural aspect to gossip in some societies was reflected in Pitt-Rivers's work among Spanish Andalusians, where a 'sabia', or woman who could perform magical acts, was also regarded as an 'alcahueta' or a gossip.[36] Patricia Meyer Spacks offers the interesting observation that 'Like the notion that taking a photograph of someone endangers his spirit, the view that saying something bad has the force of *doing* something bad wells from pre-rational depths ... Anyone can invoke the dangerous magic of language; a weapon for the otherwise powerless, a weapon (as many have noted) usable from dark corners.'[37] Such examples, in testifying to the power of women's words, suggest how gossip's associations with women may be seen as part of a widespread mythology which seeks to prevent them from gossiping, and thereby exclude them from the power and politics of everyday living described earlier. The aim of this book is to show how working-class women evaded such proscriptions, developing verbal strategies which testified to significant forms of influence within their communities.

Gossip and women's informal power

The popular focus on gossip's capacity for damage inevitably obscures its broader function, although an historical study of the change which took place in the definition of gossip, ensuring that its negative aspects were increasingly associated with women, can give useful insights into how perceptions of women's power and influence shifted over time. In many respects, an evaluation of gossip and the part which verbal as opposed to written skills played in a working-class context is important precisely because working-class women have left such a meagre body of literary material about themselves. Less than one in ten of the autobiographies amassed by Burnett, Vincent and Mayall in their great bibliography of such literature were written by women, and this dearth of material is a tantalizing indication of the need to know far more about the 'role of women as story-tellers in the oral culture'.[38] Talk was often the only expedient which women felt they had open to them, as Kathleen Woodward ruefully acknowledged about her fellow factory workers when she observed 'painfully that while their conversation was full of complaint and revolt, it seemed strangely to leave their conduct unaffected'.[39] More particularly, as was suggested earlier, gossip provides the example of a distinct type of talk which in acquiring popular associations with women served to reinforce a distinct type of feckless behaviour of peculiar significance to the experience of working-class women. For this tendency to associate women with gossip had not only a sexual but also a class dimension, since denigration of such talk can be seen as part of the ideological undermining of working-class culture which encouraged working-class people, and women especially, to undervalue themselves and their activities.

Gossip expressed the politics of everyday living, and as such was an important vehicle for the informal power which women of the urban poor often exerted over their neighbourhoods, since they had few other channels through which to express themselves. This function reinforces the importance of a broad definition of political life if the complexity of women's political experience is to be properly understood. As Kate Phillips observed of a group of working-class women more recently in Glasgow:

> Not only does politics not reflect the views of women but the existing concerns of women come to be seen as peripheral to 'real politics'. When women discuss 'the treatment you get from the doctor these days', 'waiting for operations', 'damp in the back bedroom', and 'the price of a loaf', they are more likely to be perceived as immersed in idle gossip rather than political comment. The trade union member who complains of 'treatment from supervisors', 'fumes in the paint shop', 'cold on the shop floor', and 'cuts in wages' is viewed rather differently.[40]

The burden of domestic survival which fell on women's shoulders left no scope for weakness or vulnerability, and the political consciousness of many was grounded in these pragmatic considerations. To the 'housewife' whose paid work was of a fragmented, part-time nature or nonexistent, the ability to cope with the daily crises of a hand-to-mouth existence was likely to be more greatly prized than visionary political ideas based on the

economics of the workplace.[41] The differing perspectives of many women
and men under such circumstances may be illustrated by Ivy Corrigan,
who grew up in Salford during the inter-war years. She considered her
family to be unusual because her father handed over all his wages to her
mother, in return for 'spends' (for cigarettes). Ivy described how, when a
thrift club started at his works, her father put aside five shillings every
week so that the family could have a holiday. 'And the men that were there
were saying that it wasn't right because if the bosses thought that you
could afford to put five shillings away every week they'd think they were
paying them too much.'[42] This cynical response from the men epitomized
a significantly different attitude towards savings, whereby consciousness of
their own economic exploitation effectively precluded any discussion of the
domestic impact of their actions. As Jim Hooley sardonically remarked in
his recollections of life in Hillgate, Stockport, during the 1920s and 1930s,
women had little time to discuss the niceties of broader social issues:

> The women who lived on Hillgate at that time were more 'go ahead'
> than the men. It was their job to keep the food coming in and to think
> of various schemes to keep it coming in. The men on the other hand,
> if not working (which was often), would gather on the street corners
> and discuss the affairs of the day, both political and financial. During
> these debates one could find more comedians than there ever were at
> the London Palladium.[43]

Hooley's words patronize the working-class men they describe, yet illustrate the impulse which informed women's attitude towards life, and made
gossip such an important survival mechanism for them.

Gender differences in language

Much has been written about gossip from an anthropological viewpoint.
Interest in the subject was largely stimulated by the work of Max
Gluckman, early studies tending to concentrate on the role of gossip in so-
called 'primitive', rural societies. Later attention has focused on its manifestation in contemporary Western urban culture. Gluckman, and more
recently writers such as Patricia Mayer Spacks and Sally Yerkovich, have
explored the positive aspects of gossip, which were largely ignored in traditional literature. Sally Yerkovich suggested that 'Because it is a sociable
process, the content of the talk is not as important as the interaction which
the talking supports',[44] and pursuing a similar line of argument, biological
anthropologists like Robin Dunbar have called gossip a form of 'verbal
nit-picking' which developed from the mutual grooming which is characteristic of primate groups in general. Mutual grooming served more than a
purely hygienic function, since the time spent with another individual

serviced relationships by building up familiarity with behaviour patterns and expressing commitment, much as different forms of gossip do. 'Vocal grooming' subsequently developed among humans as a means of integrating humans into larger social groups than those common among other primates.

Large groups among primates tend to consist of around 55 individuals, and one-to-one social grooming is an important way of establishing rapport between members. However, at least 20 per cent of each day needs to be spent on such activity for it to be effective within a group of 55 primates. Early human groups tended to be larger than this, Dunbar arguing that a 'natural' size for human groups is in the region of 150, which reflects a common 'clan' size among hunter-gatherers who were often based around shared hunting grounds or water holes. (One can perhaps see the local corner shop as the working-class equivalent of the hunter-gatherer's water hole.) The one-to-one social grooming common among primates would cease to be effective in a human group of 155 individuals, where 35–45 per cent of each day would need to be devoted to such activity, presenting obvious difficulties to human groups engaged in a precarious pattern of hunting and foraging for survival. Dunbar suggests that a 'shift in gear had to take place in the mechanism for social bonding' and keeping such a large group together, which resulted in the development of language.[45]

Growing interest in the positive purpose of gossip has coincided with the growth of socio-linguistic studies which have examined apparent differences in male and female speech and started to reclaim the negative words which have been applied to women's language. Gossip, while not a uniquely female phenomenon, has been shown in certain all-female contexts to display particular characteristics which are said to substantiate arguments of a specifically supportive style in female speech. Some of these supportive aspects were apparent in the gossip of working-class women, reflecting, in part, the reciprocity which was such an important part of life in poor communities.

Sex differences in language have attracted increasing interest since the early 1970s. Early research revolved around male dominance, and the apparent tentative, powerless quality of women's language.[46] Later research has been more concerned with the power structures and relationships within which women's sub-cultures have developed. It has focused on positive manifestations of women's influence, moving away from mixed sex talk to focus on that of single sex groups. This research has stressed differences in conversational style, leading some to discern a significant difference in emphasis in how men and women talk about other people. Male conversation has been defined as an individualistic, aggressive form based on competitiveness and a preoccupation with things, while women's conversation has been characterized as a more cooperative, collective activity, concerned with people and feelings, consolidating friendship and supporting a group viewpoint rather than individual assertions. Elizabeth Aries, for example, in an early study of single sex and mixed sex talk, found that in single sex groups 'men were more likely to talk about themselves, more likely to tell stories which emphasised aggressiveness and superiority, while women talked less about themselves and more about human relationships'.[47] Mogey's interviews with men and women in post-war Oxford discovered more about the husbands than wives, due to the fact that the wives talked far more easily about their husbands – and husbands about themselves – than did husbands about their wives.[48] More recently, Dunbar's research into gossip has also revealed a self-centred tendency in men's talk, which tends to revolve more around their own relationships and experiences, while women's gossip is more outward-looking and focused on the experiences of other people. This woman-to-woman bonding, whose origins reflect the important part which relationships between females play among primates, may have played a critical role in the development of human language.

Although one should take care in using evidence derived from vastly different times, places and social contexts, it is useful to consider that although concern with the personal was deemed to be trivial, neighbourhood networks in pre-war working-class communities depended on similar interests. A barman quoted by Mass Observation in *The Pub and the People* typically emphasized the personal quality of women's talk as opposed to that of men:

> Conversation, Typical – what's in the news, sensational, sport main topic among men. Work and past events, good old days, reminiscencing. Among women their troubles, especially Marital, but of course children, mainly pride in their own Kith and Kin, gossip, scandal, in fact nothing dissimilar to what women talk about in any other place where two or three are gathered together.[49]

This anecdotal judgment was followed by details of a survey conducted by a Mass Observation observer, who took ten-minute sample counts of conversational subjects in all the pubs he visited. Although this talk is not specified as single sex male talk, it is likely to have comprised a majority of male speakers, and certainly highlights likely subject matter in a significant area of male socialization and recreation. Over 40 per cent of conversations were about sport or money (which included jobs and betting); 18 per cent were about pubs and drinking; 8 per cent about politics; 6 per cent about the weather; 2 per cent about films and 1 per cent about war. Fifteen per cent of conversations were described as coming under the heading 'personal-topographical', which 'included all kinds of personal gossip and reminiscencing – discussions that often develop from or into topographical arguments and discussion'. A contrast was made with a similar count among London drinkers whose categories although criticized as 'arbitrary, middle-class', nevertheless revealed a strikingly similar percentage of 18 per cent concerned with 'personal gossip'. (The remaining conversations were concerned with sport; money; hobbies; 'shop'; politics; topography and religion.)[50] While the manner in which such conversations were conducted was not described, and despite a certain vagueness as far as categories were concerned, their subject matter certainly suggests the lack of personal focus which other researchers have discerned in male speech. Mogey's research into pub conversation in St Ebbe's, Oxford, for example, suggested that 'preferred' topics were 'largely escapist, about horse racing and football bets, about seaside holidays and coach trips. The world of personal references is harsh and full of jokes ... However, it is a friendly world too: this way of making fantasy out of accidents and misfortunes prevents close enquiry into individual lives. This is one of the topics that is taboo and everyone is very careful to avoid direct personal questions.' Although, as Mogey was careful to point out, in a close-knit community such as St Ebbe's there was little need for such direct questioning since 'the individual foibles and much of the history of nearly every member is already well known'.[51]

More recently, Jennifer Coates has argued that the aim of all woman conversation is to 'create and maintain good social relationships', the way women 'negotiate talk' symbolizing the mutual support and cooperation which aims to consolidate friendship.[52] Gossip was not unique to women, but it is possible that some of its content and emphasis were sufficiently different from that used by men for it to make a unique contribution to the development of community values. It is useful to draw on other disciplines in making this assessment. The psychologist Carol Gilligan, for example, in assessing concepts of morality within Western value systems, has discerned a sense of moral responsibility directly related to an appreciation of individual circumstances which is 'at odds with traditional assumptions about Western values ... The people whose moral talk conforms to this pattern are mainly, although not entirely, women.'[53]

Nevertheless, it is important, as other commentators have pointed out, to avoid the creation of 'new linguistic myths' in asserting such positive aspects of women's language.[54] While all women share a subordinate status relative to men, they do not form a homogeneous group and there are many variations in language use. Socio-linguistic research has often failed to address this diversity in female experience and its refraction through the prisms of race, class and culture, just as it has tended to underplay the dynamic nature of language and the significance of its historic/cultural context.[55] An examination of the gossip of women in these working-class communities suggests the supportiveness to which recent socio-linguistic research has drawn attention. However, there are also significant areas of diversity and contradiction which makes analysis of its function no straightforward matter.

Notes

1. Spender 1986: 1987, 57.
2. Spender 1980: 1985 107. Test Match Special is a useful counter to anyone who claims that men do not gossip.
3. See, for example, Harding 1975.
4. Gluckman 1963, 307–15.
5. See, for example, E. Roberts 1993, 38.
6. R. Roberts 1971: 1974, 42.
7. Gluckman 1963, 307–15.
8. Vincent 1989: 1993, 28–29, 264, 266.
9. Vincent 1989: 1993, 180.
10. Glastonbury 1979, 181.
11. Vincent 1989: 1993, 64.
12. Hoggart 1958: 1962, 52.
13. Ong 1982.
14. Davies 1992, 70.
15. See, for example, Davies's account of Nancy Dickybird in north Manchester. Davies 1992, 70–1.
16. Spacks 1985: 1986, 232. My thanks to Roger Bryant for introducing me to this book. R. Roberts 1971: 1974, 121–22.
17. Hoggart 1958: 1962, 135
18. *Manchester City News*, 8 April 1893.
19. Lewis 1984: 1986, 54.
20. Obelkevich 1987, 51; Coates 1986, 34.
21. Thiselton-Dyer 1905: 1990, 64, from Croker's 'Fairy Legends and Traditions of the South of Ireland', ed. Thomas Wright, 235.
22. See, for example, Labov, Cohen, Robins and Lewis 1968, 41, 'males are the chief exemplars of the vernacular culture'.
23. Thiselton-Dyer 1905: 1990, 67.
24. Obelkevich 1987, 43, 45, 51. Ironically enough, given their misogynist tendency, the first such collection was presented to Elizabeth I.
25. Obelkevich 1987, 46, 50.
26. Thiselton-Dyer 1905: 1990, 68.
27. Thompson 1945: 1982.
28. R. Roberts 1971: 1974, 177.
29. Hoggart 1958: 1962, 28–29.
30. Obelkevich 1987, 47. McKelvie 1965, 249. Research based on post-war Bradford.
31. Obelkevich 1987, 46.
    Does this merely reflect the childhood perceptions of writers like Roberts, and Hoggart whose recollections drew largely upon family and neighbourhood recollections? The respondents drawn on by post-war collectors such as Donald McKelvie were largely elderly women, which redressed the bias of earlier compilers. The evidence is scanty, but tantalizing.

32. Almirol 1981, 303–04.
     Christian teaching did, of course, discourage women from sharing their disappointments and sufferings with female friends. Saint Teresa of Avila, for example, urged her nuns to follow the example of their married counterparts: 'Think also of those many married women, – I know some of them, – persons in good society, who, with serious illnesses, and cruel sufferings, dare not complain, lest they should annoy their husbands. What? sinner that I am! do we come here to be treated better than they are? See how free you are from the great troubles of the world! Learn to suffer a little for the love of God, without anybody knowing about it. Here is a woman very unhappily married, but so that her husband shall not be told that she speaks of it and complains, she suffers many miseries without unburdening herself to anyone; and should we not endure, unknown to all but God and ourselves, those evils that He sends us for our sins? Especially as complaints in no way appease the trouble.' Saint Teresa of Avila, c. 1562, 29.
33. Levin and Arluke 1985, 283.
34. Almirol 1981, 294.
35. Grimes 1991, 37. See, for example, Leviticus, chapter 19, verse 16, 'Thou shalt not be a detractor nor a whisperer among the people.'
36. Pitt-Rivers, quoted in Almirol 1981, 294. A British woman of Pakistani parentage described passing on 'juicy' pieces of gossip as being 'like a pain in your stomach until you can get it out, you've got to tell somebody about it!' This observation is based on a Punjabi saying that someone has a thin stomach; in other words, they can't keep a secret. Interview with Shakila Mir, 21/4/89. Le Roy Ladurie, in his book on the thirteenth-century Pyrenean village of Montaillou, raised the question of 'traditional secrets' and the extent to which these were passed on through the generations by women, asking, 'Has matriarchy, in western society, been the best preserver of traditional thought?' Ladurie 1978: 1980, 196.
37. Spacks 1985: 1986, 30.
38. Burnett, Vincent, Mayall 1984, xviii.
39. Woodward 1928: 1983, 97.
40. Glasgow Women's Studies Group 1983, 126.
41. For an examination of these issues, see Hart 1989, 19–47.
42. Ordsall Local History Group, IC, taped recollections (hereinafter abbreviated as OLHG).
43. Hooley 1981, 8.
44. Yerkovich 1977, 192.
45. Dunbar 1992. In modern life, research into business formation has found that face-to-face interaction works well in companies of less than 150, but becomes less efficient once that size starts to be exceeded, the impersonality of belonging to larger groups of employees leading to higher rates of absenteeism and sickness. Similarly, exclusive religious groups, such as the Hutterites in the United States, break off to form new groups once an optimum size of 150 has been reached, since peer pressure in enforcing behavioural 'norms' becomes extremely difficult after this.
46. Lakoff 1975: Thorne and Henley 1975.
47. Spender 1980: 1985, 127.
48. Mogey 1956, 61.
49. Mass Observation 1943: 1987, 186.

50. *Ibid.*, 187. 'Only definite *conversations* on the subjects were counted, not isolated references; at least three consecutive statements on a subject were necessary before the subject was counted as a "conversation".'

51. Mogey 1956, 105. Mogey largely ignored women's contribution to pub life, being of the opinion that conversation there was 'confined almost entirely to the men'. This despite the fact that they sat 'around the walls, talking amongst themselves about the area, about houses, about health, and about children'. They acted, in his words, 'as a fringe to the men and even on convivial Saturday nights, sit and sing together in a corner'.

52. Coates and Cameron 1988, 120–21.

53. Spacks 1985: 1986, 43, referring to C. Gilligan 1982.

54. Coates and Cameron 1988, 73. Crystal 1987, 21, 46.

55. Much of the empirical data, for example, has been drawn from white, middle-class examples.

CHAPTER ONE

The whisper of devilish tongues: women's words corrupted

Be she old, or be she young,
A woman's strength is in her tongue.[1]

Women's words have been criticized, abused and suspected over a long period of history and within many different cultural settings. Yet while patriarchal society worked to remove women from public affairs, women just as persistently transmuted the private sphere into a matter for public discussion through their use of gossip. Gossip's association with a community of women outside the domestic sphere challenged male ideals of submissive domestic behaviour, and conflicted with individualistic conceptions of the housewife's main responsibility being to her immediate family. Addison observed in 1716, for example, how a gossip in politics was a slattern in her family.[2] The derogatory sexual myths which became attached to gossip contrasted with the positive function which it frequently performed among women, the power which men feared in women's words being symptomatic of these more positive meanings. It is, therefore, instructive to consider how the definition of the word gossip changed within the English language, since locating these changes within the historical process illustrates a downgrading process which was common to many words which became almost exclusively identified with women.[3]

Gossip: deterioration in meaning

Over time a dramatic transformation occurred in the definition of gossip, and the largely pejorative meaning it gradually acquired when applied to women was similar to that ascribed to another 'characteristic' of female culture, 'old wives' tales', which the OED defines as 'trivial stories, such as are told by garrulous old women'. Triviality, talkativeness and matriarchal characterization are constant themes in the later history of the word.

The earliest definitions of 'gossip' were of a noun concerning the role taken by god-parents at a Christian baptism. The late Old English word *godsibb* was literally a 'relative in God', which emphasized spiritual closeness and care for the child's well-being.[4] It could also apply to an intimate friend invited to a baptism, and over time the spiritual overtones became

diluted to a more secular form of caring as expressed in neighbourliness.
Christenings were celebratory occasions, providing opportunities for feast-
ing and drinking which are still commemorated in such phrases as 'wetting
the baby's head', and in various local baptismal customs, some of which
lived on into the early twentieth century. Gossip's earliest associations
with christenings remained in dialect use until the nineteenth century,
when 'gossiping' was cited in Somerset to mean a christening feast or
merrymaking in general. Joseph Wright's *English Dialect Dictionary* gives
an example of its application in Fife where 'After the mother's recovery,
friends and neighbours assembled to congratulate the parents, and drink to
the child's prosperity. This gathering was known as the cummer fealls, or
the gossips' wake.'[5] In the mining village of Throckley in the early years of
this century, 'the period after the birth was one of much visiting, leading
up to the christening of the baby and the churching of the mother'.[6] It was
still the custom in some districts to provide a feast on the occasion of the
birth of a child for friends and neighbours who came to help or offer
congratulations.[7] Elizabeth Wright wrote in 1913 that the 'head-washing',
or 'weshin' t'bairn's head' as such convivial gatherings were known in the
north of England, was 'not so much a feast as free drinking'. This festive
aspect apparent in the earliest meaning of *godsibb* helped identify the
intimacy of a spiritual relationship with drinking and the relaxation of
the usual rules governing social behaviour. By the fourteenth century the
word's more spiritual overtones had broadened and acquired a meaning
which characterized gossip as a particularly close friend and especially as
someone who was neighbourly and took an interest in their friends' behaviour. The drinking link later ensured that those who exchanged thoughts
and feelings in a convivial, alcoholic atmosphere came to be described as
'gossips' or 'tippling companions', so that by 1580 a hard drinker could be
described as a 'gossip-pint-pot'.[8]

   All three associations of gossip – with a good friend or neighbour, with
babies and with drink – were united in the sixteenth and seventeenth
century definition of the noun, as the close female friends whom a woman
invited to attend her at childbirth. Medieval women were not expected to
give birth without the company of other women, and all social classes
commonly called in female neighbours and relatives who had themselves
had children to attest to the birth.[9] This helped, among other things, to
protect the woman, if the baby died, from any accusations that she may
have caused the death or of substituting another (male) child as her own.
By the seventeenth century the concept of spiritual witness had become
witness to the physical experience of childbirth, which was a celebratory,
collective occasion from which men were excluded. (While there was, in
the sixteenth and seventeenth centuries, an expectation that husbands
should be near at hand at the birth of their children, the presence of any

man at actual childbirth appears to have been unusual up to the mid-seventeenth century.)[10] Experienced women or 'gossips' offered valuable advice and assistance should there be any difficulty in labour, and helped pass on practical information on obstetrics in circumstances where poor women were unable to afford the ministrations of a formally trained midwife. They also provided moral support and an excuse for tension-relieving festivity as a woman went into labour, since they brought food and drink which she was encouraged to share, as 'alcohol was widely believed by public and doctors alike to have great medicinal and strengthening properties'.[11] Withdrawal to the 'lying-in room' where childbirth occurred established a specifically female space in which the needs of the pregnant woman were paramount and where, after the baby was born, she was allowed to rest and recover free from the normal demands placed upon her sexuality, time and physical energies. The presence of other women ensured the effective policing of these strictures. It also made them privy to many family secrets which husbands may well have preferred to remain hidden. In France, male curiosity about the titillating conversation reputed to take place on such occasions gave rise to a distinct form of popular literature called *Les Caquets de l'Accouchée* (Chatter at the Lying-In) based on the eavesdropping of men who, secreting themselves behind the bed curtains, 'gleefully' passed 'on tales of erotic adventures, remedies for unwanted pregnancies, and various hot tips for lovers'.[12] The ribaldry which often characterized such occasions was absorbed into the definition of gossiping, which came to describe not only a christening feast but any merry gathering where bawdy conversation was likely.

> At gossipings I hearken'd after you
> But amongst those confusions of lewd tongues
> There's no distinguishing beyond a Babel.[13]

Abel Boyer's French-English Dictionary, published in 1700, gives an interesting insight into the negative associations with women which seem to have been well established in the use of the word gossip by the end of the seventeenth century. The translation of the noun was traditional enough, which was given as *commère* and *compère*, godmother and godfather. The celebratory overtones of the verb, defined as to rejoice like a good godmother (*se réjouir comme un bonne commère*) similarly retained a baptismal connection. Gossiping was translated as the merry making of women who eat and drink together (*rejouissance de femmes qui mangent et boivent ensemble*).[14] It was the adjectives attached to the noun which really pointed the way to the future – gadding gossip, drinking gossip and prating gossip. A drinking gossip was a good godmother, but also drunken woman or fuddling gossip (*yvrognesse*). A prating gossip was translated as a *causeuse* (prating or prattling woman, blabber, blab), a *caqueteuse* (a talkative gossip, a pratling woman, twatler or prattle basket), and a *becqueno* (young prating wench, prattle basket).[15] (Prattle basket, as a comment upon women's activities, presumably as they shopped together, was echoed in the dialect description of a two-handled pot, which was called a 'gossiping-pot' because two people were required to carry it, bringing them into such close contact as 'allowed them to indulge in gossiping as they went along'.)[16] Such associations suggest how gossip gradually acquired a gender-specific meaning as idle, inconsequential female talk which in the eighteenth century received dictionary recognition from Dr Johnson who supplied a definition which 'for the first time' connected gossip unambiguously and officially with women as 'One who runs about tattling like women at a laying-in'.[17] By the nineteenth century the gossip was well established as 'a person, mostly a woman, of light and trifling character, especially one who delights in idle talk', 1811 seeing the first conversational definition of gossip as 'idle talk, trifling or groundless rumour, tittle tattle'.[18] As childbirth began to lose many of the ritual aspects by which it had formerly been characterized, the positive contribution made by a woman's gossips was belittled and marginalized, the same dismissiveness being applied to any opportunities for women to socialize together.[19] Indeed, in some circumstances groups of women meeting together came to be regarded suspiciously because of their very rarity, such opportunities being relatively restricted outside a domestic setting. In 1816, for example, the Reverend J. King observed, 'It is true that the ordinary person, especially the female, never went to a gathering larger than could assemble in an ordinary house except when going to church.'[20]

However, it was the gadding gossip whose reputation most identified the gossip with the community of women outside the home, for the bustle and female collectivism of the events surrounding childbirth and the part which visiting and neighbourliness played in the proceedings were reflected in the frequency with which the adjective gadding was applied to the gossip. (In 1611, for example, 'To gossip it' was also given as to 'goe to visit neighbours'.)[21] A gadding gossip was translated as a *coureuse*, a gadding house-wife, a rambling or gossiping woman who loved company and was not able to keep it in her own home (*qui ne peut pas se captiver chez elle*). The wanderings which led a woman away from the domestic hearth in search of companionship had a significant sexual implication, mirrored in the other definition of *coureuse*, which was prostitute.

Gossip, gadding about and neighbourliness

The indisciplined associations represented by the gadding gossip, self-indulgent and preoccupied with sexual conduct and scandal, reflected a broader concern with loose talk and lax sexual behaviour among women, since the seventeenth and eighteenth centuries were periods when such criticism was directed against many types of women.[22] 'Gadding abroad' to visit friends and neighbours consequently acquired connotations of both sexual laxity and exposure of intimate secrets about family life and gender relations, since assaults on women's language helped link visiting and calling not only with wandering but also with sexual impropriety. Attacks on gossip in the sixteenth and seventeenth centuries conveyed distaste of the visiting and calling customs which took women away from their household tasks and from the more privatized family life which was becoming a necessary feature of respectability. William Mompesson, Rector of Eyam in Derbyshire, highlighted an aspect of this in 1666 when lauding the piety and meekness of his wife who had recently died of the plague. 'She never liked the company of tattling women and abhorred the wandering custom of going from house to house, for she was ever busied in useful occupations.'[23] Mompesson's observations indicate the impact of Puritan objections to gossip, whereby the pleasures of casual social contact were denied in favour of more 'instructive', productive company. As tea drinking became popular, it attracted similar censure as a focus for trivial socializing.

> There is old mother Jones and dame Jenkins
> They are the two best in the town
> They'll sit and chat over the tea-table
> And run all their poor neighbours down
> They'll sit for two hours or more
> Talking of this and that,
> While their husbands are hard at work
> They are at the tea-table chat.[24]

Women's words spoken in communal, public locales consequently became immodest and worthless, while diffidence and reserve was expected of their private speech. An English exercise from a grammar book of 1824 which was 'Designed to improve the Juvenile Mind in Spelling and Grammar' urged:

> The modest woman is not the first in conversation, neither does she drown the voice of her companions by the strength of her one. She reserves her sentiments till they are required; but she closes not her ears to the judgement of another.[25]

James Buchanan defined the gossip, in 1757, as 'One that goes too often a visiting, and talks of other people's concerns', and such allusions helped identify the female neighbour generally as someone to whom unnecessary revelations were made, and who threatened to place a wedge between a wife and her domestic duties.[26] 'Gadding gossips' were said to 'dine on the pot lid', and the fact that so many proverbial sayings criticized women's wandering habits suggests the extent to which women actively sought each others' company outside the home.[27] Indeed, the old English proverbial phrase that 'She will stay at home, perhaps, if her leg be broken', implied that only compulsion was likely to curb a woman's sociable tendencies. A Yorkshire nickname for a gossiping woman who spent her time in going from house to house was a 'rouk-town', whose reputation was summed up in the saying, 'A rouk-town's seldom a good housewife at home'. There were many other similar sayings, emphasizing the need for a woman's domestic attentions to be securely tethered. For example, Thiselton-Dyer cited 'A window wench, and a trotter in street, Is never good to have a house to keep', while a 'good wife' was said to be away from her house three times: when she was christened, married and buried. Marriage itself represented incapacitation, as in

> The wife that expects to have a good name
> Is always at home as if she were lame
> And the maid that is honest, her chiefest delight
> Is still to be doing from morning to night.[28]

Ballads like 'The Gossiping Wife' typically dwelt on the disruptive effect which such talk supposedly had upon a woman's domestic duties, leading her to neglect household responsibilities for chatter 'At some neighbour's door, with a dozen more'.

> A gossiping wife's gadding about,
> Click clacking, never at home,
> Every one's business minding abroad,
> And never minding her own.

Such talk was depicted as being so trivial and self-centred that the participants hardly listened to each other in all the noise and clatter, so that 'when they've all done, scarcely one Knows what they've been clacking about'.[29]

'The Gossiping Wife' drew an interesting counter attack typical of the ballad convention in a companion broadside entitled 'The Gossiping Husband', which while shadowing some of the original, also provided an interesting counterpoint to it. Unlike 'The Gossiping Wife', whose talk was a collective activity which took place with a large group of neighbours at the street door, the husband's gossip was portrayed as a much more private affair conducted with a companion at the public house. It also had a literary dimension, centring partly upon what was read in the newspapers – a link with the broader world of public affairs – which contrasted with the wife's gossip, was purely oral and local in origin.

> For in the morning when he rises and has his breakfast done,
> Instead of going to his work, to the public house he'll run,
> Good morning Mr Talkative have you seen the paper,
> Oh then a gossiping they all begin about their neighbour
> Oh no sir, I've not seen it yet, but for that thing I come,
> To hear the news and gossip too before that I go home,

Then sit you down by side of me and have a drop of gin,
To read the news of all the week the gossips do begin.[30]

The image of gossip represented in 'The Gossiping Husband' is of a far less communal activity, one which undermines trust between companions and cuts the gossip off from society, since 'A gossiping husband brings many foes, very few real friends'. It also conveys the impression that male gossip is ultimately a more significant activity since it has the power to destroy a man's trade and business.

For if the women gossip surely there's no harm done,
But a gossiping husband neglects his work and will to ruin run.

The intimacy of gossip between women ran counter to their expected family loyalties, and the fact that their first responsibility was towards husband and family automatically made meeting with other women a denial of domestic commitments. Perhaps more significantly, it threatened to draw them into an alarming sphere of public (and subversive) revelation.[31] The gossiping wife was, as usual, a liability because she refused to stay indoors.

She's never at home but to eat and drink
At breakfast, dinner and tea,
But when it's o'er and my back is turned,
Away out of the house is she.

Interestingly enough, this type of portrayal placed men in the passive position more usually attributed to women, and gave women far more impact within the public sphere. The ballad entitled 'Be Careful in Choosing a Wife' shows that women had vigorous expectations of domestic life, and balanced the stresses of looking after young children with an understandable tendency to get out and talk with friends.

The dinner time comes to my home I repair
'Tis a thousand to one if my wife I find there
She's gadding about with the child on her knee
And the devil a sign of a dinner for me ...
At night when I come sadly from my work
When I open the door she let's fly like a turk,
Take that young squalling brat and get it to sleep
For all the day long no peace can I keep,
And if I should offer the job to refuse,
With tongs or the poker she would me abuse.[32]

The visibility of women

While moralists have, since the Middle Ages, cited biblical authority to prove the dangers of talk about other people, the apparent growth of comment upon gossip and particularly its associations with women in the seventeenth and eighteenth centuries may have reflected in part specific changes in the visibility of upper-class women, as many began to enter the 'public' realm via their writings.[33] Lacking access to education and an economic role, such women had time and leisure for conversation and social observation which was channelled into popular literature. The eighteenth century saw a number of literary innovations to which women made an important and, until recently, neglected contribution. They wrote most of the novels at a time when in Spender's view 'popular literature was seen as a threat to standards and order ... These new books, which masqueraded as true accounts of real happenings, or which were fanciful versions of "gossip"', attracted considerable criticism since they offended men with a classical and formal education by subverting the established literary traditions normally seen as an upper-class prerogative. Indeed, Delariviere Manley created 'one of the first comic characters in fiction' with Mrs Nightwork, the gossiping midwife who 'regales the reader with secrets'.[34] Spacks, drawing the same analogy as Spender between literature and gossip, emphasizes the creative part which the oral tradition played in the development of these literary genres based on character and human relationships:

> The novel, biography, autobiography thrive on their exploitation
> of 'female values': attentiveness to the minute, the personal, the
> human. In other words, exactly those features which were attributed
> to gossip.[35]

The gossip of upper-class women and its literary expression in the novel presented a challenge which stoked male fears of a powerful female domestic society over which they had little control. However, it is useful to remember that sexual stereotypes were being challenged in other social groups in the late eighteenth and early nineteenth centuries, for while wealthier women were asserting their literary skills, other less educated women were also exerting their independence in the newly emerging industrial districts.

It has been argued that in the sixteenth and seventeenth centuries, women's gossip about courtship and marriage came to be particularly feared in close-knit pastoral and quasi-industrial communities where 'small farming co-existed with industrial pursuits', and which took their identity (and personal reputations) from peers rather than the church or gentry.[36] As the range of craft and agricultural activities which became available to women in the pastoral and industrial areas of the north and west enabled those without a male partner to support themselves independently, paid labour for young people generally and women in particular helped modify many patriarchal domestic arrangements by weakening the fear of parental and family censure while reinforcing sensitivity to peer pressure. At the same time, the frequent preponderance of male immigrants in expanding industrial districts meant severe competition for those women who were available for marriage, and great hostility to potential courtship from outsiders, which encouraged a strong sense of communal identity. Young women in the North Wales Ceiriog Valley who betrayed an interest in external suitors, for example, were brought into line by the critical gossip of the local young men's mothers, the young men themselves often taking more extreme measures against the non-conforming female if such gossip failed. This competition and the alternatives possible for an independent economic livelihood gave many women in these areas a new authority, since it was no longer a question of inheritance but their earning ability, strength, health and, by implication, fertility which had become the measure of their 'worth'. Such changes encouraged women to take the offensive in various forms of social protest in the late eighteenth and early nineteenth centuries. These manifestations of female independence, which were often inspired by gossip and rumour, helped to fuel the kind of male anxiety which was also apparent in the literary arena.[37]

Gossip and mischief-making

Mary Chamberlain has described the frequency with which accusations of witchcraft were levelled at 'outspoken women', or scolds, in medieval times: 'Constantly recurring phrases in the accusations of witchcraft are "a busy woman of her tongue", "devilishe of her tonge"'.[38] Chamberlain's litany of outspokenness highlights how women's language became in this medieval context a critical force identified with unsettling the status quo and part of a power struggle over who had the authority to heal and support life, for witches were often midwives and healers and their persecution coincided with the start of the movement of male medical practitioners into areas of health and childbirth traditionally associated with women. Groups of gossiping women were similarly suspected in the seventeenth century, when their tongue ripe disposition allegedly made them more susceptible than men to witchcraft.[39]

Spacks observes of criticism of gossip in the seventeenth and early eighteenth centuries that, 'Attacks on tattling addressed to female audiences, unlike those for males which stress the dangers of victimisation, emphasise women's tendency to indiscretion.'[40] She argues that analysis of these strictures against women's language needs to be placed in the context of a male value system based on reticence which had since the Middle Ages, frequently if not invariably, revealed fears of intimacy, vulnerability, trust and self-revelation. It was an ideology of dominance echoed in a piece of proverbial-lore cited by Thiselton-Dyer, that to 'Tell your secret to your servant was to "make him your master"'. Seventeenth- and eighteenth-century moralists urged an individualistic, solitary creed which presented even male friendship as a source of dangerous exposure through thought-less talk. Mischief-making was invariably attributed to women who met together to converse, and was conveyed in the images of popular culture. A man was urged to trust his dog 'to the end, and a woman till the first opportunity', while 'He that tells his wife the news' was said to be 'but lately married'.[41] Ballads such as 'The Gossiping Wife' draw on male fears of exposure and illustrate the effectiveness of street talk in policing behaviour.

> Up comes one with her tongue a yard long,
> O what do you think I heard,
> Your husband was seen last night indeed,
> Its all true upon my word,
> You know I always speak the truth,
> Whenever we chance for to meet,
> Though all the neighbours know full well
> She's the biggest liar in the street.[42]

It is, perhaps, significant that the earliest definitions of gossip had iden-tified it with a particular type of person (and thereby with a relationship) rather than with a process of conversation, since this largely female char-acterization reproduced the insecurity which men felt when they were excluded from or threatened by the conversation of groups of women.[43] In the sixteenth century, for example, the surgeon Percivall Willughby failed to act as experience told him he should during the delivery of a baby through unease at what the women in attendance might say, even though he regarded their views on childbirth as superstitious nonsense.

> Alice Smith of Darby, dwelling at Nun-Green, was disgusted by her ignorant, perverse midwife, for the space of ten dayes. After which time, being ill, and fainting, her neighbours laid her on her bed, supposing her to bee dying, whilst that some others of them came to my house for mee ... The inhabitants of our town, being foule mouthed, and apt to censuring, and the midwives of nogood disposi-tion, ever thrusting their ignorant carriages upon others, made me unwilling to use the crochet, although, in my thoughts, the child was departed, and did somewhat smell. [The woman died][44]

As was suggested, the negative connotations which were formally attached to gossip in the eighteenth century coincided with a period when childbirth was becoming increasingly subject to medical intervention and male involvement, as medical practitioners attempted to undermine women's skills in health matters and augment their own claims to medical status. The ceremony of childbirth and subsequent 'lying-in month' reversed normal patriarchal power relations between wife and husband,

and as the social context in which such ritual took place itself became more unsettled there were increasing suspicions about the opportunity it provided for hostility to male society.[45] As the anonymous male author of *The Woman's Advocate* wrote in 1683,

> for gossips to meet ... at a lying-in, and not to talk, you may as well dam up the arches of London Bridge, as stop their mouths at such a time. 'Tis a time of freedom, when women ... have a privilege to talk petty treason.[46]

The French historian Delumeau has observed how rumours spread by women played a key role in insurrections between the fourteenth and eighteenth centuries. Women were in the front line of attacks upon living standards or scares about children's wellbeing, and in communicating their concerns to neighbours mutually reinforced each other's anxieties, thereby fuelling rumour and its expression in riots and even revolution.[47] The authorities were not unaware of such potential for disorder; an ordinance promulgated in 1789 on St Helena illustrates just how the subversive potential of gossip could be perceived at times of social or political uncertainty:

> Whereas several idle, gossiping women, made it their business to go from house to house, about this island, inventing and spreading false and scandalous reports of the good people thereof, and thereby sow discord and debate among neighbours, and often between men and their wives, to the great grief and trouble of all good and quiet people, and to the utter extinguishing of all friendship, amity, and good neighbourhood; for the punishment and suppression thereof, and to the intent that all strife may be ended, we do order that if any women, from henceforth, shall be convicted of tale-bearing, mischief-making, scolding, or any other notorious vices, they shall be punished by ducking, or whipping, or such other punishment as their crimes or transgressions shall deserve, or the Governor and Council shall think fit.[48]

'Home Front' propaganda during the Second World War displayed similar alarm at the seditious possibilities of women's conversation, although policies to deal with it were developed within a context which regarded such words as an indication of women's woolly-mindedness. One of the earliest campaigns planned by the Ministry of Information in 1939 was that against 'Careless Talk' which targeted the destructive role of 'gossiping housewives'. The same patronizing tendency pervaded a speech which A.A. Milne drafted for a royal broadcast in 1939, in which the Queen was to speak 'as a wife and mother to other wives and mothers, and as a woman to all other women', which recommended ways of keeping up morale: 'Men say we gossip. Well, perhaps we do. It is nice sitting cosily with a friend and saying "Did you hear this?" and "Did you hear that?" But please, please, don't let us gossip now. Don't tell each other what the milkman said – it isn't true; how would the milkman know? Don't say to your friend, "My mother knows a man who knows a man" – and then repeat some silly story of a German atrocity or take in some lying story of a British disaster. You will help so much if you remember this; and perhaps it will help you to remember, when you are tempted to spread these rumours ... just to say to yourself "The Queen asked me herself not to. She asked me."' Although this condescending little missive was never broadcast, it was complimented by the director general for its admirably human touch.[49]

In 1940 the government initiated an 'anti-gossip' campaign to counter public defeatism after the fall of France and rumours of invasion encouraged by propaganda warnings against a 'fifth column'. Letters contained in Home Office intelligence files 'blamed colleagues at work or wives' "tittle-tattle" for spreading alarmist stories'. As the attack upon 'defeatist talk' intensified, social workers and observers reported 'increasing suspicion and unneighbourliness', which prompted a less strident campaign around the catch-phrase 'keeping mum', whose several variations invariably involved a diminished conception of women, notably in the phrase 'Be like Dad, keep Mum'.[50]

Men were, of course, also targeted in these campaigns, the early 'Careless Talk' propaganda posters and cartoons by Fougasse showing both women and men in gossiping situations. Nevertheless, their deliberately light-hearted message, intended to discourage panic, was firmly rooted in the idea of the 'gossiping housewife' which reflected the reality of an established comic convention and the belief that women were a more likely vehicle for hysteria and scaremongering than men. Mr Pride in Prophecy, the male counterpart to female propaganda figures like Miss Leaky Mouth and Miss Teacup Whisper, had a rather different emphasis, his name encapsulating the altogether greater weight of male opinion.[51]

Class distinctions and assumptions

This book is largely concerned with the role that gossip played among working-class women, but its middle-class manifestation was also used to trivialize women. The comments on gossip which appear in Rowntree and Laver's investigation into leisure habits in the early 1950s, for example, were partly used as a way of implying that the middle-class wife was parasitic. The case histories of 200 people over the age of 20 appear at the beginning of the study, where the sprinkling of references to gossip and talkativeness draw rather more on middle-class than working-class examples.[52] These were impressionistic, thumbnail sketches whose style approached that of gossip and reflected the manner in which the research had been conducted; their patronizing commentaries on the people who unwittingly disclosed their lives were as revealing of the researchers' attitudes as of the respondents'.[53] Mrs R., in her early forties and married to a country solicitor, was mainly interested in the 'little daily happenings to her friends', and gossip about them. She led 'a completely empty, harmless but useless life' and had 'no interest in world affairs, no interest indeed beyond the narrow circle of her own acquaintance and class'. Mrs T., in her late thirties, was a doctor, although she no longer practised. Married to a professional, she was described as rather a stupid woman who could scarcely have inspired much confidence as a doctor, and like Mrs R., was not greatly interested in anything outside her home other than the doings of friends of equal social standing and their children. Mrs L., another woman in her early forties, was married to a 'worthy but rather stodgy' professional man. Her child, dog and friends were her main interests, her greatest entertainment being to meet a group of female friends and exchange gossip about their various acquaintances and families. She wondered why her husband did not advance in his profession. 'Her method of helping him is to get to know people who she thinks might be useful to him and their wives, but her tedious prattle probably does her husband a good deal of harm.'[54] Mrs S., about 43, was married to a professional with two children, aged six and two. They lived in a moderate, detached suburban house which was scantily furnished, and admitted to being very hard up, 'less due to absolute lack of money than to the fact that they both lack any ability to spend wisely'. Mrs S. liked to go to the cinema but seldom had a chance because of her children. Her greatest pleasure was 'in tea parties with other women of her class, where they can gossip and talk about their acquaintances and their children'. Despite the cursory characterization, one can discern the frustration underlying the lives of several of the married middle-class women who had no work outside the home. Mrs X., married to an accountant, was in early middle age, with two children who were 'pretty wild since she had no control over them'. She was keen on visiting friends' houses, meeting them in a public house or entertaining at home.[55]

There were few accounts of male gossip, either overt or implied. Mr A., a customs clerk, aged 35, was extremely kindly but garrulous and his 'superficial' conversation was largely about his work. Mr S., another happily married clerk in his mid-forties, went to the pub every evening before going home, to meet up with a few old friends who were somewhat unusually described as sitting in a corner for an hour 'gossiping'. The only example of malicious male gossip was Mr R., 72, a retired railway worker who supplemented his pension by growing and selling vegetables and fruit, and was perhaps as much an example of religious hypocrisy as male inadequacy. A regular chapel-goer, teetotaller and non-smoker, he had a rather malicious tongue and 'appeared to delight in telling endless, often rather unkind, stories about neighbours and acquaintances. He says openly that the customers for his vegetables call him a skinflint, and he admits that he takes a pleasure in out-smarting them. Mr R. clearly has faith and hope, but the charity is not so certain!'[56]

The other examples of malicious gossip were from interviews with middle-class women. Miss F., a middle-aged spinster, was a companion whose trivial outlook on life was 'bounded by games of patience and bezique, hot-water bottles, taking the dog for a walk, fetching cushions, reading old-fashioned novels aloud, and all the similar tasks of a middle-aged companion'. She neither smoked nor drank, and went to church every Sunday. She enjoyed a good gossip about her acquaintances and liked a spice of malice to add flavour to the gossip, although there was no harm in her – 'only an abysmal emptiness of life'. The same was not true of Mrs Z, another single woman, aged about 50, who was a widow and had lived for many years in India. She was very 'pukka Memsahib', a terrible gossip and an insufferable bore. 'Her tongue has a barb to it and much of her gossip is malicious.' A regular churchgoer, she was not 'the sort of woman to suspect of sexual promiscuity – she probably does not stop talking long enough to enable a man to make improper advances!'[57]

As examples such as this imply, denigration of women's language transcended class boundaries. The tendency to disenfranchise women's talk was well illustrated in 1888 by a *Daily Telegraph* writer who criticized the idea that men and women should remain in each other's company after dinner rather than separate for segregated talk. 'Feminine frivolities were judged to be the substance of women's conversation, in contrast to politics, the Turf and sometimes a grave scandal or two which could be more rankly alluded to when men were the only listeners.'[58]

Nevertheless, this general disdain should not obscure a clear class distinction which also became apparent in attitudes towards the subject, as a *Spectator* article revealed in 1888. This centred on a recent debate at North Hall, Newnham, which had asked whether life was worth living without gossip, 'if by "gossip" we are to understand the pleasant chat which is one of its many meanings'. Significantly this particular definition was one which excluded the lives of working-class women. 'Easy conversation, sprinkled with allusions to persons, yet not confined to personalities' was advanced as an intellectual enjoyment possible only to those who lived under and shared in 'a developed civilisation'.

> It is deliberation made piquant by brevity of speech and by an underlying knowledge assumed on all hands, which of itself indicates at once the cultivation and the equality of the talkers. The uneducated never gossip in this sense, they only narrate and argue.[59]

Gossip, according to this middle-class definition, conveyed broad intellectual interests and a widish range of knowledge 'however superficial'. It
was also taken to indicate quick-wittedness, the personal talk of gossip
again being likened to the revelations of a good novel, since it was 'the
way in which the many, who do not discern quickly, gain their insight into
character'. However, there was still a sense in which such seductive talk
had to be reined in and disciplined, too much making the mind 'impatient
of any other conversation ... till in the vulgar, the desire for gossip
becomes almost a mania, and is indulged at any risk'.

Despite such reservations, the author of the piece felt 'social moralists'
underestimated 'the intellectual value' of discussing one's neighbours,
and that eighteenth-century 'pedagogues' 'had diffused among two generations an impression that gossip, the coffee of the mind', was intrinsically
bad, a conclusion which bears out Spacks's own observations about
the period.

The attempt to lift middle-class gossip above the level of talk generated
by the hoi polloi denoted a common Victorian view of the 'lower classes'
as lacking the capacity of their social superiors to discuss ideas. Working-
class language was often subject to the distorting lens of middle-class
assumption. The district nurse Margaret Loane commented on how the
number of words in common use among the 'lower classes' was greatly
underestimated.

> Learned men, in making their calculations, do not seem to grasp that
> the wily villager is deliberately choosing such words as he is sure his
> interlocutor will understand, and rejecting all those he thinks he will
> not.[60]

Such judgments owed much to the scientific and technological developments of the nineteenth century which had an undoubted impact on (male)
middle-class language with corresponding conceptual repercussions. It has,
for example, been argued that the 'public' language of Elizabethan
England, being 'anecdotal, descriptive, (and) metaphorical', was generally
accessible to all strata of society (at least to those in London), but that this
openness was gradually superseded by a greater linguistic segmentation
and elitism which affected all types of language.[61] Richard Hoggart
pinpointed some of these differences in speech when he wrote that
'Working class people are enormously interested in people: they have the
novelist's fascination with individual behaviour, with relationships –
though not so as to put them into a pattern, but for their own sake. "Isn't
she queer?"; "Fancy saying a thing like that!"; "What do you think she
meant by that?" they say; even the simplest anecdote is told dramatically,
with a wealth of rhetorical questions, supplementary illustrations, significant pauses, and alternations of pitch.'[62] This linguistic elitism encouraged,

among other things, the view that upper-class chatter about acquaintances was superior to the casual talk of working-class people, so that although club and after-dinner exchanges functioned in exactly the same way as talk at the street corner, any similarity was invariably rejected.

These reflections raise a number of interesting questions, not least about the nature of intra-class relations, particularly as revealed in the language which women of different classes exchanged between themselves. We have described the tendency for women's language to be particularly concerned with human relationships, which was rooted in the structural and social basis of their lives. It was this very concern with caring, nurturing and servicing which led many middle-class women to enter the caring field as social workers and health visitors, and into direct contact with their working-class sisters. Such middle-class women were certainly not immune to derogatory views of their own language, and the early twentieth century debate about the role of women in health visiting stimulated familiar doubts about what happened whenever women got together. Mr John Robertson, discussing a 'threatened appointment' before the Dundee Sanitary Committee in 1901 was 'in great form' as he asked: 'What good … would the citizens receive from two women gossiping from door to door, which would be the chief part of their occupation.'[63] Women in the field of public health could themselves be somewhat bemused by the important part which sympathetic talk played in their work, feeling that such intimacy was somehow unprofessional. A district nurse, working in an agricultural district during the 1930s, described how her patients, without asking, told her all their 'joys and troubles … aches and pains … hopes and family histories', to such an extent that 'I sometimes wonder what my job really is.'[64]

Such remarks betray not only assumptions about women's behaviour but also a lack of understanding about the nature of gossip. Many charities preferred using women to visit the poor 'because they alone could advise other women on housewifery, nursing and childcare'.[65] Indeed, more astute workers in the social work/nursing field were well aware of the importance of developing careful interrogative techniques to encourage their clients to reveal more about themselves and their families than was available through direct questioning. Margaret Loane, former district nurse and later superintendent of nurses, felt it was useless to ask direct questions in dealing with 'uneducated people', whose suspicions had to be countered through 'more informal methods':

> When one needs to know the past history and present circumstances of persons apparently in need of outside help, the best way (and by no means the slowest) is to encourage them to talk until one has all the family ramifications at one's finger's ends.[66]

While such advice on how to establish a 'confidential footing' with members of the working class was not confined to relationships with women, it is illustrative of how female professionals were encouraged to develop manipulative and linguistic skills which were highly suspect in more masculine environments.

Yet shared sexual identity did not necessarily mean class acceptance, particularly if it was accompanied by a sense of class superiority. Loane, despite her confidence in allaying the suspicions of her working-class clients, nevertheless accepted elsewhere that the 'scraps' of conversation she reported only touched the surface of their lives, and could be seen as 'merely those between a foreigner and a native'.[67] 'Any working man's wife would more readily confide her private affairs to the neighbour with whom she has had bitter, year-long quarrels, than she would to the kindest and most discreet of nurses or district visitors.'[68] A mechanistic and moralistic approach to social problems easily obscured the social and economic importance of informal talk at the street door, which was well understood by local traders like Scotch drapers who had close commercial relationships with their working-class clientele. For gossip helped ensure the acceptance or rejection of outsiders. It was a central social activity among women in working-class communities, amongst whom silence could be just as much an act of resistance as the apparent garrulousness which Margaret Harkness and Florence Bell described. Werner Picht, in his book on the Toynbee Hall Settlement, wrote that the friendship offered by settlers merely met with a 'quiet refusal' from the respectable working class, which was scarcely surprising given that one aspect of the public side to working-class life was the assumption that it entitled middle-class charity workers to descend unannounced upon the families of impoverished 'clients'.[69] Toynbee Hall was a male settlement, and Picht admitted that it was easier for members of womens' settlements such as the WUS in Southwark to enter into neighbourhood life, although even there he noted the patronizing tendency that Leonore Davidoff forcefully described when she remarked how 'Any middle class or upper class person felt free to visit a working class home at any time, to walk in and at once become involved in the life of the family by asking questions, dispensing charity or giving orders ... there was an unquestioned right to act in this way.'[70] While the visitors' ringing comments on how such women conducted their lives frequently survive, there is much less about how working-class women actually felt about such high-handed behaviour. Maud Pember Reeves describes the suspicion and reserve encountered by members of the Fabian Women's group when they were embarking on their sympathetic survey of working-class women's lives which culminated in Round About a Pound a Week. 'At the beginning of each case the woman seemed to steel herself to sit patiently and bear it while the expected questions or teaching of something should follow.'[71] The same Fabian 'visitors' encountered similar passive resistance when they attempted to spread 'a gospel of porridge to the hard worked mothers of families in Lambeth. The women of Lambeth listened patiently, according to their way, agreed to all that was said, and did not begin to feed their families on porridge.'[72] As Margaret Loane sardonically remarked, 'People who wish to know the effect of their kindly meant visits among the poor would be mortified to know how often the result is pure amusement.'[73]

Another insight into the feelings behind such apparent passivity is supplied by Ada Nield Chew, the working-class political activist whose fictional vignettes of working-class behaviour and language are nevertheless strongly rooted in her own background and experience of hardship. We may be lacking direct accounts of women's conversation, but her reconstructions often give a rich flavour of its likely form and substance. In an article describing the unrelenting flow of domestic life for a working-class woman, the subject, Mrs Turpin, recalls, 'Miss Seaton, who came hindering yesterday', asking

> if she knew that milk contained all the necessary elements to sustain life; and hoped she gave her children a good milk pudding every day. Of course she said 'Yes, 'm,' it was easiest to get rid of her that way, especially when you wanted to be getting on with your work; but she (Mrs Turpin) would like to know where the quart of milk per day (and a quart wouldn't make a pudding big enough to feed her five, leaving out herself and the baby) was to come from. Two shillings a week for milk puddings, when all she had to do upon, all told, was 28 shillings per week![74]

These examples suggest the extent to which the language and way of life of working-class communities were frequently distorted by middle-class assumptions, and how social workers, health visitors and teachers who attempted to impose their own standards on them were confronted by the cultural authority of working-class women whose very different social and moral traditions were powerfully articulated in gossip. The fact that a woman might claim never to mix with her 'rough' neighbours could also indicate a rather different 'truth' to the one expected, since it implied a sensitivity to the kind of disparaging judgments which outsiders often brought to the working-class way of life. As Alexander Paterson observed, 'the attitude of the family to the other families in the same street is always a little puzzling'. A woman would claim to have nothing to do with others who lived nearby, yet on a subsequent visit 'will be found deep in conversation with three despised neighbours, all united by expressions of mutual admiration and endearment against some interfering official'.[75]

Gossip and working-class stereotypes

Neighbourliness evinced a caring, intimate, supportive approach to relationships which was apparent in the earliest definitions of gossip. The derogatory overtones which it subsequently acquired not only denigrated female language, but also undermined the very concept of neighbourliness by criticizing the gossip's relationship with other women. The stereotype of noisy, feckless womanhood established in the seventeenth and eighteenth centuries eventually acquired a particular resonance in a working-class context, where it became associated with the public lives of poor working-class women. Poverty, and the apparent markers of poverty, were only deserving of sympathy if tidily hidden away. The lives of poor working-class women were too visible and their voices too loud, so that their speech became a comment upon their alleged irresponsibility. Poverty helped intensify the identification of neighbourliness with nosiness and talkativeness and reinforced the stereotype of the working-class woman gossip. (A feckless, weak male partnered by a loud-mouthed, overbearing woman was a feature of the working-class male myths which Jerry White describes in *Campbell Bunk*, while '"Mother Goose-Gob" or "Old Mother Murphy" with their "thin pointed nose between the aspidistra and the nets" were familiar despised characters' in working-class neighbourhoods).[76] Talking was not allowed on the communal staircases of the sought-after accommodation which Peabody buildings provided in London, and Carrie Telford, born in 1912 and brought up in Waterloo, vividly described the distinction between 'good' and 'bad' working-class neighbourhoods.

> Roupell Street, Whittlesea Street, Thede Street, was three streets known as the white curtain streets of Lambeth. Supposed to be the posh part. You wouldn't see them standing at their doors talking in this street. But in the back streets, Ethelm Street, they used to call that 'Kill 'Em and Eat 'Em Street', well, you'd see all the women there with their arms folded, their sleeves rolled up, outside the doors jawing to one another, you know.[77]

Women's respectability became associated with private words, so that 'respectable' working-class women were disinclined to join with the talk which took place between women in the street. Walter Greenwood's mother, for example, 'While being anything but unfriendly ... as a general rule, disapproved of standing with groups of neighbours exchanging tittle-tattle in the street.'[78]

> The lower middle classes and some well-to-do professional people had their solid homes round the park and, as a buffer between them and our rough and ready district, there intervened streets inhabited by those who would have been offended to be termed 'working class'. It

was customary here for front doors to be closed when men returned
from work, and their wives were not to be seen gossiping in friendly
neighbourly fashion. The district had an inhospitable look, an empty
air of bleak respectability.[79]

As a woman who grew up in Sale observed, 'there were some that gossiped
and some that didn't. In the main they kept themselves to themselves, you
know, there was this sort of desire not to waste time, you'd got enough to
do if you were running your house properly ...'[80] The working-class
woman who spent all her time gossiping was considered to be almost as
bad as the spendthrift because she could have been using her time more
productively by attending to domestic tasks. Clementina Black believed
that gossips were recruited from the women of what she called Class A
(those whose family income was inadequate but who did not earn themselves) and amongst whom were to be found the largest number of
neglected homes and children. 'A woman who is extremely poor and
whose furniture and appliances are reduced to a minimum has not enough
household work to occupy her time, while the fact of her poverty denies
her most of the means by which the better-off beguile the dangers of
vacant hours. It is from Class A, rather from Class B – in which wives do
earn – that the gossipers at doorways and the frequenters of public houses
are recruited.'[81] Beatrice Webb typically observed how if a woman 'be a
gossip and a bungler – worse still a drunkard – the family sink to the low
level of the East London street', while Lillian Beckwith, whose parents ran
a corner shop in the inter-war years, described how disparagingly her own
mother viewed such pastimes:

> 'Canting' was just talking or gossiping and was what, according to
> Mother, many of our neighbours did most of the day long. Wearing a
> clean apron to signify that household chores were finished, they liked
> to stand on their front doorsteps for hours on end, scrutinising and
> commenting on all the activities of the street.[82]

The verbal skills of working-class women

Despite Beckwith's disapproval, the form which this engagement with
street life took played a key role in developing the verbal skills which
working-class women used to help them survive their daily lives. This
proficiency ranged from deliberate silence to garrulousness and subtle
forms of linguistic mediation. One man, for example, described his mother
as 'a born diplomat' in the way she shrewdly dealt with the many tensions
and upsets of family and street life, while Joyce Storey's relationship with
her husband during the 1940s suggests the linguistic paucity and boorish
behaviour which characterized some men, particularly when they had to

accept a favour. Rather than being pleased at unexpectedly being invited to share a meal with their landlord and landlady, he 'got angry, childishly accusing' his wife of becoming lazy enough to expect other people to do her work. Despite subsequently getting stuck into the dinner provided, all he could manage by way of thanks was a grunt of satisfaction 'as he laid down his knife and fork', leaving the room 'with a curt, "See you tonight"'.[83]

Men did not have the same need for the complex verbal strategies which women were often forced to employ, as Stuart Macintyre indicated in his observations on domestic violence in Welsh and Scottish coalmining villages during the 1920s, where wife beaters typically justified their activities by claiming 'provocation', in the form of the woman's refusal to give over money or her offering offence with word or manner: 'Reported conversations point to an opaque language of personal relations in which the wife was often more articulate than the husband; but his ultimate recourse was to his physical strength.'[84] As David Graddol and Joan Swann have observed, 'in a context in which people routinely had recourse to physical violence, perhaps a dominant person could afford to be a man of few words'.[85] A woman, by contrast, had to develop other more elaborate skills, whose public expression Margaret Harkness touched on when she described the various verbal strategies women employed against male authority:

> if there is a sight on earth prone to move a man to wrath, it is an East End woman in the witness box. The female witness has not changed her character since the days of the famous Mrs Cluppins; she still enters into a dissertation on her domestic affairs, and informs the court about the decease of her late beloved, the illness of her last baby, and the wickedness of people in general. It is impossible to make her stick to business ...[86]

Such prevarication, so readily attributed to stupidity, more likely reflected both a desire to distract attention away from the matter in hand and a justification of activities by establishing a broader context in which to judge them. It was the approach of women who were well used to having to fend off masculine dominance at home with quick-wittedness rather than physical strength.[87] Of course, physical violence was not the main determinant of women's verbal skills, which have been observed in many social and cultural settings. In 1913, for example, Ada Nield Chew described a fictional conversation on the subject of a 'woman's sphere' between Mrs Stubbs, an extremely able and intelligent 'housewife', and her husband, who was a 'working' farmer on the Cheshire/North Staffordshire border.

> 'Tha makes me yed warch (ache), wench,' he said, 'wi thi "who says this" and "who says that". But it's allis like that wi wimmin. You

conna argue wi' em. They wun goo ramblin' aw o'er the show, astid
o' stickin to point.'

This countryman's grumbles about women who failed to give him the
quiet life he felt was his due are reflected in the proverbs and folk stories
of Irish peasant society, whose 'stock' characters are the scolding wife, the
shrewish wife, and the 'woman unruly as a hen'.[88]

Women's verbal skills – whether in argument, gossip or manipulation –
commonly feature in accounts of working-class life. Their proficiency was
tacitly recognized if frequently disparaged, and meant that women were
largely expected to mediate with the representatives of public life who
intruded into working-class neighbourhoods. 'If a stranger calls, he will
leave it to his wife to represent the family interests; and if there is any need
for diplomacy, the case will be safer in her hands. For she has the readier
tongue and quicker grasp of an advantage.'[89] 'Go getters' was the phrase a
Stockport man used to describe his mother and most of the women in the
district where he was brought up: 'they were the people that really
mattered, the women. Most of them was hard cases but still they were
doing the job that they were intended to do, you see ... None of them was
behind the door, they was always ready to get something if there was
anything going, you see, regarding charities and things like that.'[90]

Alexander Paterson characterized the calculating drama and subterfuge
with which many such women learnt to impose their frustration on the
outside world. As he disparagingly put it, by the time a working-class
woman was 35, 'frowsy and shapeless', 'She has begun to act a part to every
well-dressed person she meets, and to teach the children a policy of grab
and gratitude when in touch with philanthropy ... Her voice has grown
shrill, her patience declines, and she learns to whine and rage. Her arguments are a tissue of exaggeration and untruth; she accuses wildly and
defends herself volubly.'[91] Florence Bell also reproved the undue use which
working-class women in Middlesbrough made of what she describes as
their 'chief weapon', their tongues. 'It must be conceded that most of the
women have not the slightest idea of self-control, of not saying the thing
that comes into their head, either to their husbands or to one another, no
matter what it may be. And in moments of annoyance it is often something
which is very undesirable to say: the only hope is that it should not occur
to them to say it.'[92] Such judgments enabled women's resentment to be
presented as an hysterical aberration lacking real foundation, particularly as
the responses of largely male waged labourers to inadequate work conditions traditionally attracted more attention than women's domestic griev-
ances. Caricature more frequently substituted for analysis of the verbal
'characteristics' described here, which were rarely seen in terms of what
they actually represented: anger, worry, frustration and astute calculation.

Stereotyping of women's language: a hidden oral culture?

As was suggested earlier, great problems attend an historical examination of this oral culture, for while women's written words 'have some hope of retrieval' their 'spoken language is known to us chiefly through the written words of men whose comments are often based ... on stereotyping rather than observation or – more typically – on the pervasive view that women make no contributions to language'.[93] Harold Orton's *Introduction to the Survey of English Dialects*, for example, glossed over the linguistic contribution of women with the observation that 'men speak vernacular more frequently, more consistently and more genuinely than women'.[94] Edward Shorter indicates the difficulties of piecing together disparate comments on women's words in his book, *The Making of the Modern Family*. Shorter observes how a late nineteenth-century description of the veillée, or 'married women's solidarity group' in a Breton village was limited by the fact that the 'observer's resolute male chauvinism – which assumes that females just 'naturally' drift together to gossip maliciously – erases the detail'.[95] Women's own perceptions of themselves could be equally negative, as Mary Chamberlain observed of the Fen women whom she interviewed, who had

> little confidence in their skill at story-telling. They see this as the man's prerogative and are silent when their men are around, leaving the talking to the 'professionals'. Few people hear a woman's tale, remembering instead the old rustic character who entertained them so well around a pint, for pub going is not a woman's tradition. But gangs of women working on the land and mothers' stories to their children provide as great a creative field for story telling as the old boy in the pub.[96]

Occasionally one receives a glimpse of the creativity which could colour women's everyday conversation, as when Edith Hinson explained how her 'Mam invented some of the funniest words to describe things', the few she cites not unnaturally referring to food and aspects of her mother's domestic life.[97] There are similarly tantalizing instances of the 'traditional secrets' which circulated among women and to which Ladurie refers in *Montaillou*. Northamptonshire women were said to have a 'little publicised belief', 'whispered from mother to daughter', that the most virile men tended to have daughters. 'The father of a baby boy born in the 1950s was told that he had not *proved his manhood*. There was general approval for a *pigeon pair*, a boy and a girl. There would then be no need to *fill the house with boys, trying for a girl*.'[98] Virginia Woolf, writing about members of the Women's Co-operative Guild, certainly recognized the untapped creative force which resided in the language of some women:

How many words must lurk in those women's vocabularies that have faded from ours! How many scenes must lie dormant in their eye which are unseen by ours! What images and saws and proverbial sayings must still be current with them that have never reached the surface of print, and very likely they still keep the power which we have lost of making new ones.[99]

Yet the strength and vitality of these working-class women was seen in terms of a middle-class romanticism which obscured a more pragmatic use of speech, since just as important was the part which personal observation played in their everyday talk and gossip. Edward Shorter cites the disappointment of a French observer in the late nineteenth century, who was hoping to witness Breton women sharing some Celtic fables while coming together for a gossip during the veillée or 'married women's solidarity group'. The local women gathered together in the warmth of the stables during the winter months, where lighting made it impossible to sew and difficult to knit, and the Frenchman found to his dismay that their conversation had more to do with apparently inconsequential chatter than the romantic past. 'One should have liked to hear the stories of yesteryear, the old legends of a region rich in them. But the talk doesn't rise above scandal and chit-chat.'[100]

In reality, such disappointment effectively hid the real significance of gossip which lay in its observational function. It was this which could give its practitioners such influence, and helped contribute to women's intuitive reputation. Gossip also had a misrepresented yet undeniable recreational function which certainly deserves more detailed consideration than it usually receives given that working-class women usually had neither energy, money nor inclination for formal leisure activity, and the poorest frequently lacked both time and education to pursue reading as a form of relaxation. There was a tendency for women to read less than men in the late-Victorian and Edwardian periods and, indeed, some were actively discouraged from such activity. 'Very many' among the middle aged and elderly working-class of Edwardian Salford continued a 'veto' their own parents had laid down, forbidding all books and periodicals at home 'on the grounds that they kept women and children from their proper tasks and developed lazy habits'.[101] Florence Bell, writing of Middlesbrough in 1907, observed how the working-class women she visited read less than their husbands, which largely reflected their lack of defined leisure time, although there was also a higher number of women who lacked literacy. 'More than one would expect of the women between fifty and sixty cannot read: even some of those of forty.'[102] Flo Whitall was not unusual in admitting that it was a long time before she let her parents see her reading the Sunday paper. 'I was really cloaked – you know– kept like you mustn't get to know this. I learnt what I had to get to know outside. I never got to know anything at home.'[103] Observation of and comment on other people's behaviour consequently remained powerful precisely because of this relative lack of external influences. Gossip provided something of a creative outlet for women denied participation in the wider male world of status and recognized activity, yet also played a more complex part in their daily lives than concentration on its purely recreational aspect suggests. To get some sense of this broader significance we need to assess the context, characteristics and structure of gossip as it took place at the street door and in the casual encounters of everyday life.

Notes

1. A Welsh saying cited in Thiselton-Dyer 1905: 1990, 68
2. Murray 1901, 311.
3. While writers such as Dale Spender have highlighted the negative connotations of words which are associated with women, rather less attention has been paid to the historical context in which these changes occurred. Patricia Mayer Spacks's book, *Gossip*, certainly has an historical dimension, but is more largely concerned with gossip's literary manifestation in biographies, letters, novels and drama and consequently has an inevitable middle-class emphasis. Spacks 1985: 1986.
4. The French word 'commerage' or gossip, has similar roots in 'commater' or godparent. Kapferer 1987, 115.
5. J. Wright 1900, 690–91.
6. Williamson 1982, 141.
7. E.M. Wright 1913, 267.
8. Murray 1901, 311.
9. Another ballad, from the collection at Manchester Central Library also suggests childbirth's association with talk and chatter: 'And when your wife is with child, and ready to lie down, Then she will go a gossiping to every house in town'. Ballad, 'A Single Life's the Best', Manchester Central Library, BR, f821.04, Ba 1, Vol. 1, 19.
10. Pollock 1990, 53.
11. Donnison 1977: 1988, 3. Dr Johnson offered 'tippling companion' as one meaning of gossip in the mid-eighteenth century, Spacks 1985: 1986, 25–26.
12. Warner, 'Provocations: Marina Warner on Gossip', *The Independent Magazine*, 1 May 1993, 22–23.
13. John Fletcher (1579–1625), Rule a Wife and Have a Wife, iv, 1, cited in *The Century Dictionary* 1889: 1899, 2, 582.
14. Boyer 1700: 1971.
15. Twatler is given elsewhere in the dictionary as twattling housewife.
16. A.E. Baker, *Glossary of Northamptonshire Words and Phrases*, 1854, cited in Wright 1900, 691.
17. Johnson 1755. Spacks 1985: 1986, 26–27.
18. Spacks 1985: 1986, 26. Adrian Room suggests that Shakespeare has the first recorded use of the word as a verb, when in the *Comedy of Errors* (1590) the Duke says, 'With all my heart I'll gossip at this feast'. Room 1986, 129–30. *Oxford English Dictionary*.

For a twentieth-century version of this kind of 'social stereotyping' of women, see Oakley 1974, quoting from L. Tiger and R. Fox, *The Imperial Animal*, London, Secker and Warburg (1971), 200–01: 'Few would dispute that women excel at gossiping ... In the seemingly endless, and to male ears repetitive, chatter that goes on among women ... a massive and encyclopaedic confidence is built up in the gossipers ... gossip serves exactly the same grooming functions for the women as poker for the men.' The extract while disparaging, recognizes the importance of such talk in building women's self-esteem and mutually reinforcing their confidence.

19. Cf *Tea Drinking Wives*, Manchester Central Library Ballad Collection, q. BR, f821.04, Ba 1, Vol. 1, 1.
20. P.P. 1816, IV, 229, Rev. J. King, quoted in McCann, *Popular Education and Socialisation in the Nineteenth Century*, 1977:1979. Also B. Madoc-Jones, 'Patterns of attendance and their social significance: Mitcham National School, 1830–39', 63.
21. Murray 1901, 311.
22. Spacks 1985: 1986, 56.
23. Letter of William Mompesson, Rector of Eyam during the plague, to his children, following the death of his wife, 31 August 1666.
24. *Tea Drinking Wives*, Manchester Central Library Ballad Collection, q. BR, f821.04, Ba 1, Vol. 1, 1.
25. Hornsey 1824, 25.
26. Buchanan 1757: 1967.
27. Hazlitt MGMVII, 160.
28. Thiselton-Dyer 1905: 1990, 12, 164, 165, 169.
29. Ballad Collection, Manchester Central Reference Library, f398.8, B1, 71 (cited hereafter as *The Gossiping Wife*).
30. Ballad, *The Gossiping Wife*.
31. Glasgow Women's Studies Group 1983, 126.
32. Ballad Collection, Manchester Central Reference Library, q. 821.0432, Vol. 2, 156.
33. See, for example, references cited in Gelles 1989, 667, 679.
34. Spender 1986: 1987, 4, 76.
35. Spacks 1985: 1986, 263.
36. For example, mining, fishing, weaving, quarrying, and metal working districts.
37. Gillis 1985, 79, 122, 124, 159.
38. Chamberlain 1981, 64. This returns us, of course, to the supernatural powers attributed to the Andalusian 'alcahueta' or gossip mentioned in the Introduction.
39. Oakley 1974, 16. Her seventeenth-century reference is from C. Hole, *A Mirror of Witchcraft*, London, Chatto and Windus (1957), 30. Also see Demos 1982.
40. Spacks 1985: 1986, 39, 267.
41. Thiselton-Dyer 1905: 1990, 109–10.
42. Ballad, *The Gossiping Wife*.
43. Almirol 1981, 294.
44. Willughby 1863:1972, 79–80. Willughby, 1596–1685, gives a valuable insight into the practice of midwifery in the seventeenth century, although the fact that he was invariably called upon to deal with complications in labour gives him an unsympathetic view of midwives. His own views on the number of

people attending at childbirth are an interesting sidelight on the collective nature of the experience at this time. 'And, for the labouring woman's chamber, let it bee made dark, having a glimmering light, or candle light placed partly behind the woman, or on one side, and a moderate warming fire in it, and let it not bee filled with much company, or many women; five, or six women assisting will bee sufficient.' Willughby 1862:1972, 305.

45. See Wilson 1990.
46. Quoted by M. Roberts 1985, 154–55.
47. Dulumeau 1978. Kapferer 1987.
48. Thiselton-Dyer 1905: 1990, 68.
49. Public Record Office, INF 1/670, quoted in Yass 1983, 7–8.
50. Public Record Office, INF 1/265, quoted in Yass 1983, 22.
51. Yass 1983, 22–25. While work colleagues were also blamed for spreading 'alarmist stories', wives' 'tittle-tattle' featured strongly in letters contained in Home Office intelligence files.
52. Rowntree and Lavers 1951.
53. A system of 'indirect interviewing had been used, which consisted of "making the acquaintance" of an individual ... and developing the acquaintance until his or her confidence is gained and the information required can be obtained in ordinary conversation without the person concerned ever knowing that there has been an interview or that any specific information was being sought. Such a method is laborious but effective.' Rowntree and Lavers 1951, xii.
54. Rowntree and Lavers 1951, 64, 106.
55. Rowntree and Lavers 1951, 22. See also 3, 18.
56. Rowntree and Lavers 1951, 69, 94–95.
57. Rowntree and Lavers 1951, 36, 72.
58. *Daily Telegraph*, 3 March 1888.
59. *Spectator*, 15 September 1888, 1254–55.
60. Loane 1908, 80. Margaret Loane, 18?–1922, was born in Portsmouth, trained at Charing Cross Hospital, London, and worked as a nurse in both urban and rural England. For discussion on the validity of Loane's obervations about working-class life see Ross McKibbin, 'Class and Poverty in Edwardian England', in McKibbin 1990: 1991, 167–96. See also Patrick Joyce on 'the manifold strategies of popular speech' in Joyce 1991: 1994, 201.
61. Jackson 1968: 1972, 12–13.
62. Hoggart 1958: 1962.
63. Davies 1988, 50.
64. Spring-Rice 1939: 1981, 68.
65. Vicinus 1985, 22.
66. Loane 1910, 12–13.
67. Loane 1905, 107.
68. Loane 1907, 79.
69. W. Picht, *Toynbee Hall and the English Settlement Movement*, rev. edn, trans. Lilian A. Cowell, 1914, 131, cited in Vicinus 1985, 347.
70. Davidoff 1973:1986, 46. My thanks to Mike Rose for comments on Toynbee Hall.
71. Pember Reeves 1913: 1979, 16.
72. Pember Reeves 1913: 1979, 55.
73. Loane 1908, 65.
74. 'All in the Day's Work: Mrs Turpin', *The Englishwoman*, July 1912, reprinted in Chew 1982, 154.

75. Paterson 1911, 44-5.
76. White 1986, 141; Bourke 1994, 142, 234.
77. Chamberlain 1989, 20–21.
78. Greenwood 1967, 13.
79. Greenwood 1967, 34.
80. MSTC, Tape 803.
81. Black, 1915: 1983, 1–2. Black divided the mass of working-class married women into four groups: '(A) Those who, although the family income is inadequate, do not earn; (B) Those who, because the family income is inadequate – whether from lowness of pay, irregularity of work or failure in some way, such as sickness, idleness, drink or desertion on the part of the husband – do earn; (C) Those who, the family income being reasonably adequate, do not earn; (D) Those who, although the family income is adequate for the supply of necessities, yet earn.'
82. Booth 1892, I, 197; Beckwith 1982, 107. An Ordsall woman supplied a more scandalous definition of the word: 'not that people neighboured as such, they didn't go into one another's houses, in the vernacular, canting. You know what canting is? Gossiping, sitting and drinking tea and pulling one another to pieces in other words. There was very little of that went on, but if somebody was in trouble they helped one another out. MSTC, Tape 493.
83. Northampton interviews, Mr. Billingham. Storey 1990: 1992, 18–19.
84. Mardy (South Wales), Lumphinnans (West Fife) and in the Vale of Leven, Dumbartonshire. Macintyre 1980, 142. Deborah Gray White, in her book on female slaves in the Plantation South, describes how 'according to an Alabama woman, men often resorted to an antidote for verbal abuse called "hush water." It was "jes plain water what dey fixed so if you drink it you would be quiet an' patient. De mens would get it to give dey wives to make 'em hush up."' White 1985. Thanks to Lou Kushnick, Manchester University, for this source.
85. Graddol and Swann 1989, 74. Harding 1975, 292–93: 'To penetrate the privacy of their husbands, wives become skilled at asking them questions, tiny and discrete questions, about their actions and activities. ... Husbands come to think of their wives as verbally cunning and manipulative, and collectively men imagine that these are natural characteristics of women. But skills of verbal finesse and subterfuge are a function of, and an adaptation to, women's subordinate and dependent position with regard to control over resources.' Jacqueline Jones suggests that the family responsibilities of female slaves meant that they were less likely than men to run away and more likely to engage in 'verbal confrontations and striking the master.' Jones 1985. She highlights the wider importance of this verbal skill in describing how 'the institution of bondage in the American South was a unique form of capitalist exploitation that elicited from its female victims unique strategies of resistance. Slave women engaged in discreet acts of sabotage in the fields and in the Big House, and they honed their skills of verbal aggressiveness to a raw, biting edge.' Jones 1985, 323. Given the 'revered place' which 'sassy' women have in Afro-American culture, 'it was not surprising that many acquired a reputation for verbal aggressiveness in dealing with managers, union officials, and rank-and-file workers' in the 1940s and 1950s. Jones 1985, 251.
86. Law 1899, 180–82.
87. William Fishman has observed how 'wife-beating was common practice, an intrinsic part of the East End's unsavoury image'. Fishman 1988, 120–21.

Slang, for example, has traditionally been defined as a largely male preserve, although many women's communities seem to have generated their own vocabularies which have either been hidden from view or withheld from male observers. Leonore Davidoff, for example, has suggested how the balls and dances through which aristocratic young women were introduced into society engendered their own 'trade' language, so that 'a socially eligible young man was a "parti" (from bon-parti) while his opposite was a "detrimental", a "squash" was a function that young girls attended out of duty rather than for their own interest or amusement'. Davidoff 1973: 1986, 50; Kramerae and Treichler 1985, 56, 423.

88. Lees 1979, 146–47.
89. Paterson 1911.
90. MSTC, Tape 604.
91. Paterson 1911, 44–46, 211.
92. Bell 1907: 1985, 239.
93. Kramerae and Treichler 1985, 48.
94. Orton 1962.
95. Shorter 1975: 1977, 209–10, commenting on A. Carlier, *Un Village Breton en 1895*, Saint Pierre de Quiberon, 1949, 13.
96. Chamberlain 1975: 1977, 12.
97. Hinson 1984. Edith Hinson, the author, was born in Newbridge Lane, Stockport, in 1910. Care should be taken, of course, in generalizing from such examples. As John Widdowson observes, 'Fieldwork experience teaches us a necessary reluctance to state categorically that such forms are inventions or that they are confined to a specific family. All too often further investigation reveals that they are known and used elsewhere.' Widdowson 1976.

Nevertheless, Paule Marshall has described the richness which characterized the language of her mother and her friends in 1930s Brooklyn as they gathered after a gruelling day's work in the Marshall's basement kitchen and talked: 'a form of group therapy' that was also 'an outlet for the tremendous collective energy they possessed.' The warmth of human contact transformed them from day workers into poets, as their animated conversations ranged over the neighbourhood, out into the larger world of politics, and back to the sanctity of their own hearts. They excoriated employers who paid them with only a pitiable lunch – 'as if anybody can scrub floor on an egg and some cheese that don't have no taste to it!' – and they took pleasure in their own imaginative use of language, there 'in the wordshop of the kitchen.' Paule Marshall, 'From the Poets in the Kitchen,' *New York Times*, Book Review, January 9 1983, 3, 34–35, quoted in Jones 1985, 230.

98. Ladurie 1978: 1980, 196; Grimes 1991, 4.
99. Introductory Letter to Margaret Llewelyn Davies by Virginia Woolf, in Llewellyn Davies 1931: 1984, xxix.
100. Shorter, 1975: 1977, 209–10.
101. R. Roberts 1971: 1974, 166.
102. Bell 1907: 1985, 166–67. Out of 200 respondents, 17 women and 8 men were unable to read.
103. OLHG, FW. MSTC, Tapes 42, 36.

CHAPTER TWO

Talk at the street door: the gossip exchange in working-class neighbourhoods

> They talked of the weather; of the price of coals; of their husbands; their children; their sicknesses; their quarrels with contumacious neighbours and relations; of School Boards; of marriages and births and deaths that had lately happened or were on the tapis; of funerals; of clothes and boots; of the dearness of provisions; of Mrs Nemo's new bonnet; of Mr Nemo's profligacy; of the decadence of filial love and duty; of Heaven and Hell; of the fine dinners they had eaten; of murders, suicides, fires, divorces, breaches of promise, wife-beating; the stupidity of country folk – a favourite theme; and their own sharpness and intelligence.[1]

Gossip is an evanescent subject which defies the treatment applied to a history of wage rates, say, or housing conditions. It is as elusive as the terms neighbourhood and community with which it has a close connection. Yet the 'female solidarities' of street life are no less important than more conventional analyses of male forms of support and organization.[2] The neighbourhood had both social and spatial dimensions, the essence of neighbourliness being reciprocity, or an understanding of the need for give and take in ensuring survival. Gossip played a vital part in these daily exchanges, reinforcing the sense of belonging (and exclusion) which also contributed to a shifting sense of community. This appreciation of the mutuality implicit in neighbourliness was strongest among those in poorer working-class communities. By the end of the nineteenth century many such neighbourhoods had acquired an introspective character from which gossip derived much of its strength, its power largely deriving from the intimacy and self-enclosed nature of everyday life. Its importance was indicated by Eric Hobsbawm, who aptly described the limited social and geographical horizons of unskilled workers in nineteenth-century London, where 'all that lay beyond a tiny circle of personal acquaintances or walking distance was darkness'.[3] The London labour market was extremely fragmented, entry to it being highly dependent upon word of mouth, acquaintances and recommendation. Immigrant workers and the unskilled inevitably relied upon family and friends in getting to know about work opportunities, although these networks were by their very nature limited in social and geographic scope. As Hobsbawm suggests, both men and women depended on such communication systems, for women's possession of street life was not total, and varied from community to community. Casual work and chronic unemployment often ensured that men too could be found chatting ('loafing') at street corners or taking part in gambling activities. Men also had their own support networks, although as Jerry White has pointed out, these tended to be far more limited in scope than those devised by women.[4] They also gossiped in their pubs and clubs, in the street, at the barbers. Ted Furniss, who was a barber in Sheffield during the inter-war years, recalled how

> Gossip would spread in the street like wild fire, via the barber's shop, because they always used to tell me any scandal that was going on, whilst they were having their hair cut. I always tried to be diplomatic about these things and believed in the old theory that a still tongue makes a wise head. Anyway, it saved me many a thick ear that I would have got through opening my mouth.[5]

Furniss's stress on the need for professional reticence in dealing with the scandalous preoccupations of his male customers is a useful counter to the popular stereotype of the female gossipmonger.[6] Yet although significant in its own context, such male gossip did not have the same formative effect upon local mores, since it was directed out of the neighbourhood, channelled into paid work and more organized leisure pursuits and thus dissipated. In the broader flow of talk and information which was essential to the effective functioning of neighbourhood life, male gossip was largely marginal.

The role of older women

The nature of women's lives made gossip much more apparent in their activities than men's, and the sexual segregation which came to characterize substantial parts of men's and women's experience helped reinforce gossip's largely female profile. The bonds of family life and kinship became powerful forces for stability and conservatism in these working-class communities, and the inhabitants were united by strong expectations of public behaviour and individual responsibility. Older women acquired an important voice in the maintenance of social and moral sanctions, and writers such as Carl Chinn have dwelt on the role which a 'hidden matriarchy' played among the urban poor, usefully chronicling the ways in which women manifested their authority.[7] This matriarchal focus had complex origins and its significance was ambivalent. The formal tie of marriage became more accepted by women from the mid-nineteenth century, partly because of the legal security and attendant (if tenuous) hold it gave them over their husbands.[8] At the same time, the industrial and economic pressures that increasingly forced men into the role of principal breadwinner also increased the dependency of many working-class women as 'wives and mothers' because of their reduced access to the kind of jobs which paid enough to give them an independent livelihood. The influence of the evangelical movement, missions, social workers and school boards all encouraged the tendency for sexual relationships to become more conformist in nature, thereby ensuring that questions of 'family morality' became a lively issue for local gossip: illegitimacy which had once found tacit acceptance was now severely censured, while chastity became an essential element in aspirations to higher social status.[9] Despite distinct regional differences in the degree of segregation which developed between the sexes, men and women tended to develop clear cultural spheres as a result of such trends. Where men worked away from home and were largely divorced from the domestic scene, women's voices necessarily acquired a social and moral authority within working-class neighbourhoods, and in becoming more visible women inevitably attracted greater opprobrium from outsiders, who tended to judge them from both the class and sexual standpoint which was described in the previous chapter.

Depictions of powerful and frequently meddlesome older women often occur in representations of working-class life, and are testimony to the commanding presence which older women often had in long-established, introspective neighbourhoods. Indeed, the conventional stereotype of the gossipmonger was that of the older working-class woman epitomized by such caricatures as Florrie in the Andy Capp cartoon strip and Ena Sharples of Coronation Street.[10] Evelyn Haythorne typically portrays just such a character in her book *In Our Backs*, which although fictional, is based on life in a Yorkshire pit village. Despite being set in the early 1950s, her depiction of 'old Ma Barrowcliffe' nevertheless has echoes of the pre-war years. Partial to her drink, she was generally known as a 'right old tartar', and had a house conveniently situated at the end of the 'backs', where she regularly took up position on the dustbin outside next to the gennel.[11] This gave her a good view of the comings and goings and was an ideal spot from which to 'stir up trouble'.

> No-one came or went without ma's observation and no-one got by Ma until she had her gossip. Most were ready to talk, the walls were paper thin, so they'd be daft not to, but a lot genuinely wished to share their troubles and worries. Others just passed the time of day but few willingly crossed her, for she had a great knowledge of what went off in the backs. Usually, though, she didn't spread and one could trust Ma. If you were genuine you were all right, but she 'adn't time for petty illnesses or for nit picking, though she had a great sympathy for real heartaches.[12]

It is important to distinguish the character (and caricature) of the gossip from the actual process involved in such communications. An interviewee, for example, made a useful distinction between 'chit-chat', which she thought was generally good and friendly, and 'tittle-tattle', which was more likely to be malicious and was often identified with groups of elderly women who had time on their hands, 'old tabby cats' who generally 'had a field day' whenever a respectable family was disgraced in some way.[13] This particular stereotype was not, of course, confined to a working-class setting, and in some respects the gossip which took place in a middle-class milieu had a particular capacity for malice given its frequently pronounced social role and the restrictive effects of religious conformity and morality. (Such attitudes were classically portrayed in the portrait of the narrow backbiting Welsh chapel-going community, Llaregyb, in Dylan Thomas's *Under Milk Wood*.)

As Brian Jackson observed, older people tended to be most influential in groups and communities whose tradition and lore were oral, and where gossip consequently played a strong, cohesive role. Loane observed of Edwardian London that while the 'upper grade' of her patients had an 'almost dangerously strong faith' in anything they had seen in print, this was far from being the case among 'the more ignorant' whom she felt preferred 'even the vaguest hearsay or tradition'.[14] Robert Roberts similarly recorded the part which such talk played in Edwardian Salford, where,

> In home, street group, pub and trades club, people, using a much smaller vocabulary, conversed more in groups than they do today. Opinion in this narrow, integrated society still continued to be created and moulded far more by word of mouth than by any other medium. Here was the true oral tradition.[15]

Similar factors still played a part in the street gossip of Hoggart's inter-war youth in Hunslet, Leeds, where the working-class people with whom he was familiar still 'drew in speech and in the assumptions to which speech is a guide on oral and local tradition'. It is perhaps significant that the instances of such language which he cited were all drawn from women's talk. He picked up snippets of conversation, for example, from 'a few shops where housewives meet in the morning', and described the 'drab and untidy' mothers in the waiting room of a children's clinic, whose 'conversation dribbled on aimlessly but easily about their (children's) habits'.[16] Hoggart alluded to the slow pace of change in his former Hunslet community, commenting that people there were not troubled by inconsistencies but frequently managed to hold contrary opinions, believing and not believing in almost the same breath, repeating 'the old tags and practising their sanctions and permissions'.[17] Nevertheless, despite its limitations, the strength of the oral tradition to which both Roberts and Hoggart testify was vital nourishment to the authority which women (particularly older women) exerted at street level. Such women's involvement with their children meant the age cycle they experienced differed significantly from that of male counterparts, young women with babies and toddlers being particularly vulnerable and entrapped, as Pember Reeves and Florence Bell indicated. (The women visited during Pember Reeves's survey had either just had, or were about to have, a baby.) However, women in their late thirties and middle years, who had working children contributing to the family income were in a particular position to exert power over their neighbourhoods. The greater freedom some women had to socialize during this period of their lives is suggested by the Mass Observation survey of pub drinkers in *The Pub and the People* which found that 60 per cent of women drinkers were aged between 41 and 55 (the comparable figure for male drinkers was 47.8 per cent).[18] Carl Chinn made the similar observation that 'Those women in whom drinking in a beer house was seen as acceptable behaviour were normally older, married women, although an occasional younger wife might join them.'[19] The qualified dominance of such women was dissipated again as they entered old age and frequently sank once more into dependency, although the authority they exerted over their children was often maintained for a substantial period. Such women, who were frequently a conservative and restraining influence upon community behaviour, played a crucial part in the gossip network. Robert Roberts described the 'purselipped and censorious' matriarchs who acted as a 'public tribunal' in matters of status and respectability, making 'grim re-adjustments on the social ladder' whenever a local family fell from grace in some way.[20] Ada Nield Chew, in her sketch 'Assault and Battery', described a husband beating up his wife on a Saturday night in a Lancashire town. Hearing the angry criticisms which the woman hurled at her husband an elderly woman 'with a deeply lined face' declares:

> Hoo (she) goes too far, ... hoo ought to know as no chap'll stand what hoo says, an' it's every day allike. Hoo's nagin' at him mornin', noon an' neet. It'll not do. Yo hev to keep what you think on 'em to yersel. If hoo doesn't remember that, hoo'll hev to suffer for it one of these days.

Her comments epitomize the attitude of an older generation of Edwardian women who were used to putting up with and evading the brutality of their husbands, and illustrate the kind of conservative judgments which their conversations could promote.[21]

Geographical stability was one of the keys to the influence which such women exerted, for just as the physical landscape frequently had a symbolic meaning to families who had lived in it and placed their mark on it over several generations, so long residence in a street gave power based on largely unarticulated knowledge to the older women who lived there.

Entry into some of these secrets was the sign of a young woman's acceptance and maturity. Celia Dixon, for example, who grew up on a 'respectable' street in inter-war Northampton, described the family of a comfortably off station master, who were 'fervent Baptists'. They had a niece living with them, 'a middle-aged spinster, who wore dowdy clothes, no make-up or hair-do'. Although she had a job and worked hard for the chapel, she was treated as a drudge by her relatives, which was a source of great puzzlement to Celia, until told some years later by her own aunt that the niece was illegitimate, only taken in out of 'charity'.[22] As Flo Whitall observed of her Salford childhood, 'We was shushed all the time', while John Billingham typically remarked of his failure to get to the bottom of certain family scandals during his childhood that 'Young people ... you were seen and not heard, you didn't ask questions, so therefore you didn't get involved.' ''Cause Uncle Ted, Aunt Ena's husband, I don't think they were ever married ... I'm not a hundred per cent sure, I'm only slightly sure, but, you know, I've listened to 'em talking, I wouldn't ask questions but I've listened and sometimes I've thought, I don't know, I don't think they were married.'[23] Children in a Northumberland pit village who trespassed into adult space by trying to listen in to adult conversations were commonly dismissed with a 'get away and divvent cock your lugs here.'[24] Tom Wakefield, lingering in the local shop to hear about a recent sexual scandal, characteristically found his delaying tactics were to no avail, '"Shush, shush, sh, sh," one of the older women indicated that two children were present, me and another boy.' They were both served next, and Wakefield was denied any further gossip, despite fumbling with the door latch in the hopes of hearing more.[25] Such images testify to the strategies which children often employed to satisfy their curiosity, for shushing did not stop them from listening.[26] Henry Foulds, for example, used to love listening to his talkative aunts. 'I had big ears when I was a kid, as they used to say. They used to send me out when they were talking scandal, of course, but other times, when they were talking about the past, I enjoyed it then.'[27] Indeed, children could be very devious in listening to adult conversation. One woman as a small child, for example, was never told what had happened to her mother, who died suddenly. She consequently used to sit under the table at night, hidden by a long chenille cloth listening to her aunts 'because otherwise you got told to get out, you weren't allowed to listen or read papers'.

> I used to sit under there, listening, trying to get to know about my mother, you see. I must have been a little crafty girl. And I used to hear them saying that Edith had died, and it's very sad, she was only twenty nine, and all this, and we'll have to see about Elsie going to school, she's never been to school really, and – I was piecing things ... [28]

Well-swathed tables seem to have been popular listening posts for curious children. A table provided a similar hideaway for Walter Greenwood as he eavesdropped on 'biographical scraps' about his father's younger days whenever neighbours called on his mother for a chat.[29]

As a young adolescent, Kathleen Dayus, like many other young people, 'was reduced to listening to gossip' in an attempt to learn more about the facts of life, an experience which, on the whole, left her none the wiser. Nevertheless, girls learnt and applied the rules of linguistic engagement from an early age.[30] The very fact of their spending more time than boys at home with their mothers, listening to the talk which went on there, imbued them with the street conventions which bound their particular locality, while adults were not averse to drawing children into their intrigues. Dayus, for example, cites several occasions when she was used by local women either as a medium to pass on local news, or was pumped for specific information about something.[31] Children, of course, had a secret life of their own in which gossip also played an important part.[32]

Some neighbourhood skeletons retained their mystery, simply alluded to when someone's behaviour had to be brought back into line. The only daughter of another Northampton family, whose father had 'a good shoe factory job', was 'seemingly conformist in every way', yet got pregnant after 'two-timing' her fiancé. A rather sanctimonious neighbour

> stopped Auntie Loue, and started gossiping on about how disgraceful and disgusting — was, and how ashamed her poor parents must feel, considering the way they had spoiled her. Auntie Loue told me afterwards, 'I looked her straight in the eye and said, "She is not the first by any means, and it doesn't do for some people to throw stones". She knew what I meant, and never said another word!' I asked her why, and she said, 'I knew Nellie W. when we were young, and she knew what I meant, and I am saying no more', (and she didn't!!).[33]

As such examples suggest, this communication network was often quite subtle in its functioning. Another respondent, describing what life was like in Hulme, Manchester, during the inter-war years, referred to a woman whom she characterized as 'the boss of the street', due to the way people were influenced by her opinion. This 'street boss' was a widow in her sixties who also ran a money club for her neighbours. (This was a collective savings club, whereby members paid a shilling a week over 20 weeks towards a £1 share, which was allocated in turn to the members on the basis of names drawn out of a hat.) Although this woman was influential in her community, she was not known as a gossip, despite the fact that her judgments were evidently based to some extent on the opinions voiced through the street grapevine.

Q. Was she what you'd call a gossip?

Er, ... no, no, I wouldn't say particularly, no, no. Some of the others were.

Q. What was the difference between the people that were gossips, and somebody like her, who wasn't?

Well, sometimes, if a person's name was mentioned, other people would batten on to it, like, say, 'Ooh, do you remember when she did so-and-so?', or the like. Whereas her ...

Q. But she didn't do that?

No, no. Mind you, she didn't tell them to stop. (laughing)

Q. She just took it all in?

Yes, that's right.[34]

There was, as this observation indicates, a certain 'art' to gossiping which was well described by one of Edwin Almirol's respondents from among the Filipino community of California. She explained that 'gossip is like a butterfly; if you chase it, the more it will fly away from you, if you sit still, it will land on your shoulders'.[35] Once the landmarks and characters of the gossip landscape were well established, talk could be carried on in a kind of verbal 'short-hand', nods, winks and innuendo taking the place of more precisely detailed language. 'Supporting or elaborating' statements play an important part in smoothing the exchange of gossip.[36] Proverbial tradition appreciated the nature of this communication, which was aptly summed up in the Cheshire saying that '"Well, Well" is a word of malice'.[37] M. Jean Sant conveys, if in rather a clichéd fashion, something of the shorthand flavour of gossip in her book *To Be Continued*. 'As we turned into Fitzwarren Street we nearly bumped into a woman.

> Ey up, it's our Fran. "'Ave you been up to our 'ouse then?" "Hello Mam, hello chuck. Yes, Margaret said you was at our Florrie's. I saw our Florrie at the Royal last night". "Oh aye," said Gran. "Did you hear about Beattie Matthews?" Without waiting for an answer, she continued, "I'm not surprised at all. I told Florrie all that family's a load of tripe-hounds". "It's the way they've been brought up, Mam. Well I'm off now, it's getting a bit nippy. See you at weekend. Tarra".'[38]

This coded ambiguity, often reliant on tone and gesture which were perfectly understandable to practitioners, helped protect against unwelcome eavesdropping and the unguarded curiosity of young offspring. An Ordsall woman, for example, recalled the illness of her next-door neighbour's child when she herself was young, 'but there was never much said about her, and I found out later she died of cancer, and you didn't speak of cancer, it was always "she's not very well", you know, and that could have meant anything'.[39] The butterfly analogy also usefully captures other more sensitive aspects of gossip. Too vigorous an interest in other people's activities and behaviour was often suspect, so that those women who pursued their enthusiasm by asking too many direct questions were likely to be branded 'nosy parkers', and receive rather careful treatment. Walter Greenwood described one of the more unpopular neighbours from his childhood, Mrs Flarty, who 'was disliked by the neighbours because of her habit of backbiting. She was dumpy, swarthy, wore a man's cap and, with sweeping-brush in hand, was perpetually appearing on her doorstep on the look-out for somebody with whom to discuss other people's affairs. The objects of her malice were referred to not by name but by the number of their house: '... her at fifty-seven', '... them at ninety-six'.[40] Joan Green, from Ashton-under-Lyne, had comparable memories of a very fussy, houseproud woman nicknamed 'Titty Bick' by her neighbours, who was childless and didn't go out to work. 'Titty Bick' was known for always being on the doorstep at dinnertime, when she would 'collar' anyone who happened to be walking by.

> ... she always seemed to know everything that was going on. She always seemed to be on the doorstep, no matter when you passed. So she, if she had found out anything from you, she'd pass it on, or if she'd found out anything, she'd tell you and you'd say, ohh, I'll have to go now, I'm going to be late for work ... You couldn't avoid her, she was really, always seemed to be there ... If you weren't working, or if I wasn't at school, she'd, anybody passing, 'Aren't you working?' Which she'd know you weren't, because you weren't there! You weren't at work. Or aren't you at school. And you had to tell her! It was really funny.[41]

Most streets had such individuals whose inquisitiveness, although suspect, was tolerated for a variety of reasons, not least because the information they passed had its uses. The nickname of a well-known gossip from Mrs West's childhood, which was 'News of the World', well summed up the function she performed in her small street community. She, too, was renowned for hardly ever being in her house.

> I think she was always on the doorstep, I don't think she ever went in!
> ... And if she wanted to know anything, she was that sort of person,
> 'd go straight up, and she wouldn't be happy until she'd found out
> what it was, you see.

Mrs West, like Joan Green, found it a similar trial whenever she had to pass the nosy woman's door.

> I used to say to our mother, 'Ooh, I'm got to pass Mrs Chew, ['News of the World'], she's on the step, and she'd never let you go by, unless you stopped to talk to her, you see. And I used to think, well, I'm got to be quick now, I've got to get down home. You see, that's how she used to get to know the news, she'd ask you different things.

Her neighbours were careful not to get too close to Mrs Chew, since she was known for 'calling' people. She was hardly the sort of woman whom they would trust with their troubles, 'you'd never go and borrow a cup of sugar from her, or anything, no-one 'd never go to her for such things as that, you see. She was a different type of person, she was a nosy person, and that was it'. Her weaknesses were known and accepted for what they were, and Mrs West's mother, while being careful what she passed on to Mrs Chew, never told her to go away. Hearing that Mrs Chew had dropped by to call when she was out, she'd ponder, 'Now I wonder what she's coming up to tell me now!' (laughing). Knowledge, after all, was power, and Mrs West's mother was herself not without influence on the street, where she was known for helping out her neighbours when they were in trouble. It was as well to stay in with Mrs Chew, since after all, 'If you wanted to know anything, she'd know it all!'[42]

Gossip and women's leisure

In some respects, gossip reflected the seamless quality of many working-class women's lives, since there was often no clear demarcation between the multitude of monotonous tasks which had to be completed every day. An observer of women homeworkers in Manchester remarked how the constant interruptions of domestic life made waged work at home even more difficult. One woman had become so exasperated at continually having to lay down her work to see to the baby or some domestic task that she had given up such employment to enter a shirt-making factory. Single-mindedness over any activity was often well nigh impossible under such circumstances. As two of these Manchester homeworkers pointed out, they were apt to count gossip at the door with their neighbours as part of the time spent in finishing the work they had brought home.[43] Tom Wakefield's mother typically 'liked to have her hands busy', whether making a rag rug or knitting, and guilt or unease at having any time 'free' of household activities frequently led to even spare moments of sitting down being devoted to darning, knitting or repairing clothing, although making do and mending after the husband had gone to bed could also serve other useful purposes, as Aida Hayhoe recalled:

> See, I had three children. And I didn't want no more. My mother had fourteen children and I didn't want that. So if I stayed up mending, my husband would be asleep when I come to bed. That were simple, weren't it?[44]

Recreation or relaxation were, in fact, incidental to the main task of merely getting through another day. As a woman wrote in Margaret Llewelyn Davies's collection of letters from working women:

I often say we work twenty out of twenty four hours very often. Some
days I don't sit down hardly to snatch a mouthful of food. There
seems no time for women, but the men make time.[45]

In contrast to men who had clearly defined times for recreation and the
space to develop their own interests, women's leisure time was infinitely
more amorphous. Florence Bell remarked of the working-class women she
encountered in Middlesbrough that nearly all seemed to have a feeling that
it was wrong to sit down with a book, given the multitude of practical
tasks which inevitably pressed upon them. Reading was an individualistic
activity which cut the reader off from other family members, while chores
like sewing gave women the opportunity of a relaxing chat yet also indicated that they were readily available to the rest of the family. The women
who never read during their leisure usually gossiped, standing at their
street door to talk in preference to either sitting down or taking a walk in
the fresh air. (Bill Williamson's grandmother rarely took a walk with her
husband, on the grounds that the fresh air made her 'intoxicated'.)[46]
Rather than preaching the value of open air exercise, Bell felt it was too
easy to advocate the elimination of such standing and talking from the
lives of such women.

> There are times when it is almost essential to unburden the soul and
> compare experiences with some one else, and many of us may entirely
> sympathise with the woman who, at such a moment, stands at her
> street door, looking up and down the street, commanding a view of
> any possible incident of interest, and ready to catch the eye and ear of
> an acquaintance'.[47]

A familiar yet equivocal stereotype of working-class behaviour, particularly women's, was that of passivity, especially with regard to the numerous occasions on which they were required to wait or queue for attention
from professionals. Again, these generalized perceptions belie the positive
part which talk played in such situations.[48] Gossip was a means of drawing
women out of an unsatisfactory predicament, with its concentration less on
personal feelings than on what others were doing. As such, it could have,
as we will see in the next chapter, an almost addictive quality, giving a
sense of belonging, security and friendship. Ron Barnes's mother, who
moved from an impoverished East End flat to the 'affluence and respectability' of Clapton, desperately missed the neighbourliness of her old haunts,

> her little chats with the women when she was on her way to market
> of a morning. The journey there and back had always consisted of a
> series of short stops, as she exchanged interesting words of news, plus
> the latest local scandals.[49]

The sense of loss was so strong that she was back in her flat within six
weeks.

Nella Last, who painstakingly kept a diary for the Mass Observation survey, was by no means as poor as the women to whom Bell refers, but well described the cathartic effect of some kinds of gossip when an acquaintance dropped by for a cup of tea. 'We had it by the fire, and had a real good talk – one of those "soul satisfying" kinds of gossip about nothing very particular.'[50] One of the working-class women interviewed in Rowntree and Laver's leisure survey pinpointed the same need which many women felt for such disclosure. Described as 'extremely talkative', Mrs D. said that men didn't understand that women needed a good gossip. They are 'shut up all day in four walls and of course they enjoy a few words with a neighbour same as men do in a pub'.[51] Other more public venues for gossip offered a similar opportunity to pour out personal frustrations in a context which frequently allowed them to be temporarily diffused through laughter. Mary Turner, for example, described the atmosphere of a wash-house in Levenshulme, Manchester, where the same women had turned up on a regular basis over many years. The relationship with these weekly friends was supportive but undemanding as many had moved away from the area and only returned to do their laundry while others were in paid work outside the home during the day.

> The woman or women you spoke to could do nothing to remedy your troubles but you would certainly feel better about it. Some women had long standing problems and would do a bit of a performance every week, but they and their listeners got used to it and it would often end up laughing ... Friends wouldn't avoid you if they thought you were going to go on about it because it provided a certain amount of entertainment for which they had no responsibility.[52]

Many working-class writers and speakers, when recalling the past, describe the damp, miserable atmosphere of Monday washing day when everyone but hardworking 'mam' contrived to be out of the house if at all possible. 'Pubs and clubs were packed to the doors on Mondays by men escaping the chaos in the house.'[53] However, as Mary Turner's comments suggest, the arrival of the municipal wash-house, revolutionized the solitary drudgery of wash day for many women. In the 1930s, for example, the municipal wash-house at Harpurhey Baths was the venue for a 'regular community get-together' for some women. 'You could soon become the "talk of the wash-house" if you weren't careful.'[54] Nevertheless, despite the need for caution, drying time in the 'steamie' (as it was known in Glasgow) provided an ideal opportunity for a 'clash' (gossip) with friends and neighbours.

> At first I went to my mother's to do my washing, but then I heard women talking about the steamie and all the jokin' and gossip that went on. 'Nellie,' says I to myself, 'you're missin' a lot of fun, no' goin' to the steamie.'[55]

Structured context of gossip

Occasions for collective forms of both domestic work and relaxation provided a useful structure for the circulation of gossip. The flurry of activity which marked the start of the week's domestic routines, for example, was marked by numerous excuses for an exchange of talk, as Joyce Storey observed in describing life on a street in working-class Bristol during the 1940s.

> Monday was a real old gossip day. With so many women wielding a brush or going great guns with a polishing duster, they could pass the time of day to the neighbour over the way, or with the metal polish tins still in their hands, they would linger in little knots to discuss any recent happening in the street. Net curtains twitched as their owners peeped to see who was talking to who, and the whole street became like an Indian settlement, with gossip like smoke signals drifting in all directions.[56]

Although gossip was frequently squeezed into the nooks and crannies of a woman's daily life, to imply it was quite formless would be misleading. The disapproval of Beckwith's mother for her 'canting' neighbours, for example, failed to appreciate the extent to which the time for talk in such communities was defined, for the women's symbolic assertion of respectability in wearing a clean apron as they chatted from their doorstep was symptomatic of the structured context in which gossip frequently took place. Don Haworth, for example, described how the contents of the night's chamber pots were carried to the ash tip each morning, and that it was the custom 'to pretend not to notice anyone engaged on this errand. Two women who plonked their buckets down and stopped for a conversation were felt to be unsuited to the neighbourhood.' Similarly, women who were racing around to get the morning's shopping done before dinner had no time for diversions en route.

> It was not done to stop and talk in the street. Accosted by old people who had lost sense of time, women would say they were 'pushing'. Of any housewife who did stop it was said that she 'would talk all day'. It was nearly as bad as being 'not too particular', and indeed possibly evidence of it.[57]

'Wives who sat overlong at their thresholds enjoying the passing show' in Edwardian Salford 'contravened established rule and were roundly condemned: "Why don't the idle bitches go inside and get summat done!"'.[58] Such conventions signified a great deal, since while gossiping at the door could give the suggestion of a half completed household task, sitting down to talk had altogether different connotations, an aspect lampooned by the comedian Al Read whose dramatic monologues as a nosy and garrulous housewife were punctuated by the phrase, 'I won't take me coat off, I'm not stopping ...' This caricature was itself well established in 'proverbial lore', which recognized the strategy being employed by those who lingered long under the guise of only resting a moment, as expressed in the Dorset proverb, 'Standing gossips stay the longest'.[59] Gossip took place in many informal settings, whether at the front door or over the garden fence, at street corners or between neighbours sitting on the doorstep passing comment on strangers and others who walked by. Yet its open-ended reputation further belied the extent to which the time allocated to it often had very clear limits; the busy women who did not have time to chat in the street while they were on their way to do the morning's shopping, for instance, were often forced to slow down once they had reached their destination. Jim Hooley recalled the leisurely pace of the local grocer's in Hillgate, Stockport, which had chairs 'where the women could sit down and have a gossip'.[60] The fact that little or nothing was packaged often meant a long wait while purchases were weighed out. Customers took their time, ordering each item separately and waiting until 'the assistant had brought it back and bagged it up before beginning to consider the next. They used the intervals to hold conversations or start badinage which might spark along the line of assistants and backfire through the customers.'[61] Even shop talk had its conventions. Richard Heaton, who opened an off-licence and grocery concern in a poor area near the Salford docks in the late 1940s, found that being prepared to have a 'natter' with customers instead of rushing them out of the shop was a very useful way of building up business. Sundays were different, however, because of the brisk trade in 'oddments' like beer and slices of ham. 'There was no nattering on Sunday; the customers understood.'[62] By contrast, Sunday in the off-licence which Tom Wakefield frequented in the 1940s was 'not a day for being hasty, and the people in the shop waited. Some sat on small empty wooden barrels, others perched their behinds on upturned empty crates. People talked, it was a cheerful noisy place.'[63]

Women often took care that such talk should not spill over into their husband's time. As one Ordsall woman explained, it generally took place 'in the day: when the men came home – you stayed in your own home then'.[64] Such awareness of the distinction between men's time and women's time was particularly acute in areas where women were subject to an especially dominant form of male authority, in single, heavy industry communities where there was little opportunity of female employment outside the home, for example, as was the case in the post-war coal-mining town of 'Ashton' in Yorkshire. The expectations of a woman's domestic role were strictly defined in such districts, her household jobs being part of a 'contract' which had to be fulfilled while her husband was out of the house. Indeed, these chores were not supposed to intrude upon a husband's enjoyment of his home, and the woman's ability to complete them by the time of his return from work was 'very commonly under discussion'.[65] Given that she was expected to be fully occupied during this period, one can see how 'gossip' with the neighbours could be readily condemned by husbands as an infringement of the domestic covenant. Nevertheless, despite the expectation of constant labour within the home, women in 'Ashton' still awarded themselves time to gather in groups of three or four over cups of tea, where there was (in the stereotyped judgment of one writer) 'endless gossip about other neighbours, about their own husbands and children, about the past'.[66] For while working-class women were defined by a domestic role, their own perceptions of such work did not necessarily embody the values which outsiders assumed. A Manchester woman, for example, recalled how some women always hurried to put on an apron when their husbands were about to return from work. However, as she cryptically observed, that didn't necessarily mean that they'd been attending to their housework all day. The apron's symbolic quality was an effective screen for whatever they had (or had not) been doing during that time.[67]

The characteristics of gossip varied according to the structure of the groups which perpetuated it, and there was an important qualitative difference between gossip which took place on a fairly intimate basis among close friends or relatives, and the more superficial 'grazing' form of conversation which occurred between individuals passing the time of day with each other. There were important degrees of intimacy in gossip, and the tension-relieving exchanges which Nella Last so appreciated were very different from the 'effortless sociability' of the casual street encounters which Josephine Klein described. Women could place great value on gossip with a confidante, as Leo Kuper noted of the housebound women of Braydon Road, a post-war housing development on the outskirts of Coventry. It was an antidote to 'nerves', which tended to afflict the disempowered women of these estates; 'Everybody needs somebody they can tell their troubles to sometimes.'[68]

Gossip and local women's groups

The conversation which took place on the street, in local shops, at the wash-house and in the back yard had a fluid, organic quality whose content was constantly sifted, replenished and sometimes embellished. These casual daily contacts were a natural feature of 'traditional' working-class neighbourhoods, and had the ease of well-established familiarity. A Lancaster man observed that, 'Some person would be passing, and someone would be at the door and stop to have a chat, then somebody else would come along and then perhaps three or four would accumulate.'[69] As

Carl Chinn describes, 'One wife would join and another would leave shortly afterwards, so that the actual time any individual woman might spend as part of the group could be short.'[70] In contrast to the loose affiliations of this kind of talk was the conversation which took place in more structured groups of women, particularly those drawn together because of ostensible links with a local church or chapel. The supportive features which contemporary socio-linguistics have sometimes discerned in all-female speech were not always apparent in the talk which went on in some of these groups; members sometimes used a group's status to reinforce their own standing and exclude the socially undesirable. The Young Wives' Club which was attached to a church in St Ebbe's, Oxford, was described as having a social rather than religious or intellectual function, the women coming together to listen to a visiting speaker and more importantly to engage in friendly informal talk.

> All feel themselves to be better than the ordinary run of wives in St. Ebbe's, and contact with the church is an important reinforcement of this point of view because the vicar tends to support this attitude. The most important use of the club is to judge the quality of local gossip. One woman who moved out of St. Ebbe's but kept up her membership said she now felt out of things for she has first to collect the items of gossip that everybody in the group takes for granted in the discussion. The club is not primarily a place to exchange gossip, but a centre where it can be judged against a set of standards which the members feel to be superior to those of the neighbourhood.[71]

Geoffrey Gorer's survey of 'English character' conducted in conjunction with the *People* newspaper in the early 1950s found that the most 'assiduous' visitors to church or chapel meeting rooms were women ('in most cases poor, often unmarried, either young or old rather than middle-aged'), and that they were 'particularly censorious about the moral faults and failings of their neighbours'.[72] Members of the Women's Bright Hour Circle, for example, which was connected to a Northampton chapel, were described as 'backbiting old hypocrites, who spend all their time pulling other people to pieces'.[73] Reservations about the kind of talk which went on in the Catholic Women's Guild similarly stopped Maria Goddard's mother from joining.

> I think she tried it and didn't like it. I think she thought they were a lot of gossips! (chuckling). I think she thought they were too many do-gooders, too good Catholics, very good Catholics. Licking the pictures off the wall! (laughing).[74]

Guild members tended to have a little more money, more time and fewer family commitments than other women, and 'were a bit like social workers in a way, telling people how to run their lives as Catholics'. Some of them were 'a law unto themselves', and used to go visiting parishioners, often uninvited. Maria Goddard's mother's views on their activities were uncompromising: 'She thought they wanted to come into your house and find out all your business, and then go and gossip about it.' Similar feelings of social superiority seem to have coloured the attitudes of the 'poor, ill-educated women' to whom Gorer referred. They tended to describe themselves as middle class because their church- or chapel-going gave them higher status, and, insulated by the exclusiveness of their group membership, tended to have few complaints about neighbourly inquisitiveness.

The introspective dynamics of these more exclusive groups, where frustration at lack of status and power easily generated destructive comments about other people's behaviour, was well described by Barbara Holman, another of Mary Chamberlain's Fenland respondents who drew on the changes which had taken place in post-war Gislea. She was a village outsider, both in terms of birth and the fact that her husband had left her. On the few occasions that she had joined in local social activities, particularly with the playgroup, the time had been largely spent in 'back-biting' about somebody else.

> How so-and-so hasn't done her share and how much they have done their share. They seem to resent other people and each other. I definitely think that there's a feeling that the village is ours, those that have been born and bred here, and I'm certain they resent newcomers without a doubt. But even amongst themselves there is still back-biting and squabbling. I think it's possibly that they all feel insecure for some reason or other. And they all want to try and establish that they are better than the next person. And the only way they can, is by saying that she doesn't do as much as I do. Really, it gets down to the one basic fact that the women find it difficult to find their identity. They regard the husband as 'my man' who is superior in every way, who is the acknowledged breadwinner and even if the wife does happen to go out to work she has very menial tasks to do – they either work on the land, or do the housework round the village for other people. And that's about the sum total of what they can do.[75]

Other channels of communication: shops and traders

The volume of all this public opinion flowed through many channels, and shopkeepers were frequently at the apex of the communication networks which permeated working-class neighbourhoods since their close relationship with customers meant they were privy to much of the gossip which took place in the public domain (as opposed to that which circulated at the level of family and close neighbourly relationships). A woman recollecting life in Ordsall, during the inter-war years observed that:

> The shop was a place for gossips. Women used to come to m'mother with their troubles – If they were expecting, or about childbirth or if

the kids were ill. They'd come in for two ounces of syrup of figs or indian brandee and then start talking about what they wanted it for. She was a bit of a Ruby M. Ayres, like in the novels, m'mother, but she did know quite a bit about health and that.[76]

One woman claimed a shopkeeper she remembered from her childhood knew all the news for a radius of about three miles 'and sometimes further', and the importance of such relationships was well recognized by doorstep traders whose success in assessing creditworthiness depended on keeping up to date with the latest gossip. The training guide of a credit drapery firm in Manchester, for example, stressed that enquiries about 'removed accounts' had to be made from the corner shop and 'from any other person in the neighbourhood'.[77] George Harding, who was a police-man in a poor district of Northampton during the 1930s, recalled how he regularly dropped by to spend time with 'the dear old souls' who kept the local shops. He even got put on a disciplinary charge for idling and wasting his time drinking tea, but as he explained,

> we learned a lot by this. You go into the shop, through into the back room and the old person – usually elderly – would make some tea and we'd sit down. We would listen and they would talk. They knew everybody in the district. Who were going to have a baby, you know, the girls ... The shop was the centre and hub of everything. They all went to the shop ... If somebody was spending a few bob that he shouldn't have, they would quite readily tell the police. They didn't consider themselves grasses or informers, they just thought it was against the law, what they're doing, and you ought to know. By visit-ing these places we got no end of information.[78]

Friday pay-day meant that the small grocer's shop which Lillian Beckwith's father ran was crowded with not only those who had come to collect their weekly orders but with others who had come to glean news through the shop gossip of any jobs which might be on offer. 'In the good weeks whole families came, adding a fillip to their evening by foregather-ing inside and outside the shop and sharing in the general conversation.'[79] Concentrating on traditional male meeting places as centres of social life inevitably obscures the significance of such local institutions. As Evelyn Borland, a Salford resident, observed, 'It was almost always women in the shop, much more so than these days, occasional men – for cigarettes or beer, but they didn't stop to talk.'[80] George Orwell, while criticizing the absence of pubs on pre-war Corporation housing estates as a 'serious blow at communal life', interpreted a similar lack of shops there more from the point of view of the independent shopkeeper than from that of their erst-while (largely female) customers. Although many small shopkeepers certainly were ruined by a loss of clientele to such housing schemes, Orwell's emphasis typically neglects the role which such shops played in the limited social life of working-class women.[81] It was, after all, the combination of a good memory, perceptiveness and the invaluable vantage point of being brought up in a such a corner shop which made Robert Roberts so astute an observer of working-class life. His school inspectors, worried by his fellow students' apparent difficulty in expressing themselves, wanted to know why Roberts was so articulate. Did he, they asked 'talk at home ... in the family?' Was he actually used to something called 'conversation'? Roberts's reply aptly summed up the corner shop's creative function: 'We've a shop, sir. It's talkin' all day!'[82] Yet the very position which Roberts's family occupied as small shopkeepers inevitably coloured his own view of the world, which he defined in terms of an urban 'village' of about 3,000 people. This pattern was on far too large a scale to be recognized by most of the women who were his mother's customers, their geographical horizons being far more limited in scope. As Roberts himself recalled, one woman spoke 'wearily of never having been more than five minutes' walk from her home in eighteen years of married life', and a Glasgow woman reiterated the circumscribed boundaries of many women's daily lives in describing a move which might have been a hundred miles rather than the few yards it was in reality: 'I was twenty-one when I got married and went away to live, over three hundred yards from my mother, the other end of the village. I was terribly hame-sick because I didnae know the neighbours'.[83] Such examples reveal how powerful a medium gossip could be under confined circumstances, yet also indicate how tapping into the local grapevine could extend somewhat a woman's mental horizons beyond the physical limitations of her own back yard. Indeed, the speed with which particularly advantageous gossip could spread throughout a neighbourhood is underlined by Denis Blake Lobb who grew up in Hyde, Cheshire, during the inter-war years. Lobb recollected a friend who had come into his father's shop for a chat, and was warned by the shopkeeper that a woman standing at the door was listening in to the conversation and would repeat anything she heard 'all round the town'.

> So he said, 'Oh, will she? Right, we will have a bit of fun.
> 'I believe', said Arthur, 'that they are giving the Mayor's five shillings away this afternoon at the Town Hall.' So my father said, 'Mayor's five shilling? What's that?' 'Well', he said, 'anybody what's a resident of Hyde can go up to the Town Hall this afternoon'. He said, 'In fact, they will start queuing any minute now, but if you go up there, they will get five shillings. You have got to be a resident of the town, mind you, but they will just give five shillings'. So he said, 'Is she still watching?' My dad said, 'No, she's gone. It will be all round the town in ten minutes', he said. And half an hour after he said, they were laughing away at this, when a big shadow in the doorway and it was Sergeant Bredbury. Do you remember him? He

said, 'Now, you two buggers, I have a good mind to run you in for inciting the peace.' He said, 'We can not stir at the Town Hall, there is hundreds of folk queuing up for Mayor's five shilling. What have you been telling folk?'[84]

The bushfire spread of local scandal is apparent in an incident that Kathleen Dayus describes, when an unfortunate hop picking incident in the country resulted in her older brother stealing a pig from the farm on which they had been staying. The incident led to much neighbourhood talk, apparently inspired by two particular families, but collectively dispersed by a great many other neighbours. By the time Kathleen Dayus reached the local grocer's the theft was the main topic of conversation there, already having been colourfully embroidered by more remote inhabitants of the district.[85]

Various forms of retailing were, in fact, the arteries through which information vital to the local population was regularly pumped, although the significance of this circulation has not always been recognized. Thus, while Maud Pember Reeves's description of women's lives in working-class Lambeth poignantly pinpoints the isolated nature of much of their work at home, it too overlooks the subtle influence of the communication network which underpinned even this less public neighbourhood, although Reeves herself observed that:

> A weekly caller becomes the abashed object of intense interest on the part of everybody in the street, from the curious glances of the green-grocer's lady at the corner to the appraising stare of the fat little baker who always manages to be on the doorstep across the road. And everywhere along the street is the visitor conscious of eyes which disappear from behind veiled windows.[86]

The efficacy of this attention to other people's business was highlighted in the case of Lulu, daughter of a 'deserted' woman, who suffered from an illness which often resulted in her having to be rushed suddenly into hospital. A Fabian 'visitor' was present on one of these occasions when 'it seemed as though the whole street knew exactly what to do. One neighbour accompanied the mother and child, one took over the baby, another arranged with a nod and a word to take the mother's place at work that afternoon, and in two minutes everything was settled.'[87]

Each neighbourhood had key figures and contact points which ensured the speed of such a response in a crisis, be they corner shop, pawnshop, markets, street stalls, fish and chip shop or wash-house.[88] Edna Bold, who grew up in Beswick, Manchester, in the early 1900s described the 'Road' as a 'social centre where everyone met, stopped, talked and walked. The butcher, the baker, the milliner, the draper, the barber, the greengrocer, the pawnbroker, the undertaker, were friends, confidants and mines of information.[89] Bold's reference to 'confidants and mines of information' suggests the reciprocal element in these relationships. This double-edged aspect was particularly apparent in the pawnshop, where the very nature of the pledge transaction, and the fact that those serving behind the counter tended to be male, produced an underlying tension which was frequently expressed in banter. Olive Malvery, for example, described 'a continual fire of chaff and raillery' which was kept up between the pawnshop's female customers and male assistants.[90] The pawnbroker, in listening to the gossip which went on from the other side of the counter, undoubtedly picked up information which helped loan decisions; but women were themselves not unaware of this outside audience and the fact that it could be used in a number of ways, both for amusement and as a useful diversionary tactic. Vincent Walmsley, for example, recalled his time working in a pawnshop as a young man, when his female customers used deliberately to tell smutty stories in order to embarrass him. 'I'd not been brought up that way ... And, er, I used to blush if anybody said anything. And this ... one particular woman, used to do it on purpose to make me blush. 'Cause I was stood at the desk, and I had to overhear them, and they used to tell these smutty stories.'[91]

Although there was a fatalistic element in many working-class attitudes, women were often quick to respond when retailers overstepped the conventions which underpinned relationships with them, and when they could see an obvious remedy for their criticisms. Women were notoriously reluctant to admit to dealings with street moneylenders, for example, yet occasionally they even combined against their tormentors. In 1913 a Smethwick moneylender was successfully prosecuted for acting illegally after police had received complaints that she was unregistered. She had been 'shopped', because although people in the district were unaware of the exact amount of interest being charged, they had become conscious 'that they were paying through the nose, and had been talking about it'. The woman had got her solicitor to write to the complainants warning that she would take out proceedings against them if they persisted with their 'slanderous' statements. However, they do not seem to have been much alarmed by the letters, possibly because government concern at moneylending abuses was currently attracting substantial publicity, and a number of women gave evidence against her.[92] In a similar manner, gossip among local women was responsible for getting a Northampton butcher the sack in the 1930s after they noticed discrepancies between the prices he was asking and those charged by other butchers in other branches of the same firm. There was 'a lot of angry whispering, and looking at him at the back of the shop, and a big woman, she said, "Well, I'm going down town ..."' This woman, who was described as having a 'big mouth', waited until she knew that the district manager was due to make a visit, went into town to copy down the prices being charged in the other branch, and handed them over to him when he arrived.[93]

Women's relationships with their door-to-door traders were another significant aspect of this communication network, since they helped create social links between women as they carried community news, information and gossip from home to home. Linda McCullough Thew, describing life in Ashington, a mining village in inter-war Northumberland, observed how, 'In those days of fairly large family connections and very few telephones, the store order man often delivered verbal messages in an emergency as he went on his rounds.'[94] Ron Barnes typically described how in his East End childhood 'Any weekly callers would be asked in for a cup of tea. ... My gran used to have them all in. First the milkman, then the coalman, then the baker, insurance man, tallyman, Xmas club man, window cleaner, and God knows how many more.'[95] The insurance man, whose own livelihood depended on not breaking the intimate confidences which were frequently shared with him, was allowed across the threshold in ways that neighbours frequently were not. 'The insurance man called once a week, he was your mother's best friend ... The same was often true of the rent collector and club man whom 'you knew from the moment you could talk', and who saw 'all your life unfold from being born, to getting married and even dying.'[96] As Barnes's observation suggests, such traders were predominantly male and their easy access across the domestic threshold lent sexual overtones to their position which were readily exploited in male mythology and by the neighbourhood gossips. Women were believed to be particularly susceptible to the tallyman's 'cajolery'. Charles Booth described their influence in 'better' working-class neighbourhoods where, 'Their power of talk does it. Wives left at home all day, dull; along comes a tallyman with an oily tongue; they like a gossip, and don't have the chance of seeing many men, so they talk, and then buy.'[97] An English ballad on the Irish 'pedlar' exemplifies the sexual connotations which attached to the door-to-door salesman's dealings with his female customers (and incidentally reveals an aspect of the racial stereotyping of Irish men). With salacious delight the 'pedlar' describes the attraction which his 'spicy' wares hold for his clientele, dwelling suggestively on the appeal of his cinnamon stick and large nutmegs.[98]

Sexual innuendo played an important part in gossip, whose critical function in establishing reputation and status has been well attested by anthropological studies.[99] The enforced intimacy of the poorest working-class neighbourhoods of the late nineteenth and early twentieth centuries gave the voices of local women a particular resonance in such matters. Poverty reinforced a sense of the hostile and unpredictable among the irregularly and poorly paid urban poor, such as those of Campbell Bunk, whose female dominated 'protective culture' has been so well described by Jerry

White, and there is a sense in which the conformist disposition of older women can be seen as a means of safeguarding the neighbourhood against the questionable, unsafe world outside. The moral codes implicit in their gossip were one way of defining a social space within which local people felt comfortable, although such talk also played an important part in creating the mental parameters of people's lives, and it is to these and gossip's broader functions that we turn next.

Notes

1. E. Pugh, 'A Small Talk Exchange', in Keating 1971, 105.
2. See Ross 1983 for a pioneering article on women's neighbourhood support networks. For one of the more useful recent discussions of the problems of defining and researching concepts of neighbourhood and community, see Benson 1989, Chapter 5.
3. E.J. Hobsbawm, 'The nineteenth century London labour market', in Centre for Urban Studies 1964, 8.
4. White 1986, 76.
5. Furniss 1979, 27. Furniss was born in 1912.
6. In 1985, Jack Levin and Arnold Arluke published the results of a study which examined sex differences in 'gossip mongering' among American college students. They concluded that while the women of their survey were rather more likely than men to converse about the activities and attitudes of other people, gossip defined as derogatory talk resulted in no significant differences between the sexes. They found that while the women's talk concentrated on the people in their social networks such as close friends and relatives, that of the men concerned rather less intimate subjects such as distant acquaintances and 'media celebrities' like disk jockeys, coaches and TV personalities. Levin and Arluke 1985. Their study was conducted among 76 male and 120 female college students. Gossip was defined as 'the presence of conversation about any third person, whether present or absent from the group'. Of the women's conversations, 71 per cent were spent gossiping about others, compared with 64 per cent of the men's conversations.
7. Chinn 1988.
8. Gillis 1985, 232–33. Unlike the eighteenth and early nineteenth centuries, when heterosexual relationships seem to have been characterized by an informality which readily tolerated cohabitation.
9. Gillis 1985, 238.
10. Most contemporary soap operas have their resident 'gossip', the typical image being one of 'lonely middle aged women'. Vera Duckworth in Coronation Street is an archetypal gossip, spreading rumours, as is Martha Woodford in the Archers. Mike Rose, of Manchester University, has drawn my attention to a widely syndicated cartoon strip in the United States called 'Snuffy Smith', which revolves around a 'roughneck' hill-billy family, whose 'Maw' is always at the 'gossip fence' recounting stories to her neighbour and collecting pieces of 'gossip', which have an important exchange value.
11. Gennel or ginnel – an alley or passageway.
12. Haythorne 1986, 8–10.

13. Northampton tapes, Mrs Celia Dixon, (b). Cat, in the sense of 'a spiteful, backbiting woman' is another derogatory term commonly applied to the gossip. See also Jones 1980, who defines gossip 'as a way of talking between women in their roles as women, intimate in style, personal and domestic in topic and setting, a female cultural event which springs from and perpetuates the restrictions of the female role, but also gives the comfort of validation'. Jones divided gossip into 'four functional categories: house-talk, scandal, bitching and chatting'. Chatting was defined as 'the most intimate form of gossip, a mutual self-disclosure transaction where the skills that women have learned as part of their job of nurturing others are turned to their own advantage', 196–67.

14. Loane 1910, 89.

15. R. Roberts 1970: 1978, 183.

16. Jackson 1968:1972, 45; Hoggart 1958: 1962, 27–28.

17. Hoggart 1958: 1962, 31.

18. Of women drinkers 34.6 per cent were aged between 25 and 40. Harrisson estimated that 16 per cent 'of a large count over a long period in all types of pub' were women, although the bulk of their drinking went on at weekends rather than during the week, when most regular evening drinkers were male. Mass Observation 1943: 1987, 134–37.

19. Chinn 1988, 120.

20. R. Roberts 1971: 1974, 10.

21. Chew 1982, 181. Leonore Davidoff has described how real power and influence in upper-class society also came 'rather late' in a woman's life. Dowagers, in particular, were 'formidable social leaders' who brought considerable pressure to bear upon any lapse in social demeanour. She estimates that by the end of the nineteenth century there must have been about 4,000 families 'actively involved' in upper-class society 'which is probably about the numerical limit for this kind of face to face community held together by gossip and information exchange'. Davidoff 1973: 1986, 61, 94.

22. Dixon 1989.

23. Northampton tapes, Mr Billingham.

24. Williamson 1982, 142–43, i.e. don't bend your ears here.

25. Wakefield 1980: 1988, 62–64.

26. OLHG, FW.

27. MSTC, Tape 247.

28. MSTC, Tape 12.

29. Greenwood 1967, 16.

30. Oakley 1972, 79–80

31. Roberts 1984: 1986, 193; Dayus 1982: 1987, 1985: 1986; 1991.

32. See, for example, Fine 1977, 181–86.

33. Dixon 1989. Nellie W. was later described as a 'big, fat, red-faced woman, and a born gossip (if she didn't know about "it", no-one else did!!)'. Her husband was a little man, 'and apart from that, so insignificant that I can't remember anything else about him'.

34. Miscellaneous tapes, Miss Badby.

35. Almirol 1981, 300.

36. See, for example, Yerkovich 1977, 195: 'Closure in gossiping or transitions from gossiping to other ways of speaking may be in the form of a generalising statement made by one or more of the participants (e.g. "Well, you never know," "People do act crazy," or "Isn't that something?").'

37. Champion 1938, 34. Women were not unaware of the various verbal devices they used in such conversation, as Lady Morgan observed in her Autobiography in 1818, '"Well, my dear!" as we say in Ireland when we enter on a gossipry.' Cited in Murray Vol. IV, 1901, 312.
38. Sant 1985, 9.
39. MSTC, Tape 558.
40. Greenwood 1967, 29.
41. Miscellaneous tapes, Joan Green.
42. Northampton tapes, Mrs West (b).
43. Black 1915: 1983, 169–70.
44. Wakefield 1980: 1988, 12. Chamberlain 1975: 1977, 77.
45. Davies 1915: 1978, 190.
46. Williamson 1982, 131.
47. Bell 1907:1985, 167.
48. For e.g. see Macintyre 1980, 139.
49. Barnes 1976, 46.
50. Broad and Fleming 1981, 36.
51. Rowntree and Lavers 1951, 32.
52. Turner 1988, 1–2.
53. Slawson 1986, 60.
54. Kay 1990, 11.
55. Blair 1985, 143–44.
56. Storey 1990: 1992, 112. Storey was born in 1917.
57. Haworth 1986, 35, 81. Haworth was born in 1924, in Bacup.
58. R. Roberts 1970: 1978, 84.
59. Champion 1938, 30.
60. Hooley 1981.
61. Haworth 1986, 35–36.
62. Heaton 1982, 23. Richard Heaton was born in Salford in 1901.
63. Wakefield 1980: 1988, 62–63.
64. OLHG, DM. See also E. Roberts 1984: 1986, 196.
65. Dennis, Henriques and Slaughter 1956, 181.
66. Dennis, Henriques and Slaughter 1956, 203.
67. Miscellaneous tapes, Maria Goddard.
68. Kuper 1953, 7, 44.
69. Oral History Archive, Lancaster University, Mr CIP.
70. Chinn 1988, 116.
71. Mogey 1956, 107–08.
72. Gorer 1955, 66.
73. Dixon, 1989.
74. Miscellaneous tapes, Maria Goddard, (b).
75. Chamberlain 1975: 1977, 166. Erica Wimbush, examining the role of leisure among women with pre-school age children in Edinburgh during the 1980s, found that some 'kept away from the local mothers' circles (e.g. mothers and toddlers, coffee mornings) because they felt themselves to be outsiders to the 'happy family' stereotype which prevails in these groups. They were often wary of the controlling aspects of gossip within these networks. What are often regarded as private family matters – such as marital relationships, child-rearing practices, children's clothing and appearance – were more vulnerable to critical scrutiny in these groups. Thus women who preferred to keep away from mothers' groups included those without male partners, those with

marital or domestic problems, an older mother in her forties and women from low income households (including unemployed families).' Wimbush 1988, 65.

76. Ordsall Local History Group Display, Juggling All Your Life.
77. Tildsley 1985, 5; Stewart and Sons Ltd, Undated.
78. Northampton Arts Development 1987, 99.
79. Beckwith 1982, 158–59.
80. OLHG, EB.
81. Orwell 1937: 1974, 63–64.
82. R. Roberts 1970: 1978, 150.
83. R. Roberts 1971: 1974, 49; Blair 1985, 144.
84. Interview with Denis Blake Lobb, Transcript held at Stalybridge Library. Hyde is now part of Tameside. As this example suggests, although known gossips were often people to be feared and avoided, there were ways of using their manipulative talents to advantage within a small community. This observation is based on experience of the Muslim community in Manchester. 'If you want something spreading around the community, you know where to go! You know that by tomorrow everybody will know. That system is used quite a lot actually, if you want something to get out but you don't want to pass it on yourself you go and tell it to that particular person who you know, a hundred per cent, that person will pass it on. And add ten bits to it, maybe!' Interview with Shakila Mir, 21/4/89.
85. Dayus 1982:1987, 164–66.
86. Pember Reeves 1913: 1979, 4.
87. Pember Reeves 1913: 1979, 187.
88. See Walton 1992 for the role that the fish and chip shop played in the exchange of gossip, not only for women but for adolescent boys and courting couples, 14–15, 147, 159–60.
89. Burnett 1982, 227.
90. Malvery 1907, 258.
91. MSTC, Tape 541.
92. *Pawnbrokers' Gazette*, 19 July 1913, 485.
93. Northampton tapes, Celia Dixon, (e).
94. McCullough 1985, 81.
95. Barnes 1976, 81.
96. OLHG, EO.
97. Booth 1892, Vol. 8, 83.
98. Ballad Collection, Manchester Central Reference Library, BR, f821.04, Ba 1, Vol. 3, 98.
99. Bleek 1976, 528. Such studies have often attributed a greater importance to gossip in rural rather than urban settings. (Gossip plays an important self-conscious part in radio soaps like the Archers.)

CHAPTER THREE

The knowable community: the limits of mental and social space

> You cannot live in a court without knowing a good deal about your neighbours and their concerns, even without deserving the title of a gossip.[1]

Although the power of gossip was certainly recognized in the stereotyped assumptions frequently made about its practitioners, its manifestation within working-class neighbourhoods suggests the ambivalent influence which women wielded through such talk. The adaptive strategies they developed had the capacity both to support and constrain, so that gossip's very function in the maintenance of neighbourhood values underlines its potential as a force for conservatism among women. It is also an important reminder that the undeniable strength and survival capacity of working-class women should always be seen in the context of the broader patriarchal and class forces which moulded and distorted their lives.

Information value of gossip

Robert Roberts well recognized how 'that daily feature of the slum scene, the "hen party"', did not function, as many thought, merely to peddle scandal', but 'played a vital role in a milieu where many, through lack of education, relied entirely on the spoken word'.[2] A miner's widow, interviewed about the effect of rationing upon her family budget in 1947, indicated the economic importance of the information – wrapped in gossip – which she often came across while shopping when she explained how 'round about us we have got a good shopping centre, so we are very fortunate, and I find in getting about you pick up wrinkles and swop ideas and hints (for I am not too old to learn)'.[3] A former Hillgate resident similarly suggested the extent to which poor families depended on developing a keen ear for local news in their struggle for survival.

> My mother, like I say, was always on the forefront if there was anything going. It was like the 'bush telegraph', if you understand what I mean. It spread amongst the women, 'I believe they're giving shoes away at so-and-so, I believe they're giving bundles of clothes away at such a place', and things like that.[4]

Jim Hooley, again writing of his impoverished childhood in Stockport during the 1920s, illustrated the economic value of this 'gift of the gab' in the pawnshop on Monday morning when everyone was waiting for the manager to inspect their bundles to see if the contents were worth what was being asked. As suggested in the previous chapter, it was common for the women to 'keep him talking to take his mind off opening the bundle, telling him jokes – the kind that would embarrass him. More often than not he would forget to open the bundle and would tell his assistant to make out the ticket for the sum they had asked for.'[5] Women doing their laundry at the local wash-house passed on information as they gossiped about catalogue trading, special offers, people who would do 'a quick foreigner' or could 'get things', some of which had undoubtedly tumbled off the back of a lorry.[6]

The exchange value of gossip could, in fact, be one of the most valuable assets the impoverished women of a slum community possessed. A pawn-broker remarked of his customers in a dilapidated central district of Manchester that it was not only the prospect of borrowing that attracted them to him, 'they used to come in for the chatter'.[7] Taking notice of and even encouraging such talk was, of course, also in the trader's interests since it was a good barometer of many a family's financial and economic circumstances.[8] Similarly, such close attention to neighbourhood gossip traditionally assisted many women whose economic well-being was based on servicing their own sex. In 1871, for example, Dr Charles Cameron described how professional fortune-tellers or 'spaewives' and washer-women (whose work made them privy to kitchen gossip) served as abor-tionists' touts in Glasgow.[9] Many women put the knowledge they gleaned through street talk to good financial use, since their familiarity with the local gossip helped them come up with many an accurate reading for fortune telling activities, while street moneylending also depended on good information about changing family circumstances. Indeed, the popularity of fortune telling, reading the tea leaves and fire reading among many working class women owed much to the gossip element in street culture, just as the intuitive qualities traditionally associated with women were strongly rooted in the intimate knowledge of other people's daily lives. 'You see, when anything happened all the street knew and they would come and ask, "Do you know about such a body?" Everybody knew every-body else, scandal and all sorts.'[10]

Gossip was a conduit for all sorts of useful information which countered the strains of domestic isolation, helped bond the community together, and allowed women both to store and to redistribute information 'that could be important economically to themselves and their neighbours'.[11] Robert Roberts's admittedly childhood memories of the conversations which took place in his parents' corner shop ('the housewives' club', according to

Hoggart) nevertheless give a flavour of the gossip which went on.[12] The habits of their menfolk not unnaturally loomed fairly large among the women there, particularly as far as their drinking and eating habits were concerned.

> A boozed-up husband coming in hours late would frequently complain about a meal kept warm for him, or would push it away untouched. This habit women in the shop constantly bemoaned. 'What can you do? Jack's that funny with his food. You can't please him.'[13]

Indeed, the shop conversation of women often seems to have involved running down their men in some way.[14] 'I often used to walk into the shop as I was growing up and there'd be hysterical laughter from the women, and me mam would go "Ghe ghum, go on you're not needed in here, back in the kitchen". They'd be talking about sex, you know.'[15] The Liverpool *Porcupine*, which was much interested in the talk which went on among pawnshop customers for the insight it gave into the 'domestic economy of working people', recorded a conversation as to the best course of action when a husband came home drunk and had failed to hand over any money: 'whether it's better to take it out of his pockets without his knowing – whether it's better to be good humoured with him, and joke it all out of him – whether it's better to set the children on him – or let him alone until he has had his first sleep, and then he will think of the money and tip it up like a man'. The way in which all these points were argued and the advantages each possessed, were given with considerable skill 'and exhibit knowledge which is the result of painful experience'.[16]

Gossip and reputation

Gossip helped to link women of the urban poor into a broad and supportive information network whose very nature also made it an extremely effective 'self-policing system' among some who used shaming and ridicule as effective sanctions against themselves.[17] This maintenance of group values at a street level, which could be extremely restrictive, seems to have been particularly strong in close-knit single industry communities where women had little access to work outside the home. Social activities in the Yorkshire mining town described in *Coal Is Our Life*, for example, were strictly segregated, those taking place outside the home being almost entirely male centred. Women's social contact in such districts revolved around customs of visiting and 'callin' with kinsfolk and neighbours (many wives saw one or other of their relatives every day). Most had a wide circle of family, childhood acquaintances or long-established neighbours with whom they gossiped, and the introspective nature of such communities meant that the full weight of public opinion and 'gossip' could be exerted against any woman who contravened local behavioural expectations. No 'self-respecting' young woman would go into a local public house unaccompanied by her husband or fiancé, since those who transgressed against their confinement to the home and family were 'talked about' and publicly disapproved of.[18] Any small incident which happened in a poor working-class neighbourhood was likely to attract lively speculation from an interested audience of 'nosy parkers' who were not usually averse to asking a few direct questions of anyone who might know what was going on, as Kathleen Dayus comments on numerous occasions.[19] The power of 'wagging tongues' was acutely felt in such districts, as her own mother's anguished shriek of 'Whatever will the neighbours think?' indicated when she discovered her unmarried daughter's pregnancy. Elizabeth Roberts has emphasized the importance to the working-class people whom she investigated of not getting a 'bad name', since 'They knew they would be talked about.'[20] As one respondent put it: 'I think the working-classes were more careful because the whole street knew. There used to be an expression that "the whole street will know about it".'[21] Roberts has suggested that gossip in the communities she has studied often served as a brake to more overt forms of domestic violence. For street talk, manifested at its most extreme in social ostracism, could severely inhibit behaviour which went against the grain of local standards and encourage a lasting unease at what was and what was not public knowledge.[22]

Sexual behaviour was a prolific source of gossip which could have far reaching effects upon a family's social status. Incestuous father/daughter relationships were observed in Edwardian Salford and pushed the family low in the ranks of local respectability, although little was done to prevent the abuse. 'Even to the lowest levels, in matters sexual, people strove to maintain a façade, for known nonconformity in sex could do more than anything else to damage one's prestige.'[23] Retaining face with neighbours was an important part of a woman's dignity. Even where sympathy perhaps prevented overt reference to local scandal, the protagonists were well aware of the encircling ripples of gossip, yet refused to acknowledge them. A Preston woman's father had an affair when she was a child, and when asked if the neighbours knew about it, she replied:

> Of course they did. You didn't tell them, but one told another. My dad wore clogs and they were beautiful clogs, he was as light as a dancer. He used to come home at all hours in the morning and there was always somebody heard him come home, and they used to wonder where he had been till that time in the morning. Well, my mother knew, but you just kept it to yourself and put your best face on.[24]

Women were expected to have higher sexual standards than men, and were certainly judged by a different set of rules. Francie Nichol exposed her own vulnerability as a single parent when she commented of South Shields that 'A woman on her own with kids, was no better than a loose woman in many people's eyes', since who was to know if she had ever been married at all? Who was to know, on the other hand if a man on his own was married or separated? He was, in any case, more likely to receive sympathy, as having suffered at the hands of 'a no good, idle woman' or 'slut'.[25] Another woman, recalling the inter-war years in Manchester's Collyhurst area remembered an acquaintance who took up with another man after being regularly battered by her husband. The affair was well talked about, yet she received little sympathy from other local women, who refused to lend her a black hat when her husband died because they disapproved of her sexual liaison. 'That was their way of showing how they felt about her behaviour. And this is women judging women!'[26] A more extreme example of such sexual judgment was the case of a widow who was said to be 'entertaining' the husband of a sick neighbour.

> There was a man who, who was knocking about with a woman, a widow, while his wife was sick, you see, and of course, this got round and the women got together and they put a big bonfire outside the front door, and built an image of the woman on the pole on the top of the fire. Well, we as kids, oh, that was bonfire night for us. We didn't know the seriousness of that, you see, until it was explained to us later on.
> Q. So the community had its own rules?
> A. You see, they barred this woman, it was her that caught it, not him, this widow, you see, that caught it. She was entertaining this chap in her house and his wife was bad, you see, and didn't live a couple of street apart? but, the women got together and they got all us kids to go to market, bring all these, they was going to have a bonfire with.[27]

This was an example of a practice which was rare in industrial districts by the inter-war years; ostracism, the silence of disapproval and rejection, had by then become a more usual tool in the working-class neighbourhood. A refusal to admit an individual to the local speech community was like wiping the slate clean not only of the person who had committed the misdemeanour but the crime itself. This was perhaps most notably expressed in the attitudes towards incest portrayed by Robert Roberts, which excluded the suspected household in a silence effectively precluding legal prosecution. Among the Birmingham urban poor whom Chinn describes, a woman who was cruel to her children might be ostracized or gossiped about but was rarely subjected to any other punishment.[28]

The close-knit neighbourhoods which had developed in many working-class areas by the early years of the twentieth century enabled gossip (and silence) to be used with devastating effect against those who transgressed against local mores. The frequently tightly meshed nature of local relationships ensured that married women could be extremely influential in questions of courtship and marriage and may be a reason why the fall in illegitimacy rates in England coincided with the 'establishment of settled communities amongst the poor'.[29] A young woman's sexual reputation had important implications for a whole family's good name, and the 'surprisingly large number' of slang and uncomplimentary dialectical expressions surrounding illegitimacy illustrates the impact it had upon a woman's status.[30] Silence remained a powerful tool to indicate disapproval. Tom Wakefield, writing of his childhood in the 1940s, was waiting to be served in the local off-licence when a young 17-year-old girl named Elaine Braithwaite came in. She was unmarried, and heavily pregnant after a relationship with a black American GI. As soon as she entered the shop, people began to speak more quietly and then stopped talking altogether. 'Not even a whisper. She stood at the back of the crowd. I sat on the crate and looked at her. That's what everyone in the shop was doing, looking at her ... The shop had gone so quiet and still. All that you could hear was the swishing noise of the beer pumps.'

Elaine was the last in and the first to be served, and the silence continued until the door closed behind her. As soon as she left the talk started, about the scandal of her having a black baby, how her father had beaten her on being told the news, and how her mother had threatened to throw her out. Disapproval, intensified in this case by its racist element, centred partly on her perceived lack of shame: 'bold as brass ... She were seen with him. She were warned. Now look what's it's come to.'[31] The approved convention was for the unmarried, pregnant woman to show appropriate contrition if there were to be any possibility of acceptance back into the neighbourhood. John Gillis noted how a civil wedding came to be regarded as 'a kind of penalty' in the period up to the First World War, 'an acknowledgement of indiscretion that placated those neighbourhood gossips who reserved the full measure of their contempt for those brides who attempted to hide their shame'.[32] There was a sense that the only appropriate behaviour for illegitimacy was complete withdrawal from public life, such withdrawal having the advantage of assisting in the fictions which were often perpetuated by the tacit support of the local community, as when the illegitimate child of a local daughter was raised as the grandmother's child.[33] Chinn, for example, described how 'one illegitimate child of a long-established family in the Studley Street locality learned the details of her birth only as a result of the unmeant indiscretions of a very old woman'.[34] Despite outwardly expressed disapproval, in private women could express considerable sympathy for the plight of the pregnant unmarried woman. Bill Williamson's grandmother, for example, 'told her daughters often enough if they heard of anyone falling pregnant that "it just happens to the good ones", and, invariably added, "She's not the first and she'll not be the last!'"[35] In this case gossip perpetuated the myth necessitated by patriarchal conceptions of status which depended on having a 'respectable' family life. Women protected their daughters from their father's anger while also ensuring that his self-esteem remained intact. Emily Ryder's mother lodged her pregnant daughter with relatives, and urged that 'she must not come home under the present circumstances. What would the neighbours say. Her father must not know about it. He would go out of his mind.'[36]

Gossip had the power to intimidate even such a domineering individual as Kathleen Dayus's mother, so it was scarcely surprising that it should play an important part in overseeing standards of housekeeping, children's behaviour and street respectability.[37] Nowhere was this more apparent than in the expectations of public display which attended preparations for Whitsun week in northern towns like Manchester and Salford.

> Q. Did they talk very much about other people?
> A. Well, there were some that they looked down on. If anybody hadn't got anything new for Whit Week, if the children were clad in their usual clothes, they were looked down on, you know ... Even if the clothes, the very new clothes that they'd bought themselves were having to go to the pawnshop on Monday, (well, it'd be Tuesday really), er, still they looked down on people who hadn't made the effort.[38]

Failure to wear new clothes for Whitsun reflected not so much on the church as on the local community, and even if a family was indifferent to religion, their children still walked with any church group with which they could claim a tenuous connection, be it through the parents' marriage or attendance at a particular denominational school. Inability to do so was a potent source of local talk.

> Q. So if they didn't have new clothes to walk in, they were sort of letting the church down?
> A. Oh no, no, no, not letting the church down, letting the community down, yes, the community. 'Oh, it means nothing to them', I've heard! Means nothin to her, you know. 'Just look, her children have only got what they wear every day!'[39]

Reputation was critical in such neighbourhoods, where another important status symbol was the condition of a woman's front steps and flags. John Burnett describes the frequent preoccupation in working-class autobiographies with keeping the home clean and tidy and upholding standards of domestic respectability. This sometimes obsessive desire was a 'cordon sanitaire' dividing the respectable from the undeserving dirty poor. Burnett sees such preoccupations as not only an urban 'but especially a northern phenomenon' which provided a spotless symbol of female affirmation to the dark satanic mills belching outside the home.[40] 'John O'London' made a similar observation in 1905, after a long tram ride from Manchester to Oldham, when he learnt with his own eyes 'the lesson of cleanliness and house-pride which the meanest Manchester streets offer to London ... the white lace curtains in humble windows would put St. John's Wood to shame'.[41] They were certainly signs that a woman was not so abandoned in hope as to lose both self-esteem and the public recognition which was often the only acknowledgement of her domestic struggles. In a similar way, the weekly pattern of household activities contributed an important collective rhythm to life and helped give women the psychological momentum to carry on their daily struggles. Even within the demoralizing circumstances of their material lives, women managed to assert their identity in surprising ways, domestic space itself sometimes becoming a vehicle for self-expression.

> Trying to keep the house clean was a thankless task. The houses were very neglected by the landlord, yet it was surprising how some folks managed to keep their homes bright and cheerful. I remember one young Irish woman who kept her little parlour furnished with everything bright green. All the chairs had green covers on. The curtains were green and even the mantelpiece was draped in green. It seemed strange to me, but that was her idea of cheerful colour for her home. I suppose it reminded her of her homeland.[42]

The working-class woman's exasperation and frustrations were often expressed through gossip, but there were also boundaries to this interchange. Real or potential shortcomings in her housekeeping role had to be veiled, which meant that entry into the house itself was often off-limits to all but family and the most intimate of friends. At the same time, the pavement space immediately beyond the front door was 'annexed' as an extension of the house, and became a publicity vehicle for her domestic competence.[43] Standards of housekeeping were important markers of physical space, and careful attention was paid to the doorstep, which was washed, scrubbed and carefully delineated with 'donkeystone', a rectangular shaped stone stamped with a donkey motif which came in different colours: white, brown, cream, even greyish with blue speckles, which was known as 'blue mould'. 'John O'London' described the 'gospel of brownstone' in Manchester in terms of a 'religion', since its application to 'doorsteps, window-sills, and every kind of stone jut or surface' was universal.[44] However, the geographical and spatial limitations which marked women's lives in such communities also had an important bearing upon the almost ritualistic way in which such activities were approached. Donkeystoning symbolically defined the point of entry into the home, for the doorstep was transitional space, on the border of public and private. It represented a sanctuary, from which a woman felt safe to hurl insults at neighbours without fear of being followed for retribution. It formed a natural backdrop for the street photographer, whose snapshots of working-class women usually defined them in terms of their domestic and maternal obligations, wearing an apron and attended by children. It was an important vantage point from which to view the comings and goings of street life, and as such was often a source of much discomfort to outsiders. It was a space defined by the conventions of donkeystoning. 'It was a pleasant sight to see, on a Saturday, the long line of multi-coloured pavements and doorsteps winding away up a long street: a real communal undertaking.'[45]

Thus although donkeystoning publicly affirmed a woman's sense of domestic responsibility, it also conveyed different meanings according to the family, street or period in which it took place. To those women who wished to distinguish themselves from the 'rough' poor it could certainly express their desire for cleanliness and respectability: 'It was a competition for the cleanest steps. That the house should be spick and span from top to bottom. Everything had to be tidy. Clothes had to be cleaned and washed and pressed', 'it was who can have the nicest step in the street'.[46] Some streets exhibited a stubborn uniformity: with little expression of individuality, 'everything was the same. There was no painting different colours.'[47] In other contexts, however, such attention meant more than a representation of cleanliness and thereby respectability, it became the daily assertion of a woman's right over a certain territory and even an expression of her character. Fred Davies, writing of his childhood in Hulme remembered how each house had its own permutation of donkeystone, 'Our top step was white, the one below, level with the surrounding flags, was brown and a few nearby flags were cream.'[48] Joan Green, who grew up in Ashton-under-Lyne during the 1940s and 1950s described how some women on her street

> did different patterns, and edged it with a lighter one, or they did the step lighter. And then there was a lovely sort of orangey tan colour ... Well, some people had their own designs, really, some people did it in a half moon like a hearth rug, you know ...
> Q. So there wasn't a set pattern, set way of doing it?
> A. No, I think people just did what they wanted. But woe betide you if anybody walked on anybody's front when it had been mopped ... (In our street it was called mopped)
> Q. And when would you do that?
> A. Well, most ladies who didn't work, usually did it on a Thursday. Usually it was Friday morning, I think, and me mother did it sort of Friday night, so it was all nice for the weekend.

Joan's mother, who had a full-time job, would dash home on a Friday night to mop her front, because she knew she would probably be the last in the street to have mopped it. Joan cleaned the back and toilet, but was not allowed the privilege of tending to the front until she had left school at 15, 'you really felt you'd come of age when you were allowed to do the front'.

The familiarity of such routine could also be used to channel anger, frustration and humour, as was expressed in an extreme form by one woman during the Second World War when, 'after one Sunday night raid, a woman was seen donkey-stoning her front steps of her house the following morning. Asked why she was doing this when the whole of the back of the house had been damaged, she replied with a grin – "Well! I always stone the steps on a Monday morning".'[49]

Some elderly people remember the childhood appeal of donkeystoning with an almost sensual delight. One woman recollected the frustration of being denied the 'privilege' of cleaning the doorstep: 'I'd been dying to do this with this stone, I'd never done it, I wasn't allowed. I was the kid.'[50] Another woman who 'used to love cleaning' regularly took up position on a Saturday morning to watch her neighbour clean her step, and drove her mam mad, wanting to do it like Jessie:

> she always had a special cloth, a woollen one. If you had a woollen one, it didn't scratch it you know, when you rubbed the stone on the white and the cream and then you rinsed the cloth out again and wiped it dry. It used to dry a lovely colour, oh and the way she used to smooth it after, straighten it out like. Then it used to dry lovely and I used to say, 'Oh if I could only do it like Jessie'. Oh, it was lovely ...
>   Anyway, I did it and we got into the knack of it and I always kept it that way – used to take hours cleaning the front while others 'd just put a bit of stone on and then wash it and wipe it dry and leave it. I used to be still doing it and I'd go right along, right under the window getting it perfect.[51]

As such loving explanations suggest, even techniques for rubbing in the stone could vary, 'sometimes the edge of the step alone was whitened or maybe a strip at the side of the step.'[52] In Glasgow closes women decorated the floors of their entries at the wall edges with pipe clay scrolls carefully and precisely applied in designs peculiar to each close. Such emblems signified pride in the locality where they lived. They asserted both private space and collective responsibility, failure to adhere to such communal statements being a potent source of argument and gossip:

> There was a slitter in every close didnae do her pipe-clayin' right, and splashed the walls when it was her turn to wash the entry and the stair. We'd one like that and there was a right bit of aggravation over her, I can tell you. The rest didnae get on with her at all.[53]

As use of the word 'slitter' suggests, a dirty home implied a certain sexual laxity, in the same way that too ready an occupation of public street space indicated a similar looseness in the minds of those who preferred to keep themselves to themselves. Even the state of the washing a woman hung out on the line could give rise to comments about her character: 'the good ones put it out on a Monday about half past ten and you know, you'd got a lineful, and they weren't above examining to see whether you'd got it, whether you's boiled them ... that was a thing, you know, I'm sure she never boils hers ...' ; 'you couldn't mix your clothes when you were pinning them out to dry, all towels on one line, pillow slips on another line, bedding on another line, you mustn't mix them up, you don't know how to wash if you do that'; 'I remember, I hung washing out, they were all out looking at it, I remember that. And it was discussed whether it was clean or not – oh, I remember that, and I remember putting a towel out that had a stain on it, I've never forgotten that. They were "yap yap".'[54] The ambivalent quality of this kind of gossip was alluded to by Richard Hoggart in his analysis of inter-war Hunslet when he wrote that working-class people watched and were watched in a manner which, because horizons were limited, often resulted in a mistaken and lowering interpretation of what the neighbours did:

> though the neighbours are 'your sort' and will rally round in trouble, they are always ready for a gossip and perhaps a mean minded gossip. 'What will the neighbours think?' Usually they think that two and two makes six; their gossip may 'mean no harm' but it can be unconscionably brutal.[55]

As we have seen, concerns like maintaining a well-kept doorstep which publicly asserted an ability to hold one's own were also allied with powerful expectations of being a good manager. 'You were,' as a Broughton woman explained 'expected to cope.'[56] Poor copers were looked down on, so it was important to give an impression of trying to keep up appearances, even though there was often a tacit understanding of the reality behind the façade. 'Because you didn't tell anyone if he kept you short, though a lot of the neighbours knew.'[57] Cruel judgments could be made about the appearance of a house, and some women resorted to hanging their curtains with the pattern turned to the outside as a 'statement' to the people who passed by.[58] Yet there were also sound economic reasons for upholding such fictions, since they often affected an ability to obtain credit. Louie Stride described the 'Paddy Man', selling clothing from door to door on 'tick', 'He was, of course, choosy who he gave credit to and knew everybody and all their business', while credit drapers in Manchester were advised to avoid knocking on houses with a dirty appearance. 'A house which has permanently drawn curtains below, or dirty windows will almost certainly be a bad payer.'[59] As a woman who lived in a mining village near Newcastle commonly reminded her daughter, 'People knew the inside was clean when the outside was good.'[60] Thus apparent concern with such markers of respectability did not necessarily imply an assimilation of middle class values, and although seemingly petty, such preoccupations may also be seen as a strengthening mechanism which helped sustain people against the conditions under which they lived. For conformity with neighbourhood mores not only implied a belief in the importance of shared experience, but also reflected a desire to control or at least stabilize the uncertainties of daily life. It only needed a few to ignore local conventions for relationships to start to fall apart and petty rivalries and jealousies to surface, so that pressures for conformity and control of public space were consequently a means of disciplining latent disorder. Such considerations may be glimpsed in C. Stella Davies's description of Charlesworth, a Derbyshire village 11 miles from Manchester, in 1916. The local inhabitants, many of whom were the descendants of early textile workers, were largely employed in the local cotton mills and rope works. The village itself was neglected by public services with unlighted roads and no public removal of refuse.

> Under these circumstances the village was surprisingly clean and tidy. There was a collective sense of responsibility, tied up with 'being respectable', which prevented the place from becoming squalid. Those who did not maintain the respectable standard were quickly made to feel the weight of public opinion. 'It's high time tha emptied thi closet, ar't waiting for me to do it for thee.'[61]

Michael Conway, writing of inter-war Portwood in Stockport, described how local social life was centred upon the communal yard where 'they gossiped, kept pets, played, hung out their washing, and on occasions squabbled over some trivial incident. The families of one yard were moulded into a clan, banding together in the face of any illness, accident, or disaster that befell any member'.[62] Yet a narrowness of experience and expectations could easily lead to an over-preoccupation with the minutiae of their neighbours' lives as an awareness of spatial codes did not preclude speculation about other people's affairs. Indeed, the claustrophobic nature of such housing often gave neighbourhood talk and quarrels a theatrical quality. Kathleen Dayus vividly evokes her childhood in Edwardian Birmingham and her troubled relationship with a powerful and belligerent mother who dominated life in an overcrowded court of back-to-back houses where she and possibly another 50 people lived. With little space inside the house, most social life took place in the yard in full view of the neighbours and on one occasion when a row was brewing 'all the neighbours lifted their windows and popped their heads out while some of them crowded round to watch developments more closely'. Any minor ruckus was likely to bring them to their doorsteps, and Dayus's mother, who enjoyed having an audience, tended to encourage her 'followers'.[63] An Ordsall woman recalled the public nature of such life in poor communities during the inter-war years where little remained secret for very long and neighbours' knowledge of each other could often be quite intimate:

> We were so close to one another then — your door was there — their door was there. You couldn't help but know. If you spoke loudly or had a row, your ear was to the wall and you were listening![64]

Gossip and 'community': myths and neighbourhood values

Gossip permeated Dayus's own neighbourhood, and she often portrays its practitioners in stereotypical terms (at one point calling the local gossips 'ragged ignorant women' and 'wicked old witches'.) On one occasion, when her parents returned from seeing her brother Frankie, who was ill in the local infirmary, they all flocked around, asking all sorts of questions, forming a ring, 'nodding their heads and thinking the worst'.[65] Her father, indeed, never had much to do with their neighbours 'because he thought they gossiped too much'. Unfortunately, gossip could, indeed, have an addictive aspect, which occasionally had destructive effects on women for whom gossip became an escapist substitute for a more rewarding way of life. Francie Nichol, for example, described a run-down fish and chip shop in South Shields whose owner had a purely desultory interest in her business, customers often waiting unattended while she exchanged the latest gossip.[66] Such behaviour is a reminder of the pressures which poverty and a hand-to-mouth existence exerted over women of the urban poor. The cultural patterns which marked their experience were defined by poverty, and where survival itself dominated daily life it is scarcely surprising that the immediate and familiar should be a major preoccupation.

Women with very young children, the elderly and lone parents could easily be marginalized in the gossip exchange of local neighbourhoods, a combination of being relatively unknown or having unusual family circumstances which set them outside the usual 'norms' of the district, making some people particularly vulnerable to a more embroidered form of gossip and sweeping general statements which could be very harmful.

> There was a Mrs Levi in our street, and she was a very old lady, and she used to be glad of somebody to go errands for her, because she was bad on her feet ... So everybody presumed she was Jewish and she was wealthy. Whether she was Jewish, I don't know, but she certainly wasn't wealthy. She was generous to the kids that ran errands for her. There were loads of rumours about her.[67]

Elsie Pettigrew, describing her experiences in Liverpool in the early 1920s, recalled similar talk about a lonely, retired sea captain who lived on his own. She and friends used to visit him, taking him bread which they had baked at school and doing what they could for him, washing up and tidying. 'He was a very honourable man and he never said or did anything that would cause harm or offence, but as often happens in that situation nosey suspicious neighbours warned us not to go to his house. Naturally we took no notice of them, but they reported our behaviour to the school and we were forbidden to go again.'[68] Awareness of the cruel judgments which could be made on the basis of very little information made many reticent about the amount of information they gave away about themselves. The daughter of one woman who 'kept herself to herself' and didn't want to know anyone's business subsequently admitted that 'actually, it wasn't a very happy marriage, so I don't think she wanted anyone to know'.[69] Nevertheless, there could be brakes upon even this form of talk, as Francie Nichol found. Busy putting the children to bed one night, with the door open to the street she chanced to hear the voices of women in a shop across the road describing her in a none too friendly manner as a 'brazen bitch' no better than she should be. The remark shattered her, and she eventually confessed her suicidal depression to her son, who immediately went and put the gossiping women to rights. From then on they couldn't do enough for the family, telling the rest of the neighbours of their situation, and gathering together food, coal and cast-offs.[70] Such examples illustrate not only the ambivalent quality of gossip but also the shifting sands of the so-called 'community', or 'neighbourhood' life it reflected, since as these observations suggest gossip had both positive and negative sides. Communal intimacy was invariably double-edged in the tensions it stimulated between neighbours, while the brake which gossip put on unconventional behaviour also made it an important area of social regulation within the community. Street moneylenders often used the threat of exposure through gossip to blackmail clients into compliance, and this aspect could be particularly effective in neighbourhoods permeated by rigid conceptions of respectability or in middle-class communities where women were held up as exemplars of good behaviour and custodians of morality. While gossip could play an important part in encouraging a sense of self-worth through a sharing of views and information, it became threatening once a woman's sense of her self became linked with an idealized domestic identity. As Kate Phillips wrote in her survey of women in contemporary Glasgow, 'Self-esteem is at risk in talking openly and frankly to other women. Propriety says good wives don't gossip, decent families don't argue, happy couples don't bicker over money, good mothers love their children all the time.'[71] Gossip, as we have seen, threatened the myths attached to family life, and the risks of divulging in public what had been private consequently placed both individual and collective checks on its subject matter. Conversation about others could be restrained by a number of factors, not least of which was kinship. Such talk often had to be handled with care since it could be difficult to know who was related to whom in both fast-shifting neighbourhoods and localities underpinned by complex family relationships. An elderly woman born towards the end of the nineteenth century in an isolated Fen village described the close-knit nature of the place, which had no outsiders and much inter-marriage. 'They was all married to someone in the village. You was afraid to talk of any one, because they was all relations. You couldn't get far, that's why you kept together.'[72] Similarly, an Ordsall woman described the content of talk in her neighbourhood during the inter-war years: 'You wouldn't tell them personal details – nothing like that. You'd discuss your children, your work, what you were going to have for dinner or tea – sometimes your husbands.'[73]

The verbal reticence described earlier meant there were also other areas of experience which were subject to privatizing tendencies. In particular, the harshness of working-class life coloured attitudes towards both offspring and other women in similar circumstances and caused women to put up with all kinds of physical problems because it was considered 'unwomanly' to complain. Thus, while abortifacient remedies were often passed on by word of mouth, physical complaints which stemmed from childbirth or other female ailments apparently received less sympathetic attention, possibly because they were so common. A former midwife who worked among women in a very poor part of Birmingham during the 1940s described how 'an awful lot of them put up with pain, it was part of every-day living ... these mothers used to be in long, tedious labours but very few of them made any row at all, the fortitude of pain was much higher, because they had been schooled up from that from children'.[74] Such women had known the pain of hunger while keeping the rest of the family fed, and expected to put up with the pain of physical ailments because they couldn't afford to go to the doctor or dentist: 'I've seen them with a dreadful tooth abscess and a big salt bag, used to fill a bag with salt and put it in the oven and get it hot and hold it against their faces, they couldn't afford to go to the dentist because he charged.'[75] Marie Stopes reported that 31 per cent of her first 10,000 patients in the 1920s had serious untreated gynaecological problems, and one woman writing in *Maternity*, who suffered from the 'cruel torture' of a fallen womb, only found out by accident that other women she met were not experiencing the same distress.[76] This ignorance stemmed in part from a fatalistic sense that it was a woman's lot to assume such burdens, and contributed to a culture of private pain and public stoicism which effectively closed off certain areas of a woman's life to frank, supportive discussion. A woman describing her own experiences of childbirth in the 1890s, explained how no attempt had been made to get help for her since, 'At that time it was much more usual to trust to Providence, and if a woman died it only proved her weakness and unfitness for motherhood.'[77] Although such attitudes may have been less acute by the inter-war years, Jane Lewis nevertheless suggests the persistence of such ideas when she observes there is some evidence that 'working women' in particular disliked the idea of anaesthesia during childbirth. She quotes from the Annual Report of the General Lying-In Hospital for 1932, which recorded that in the Westminster and Lambeth localities, 'a definite stigma is attached to any mother who has an abnormal confinement – that is to say, an anaesthetic'.[78]

Such examples not only suggest the extent to which such a critical area of feminine experience remained individualized and closed to frank supportive discussion, but also signify the important part which gossip played in reinforcing norms and expectations of behaviour, particularly as far as women were concerned, although even men were affected by it. As Robert Roberts declared: 'Though a man might fear the law he feared too the disapproval of his neighbours and especially the condemnation of those who through articulateness, intelligence, economic and social standing acted as moral exemplars within the community.'[79] Roberts's observation underlines the importance of talk in raising and promoting standards of behaviour, although it could also serve to keep neighbours 'in their place' by undermining personal prestige, since a woman who held herself aloof from the street gossip could be seen as self-consciously rejecting the neighbourhood value system. Thus, the niece of a Northampton woman who married into a wealthy middle-class family in the inter-war years was felt to be trying to cut herself off from her working-class relations. As a result, whenever she passed by her aunt's house she was subject to taunts and catcalls to such an degree that the victimized woman had eventually to threaten court action through a solicitor's letter.[80]

Such examples contrast with the images of neighbourliness and friendly chat which feature powerfully in many recollections of life in inter-war working-class communities, when,

> on warm summer evenings Neighbours sat out on the pavements and gossiped. The children walked on their hands, did handstands by the wall, played leap-frog, tippled, did country dancing or just sang songs like 'One Man Went To Mow'. Later on, jugs of tea, cakes and jam butties would appear. Everyone was happy and at peace. When it started to get dark, we all went inside to cheery 'good-nights'.[81]

It was, after all, 'in the warmer days, above all, that people felt a glow of "community", a sense of belonging each to each that, for the time being, overrode class and family differences'.[82] Warm summer weather was particularly important for women in the poor urban districts, since it gave them the opportunity for convivial socializing. The streets of such neighbourhoods seemed full of people at such times: '... they always used to bring their chairs outside and sit outside. The ruddy street was full of chairs. There were more chairs outside than there were inside.'[83] The extent of such clutter was described by another Preston resident. 'We lived in Harrington Street and there was one family and when anybody came on a Sunday night in summer they didn't go into the house, they brought them a chair out. We counted them one night and there were twenty-three people belonging to them, family and friends.'[84] Yet these cosy street scenes easily obscure the contradictions of enforced intimacy in many close-knit neighbourhoods, and spatial distinctions were apparent even in the midst of this easy familiarity. Jack Jackson wrote of inter-war Salford, for example, that, 'The man of the house, if he wasn't in the pub, would almost always sit in solitary state, while the womenfolk gossiped in groups of perhaps three or four, keeping an eye on the youngsters playing around them in the street.'[85] The obverse of these cosy memories was also the best forgotten tendency for cold, bad weather to push people back indoors to their individual firesides, so that 'on early Sunday evenings in winter loneliness along the streets seemed almost palpable', although the extent to which this reduced more communal forms of communication obviously varied from community to community.[86] Hilda Scattergood, for example, who was brought up in Tebay, North Westmorland, described the long winter months when both men and women joined forces 'for the big project of every winter', the new hearth rug made by pushing rag strips through a hessian backing with a 'prodder' made from a piece of bone: 'While the prodding was going on the children played their games among the grown ups' feet under the frame, visitors called and took a chair by the frame, producing their own prodders, joining in the work and the gossip.'[87] Mat making in the Northumberland mining village of Heddon-on-the-Wall, which was also done on a frame, provided a similar 'focal point for neighbourly contact'. A 'casual visit for a cup of tea would often be the occasion for friends to sit and work at the mat for a few minutes', a comment which again highlights the frequently observed need for casual conversation among women in highly regulated working-class communities to be given some practical justification.[88]

The material circumstances of their lives had a critical effect upon the way that working-class people interacted with each other and on the images which were presented to outsiders and appeared in neighbourhood myth. The friendly reluctance to go to bed in summer also owed a great deal to the deterrent effect of the bug population, which often became a 'real pestilence' in hot weather.[89] Richard Heaton described the bug infested houses of his early days in Salford before the First World War, where the summer saw people sitting outside their homes 'until well after midnight and they were tired out, otherwise they could not sleep for the infestation'.[90]

> No wonder most people didn't bother to go to bed at nights, and sat
> up instead at the bottom of the passageways, in a rocking chair or

armchair, gossiping away to each other until the dawn appeared. At least it was better than being bitten away by bugs![91]

It was scarcely surprising that the communal intimacy of poor working-class streets should be rejected for these very associations with poverty by those who had the resources to afford physical space and social distance.

The negative side to gossip, which led individuals or groups of people who failed to conform to established behaviour and conventions to be victimized, meant that unmarried and childless married couples often attracted sly speculation in pre-war communities. 'Spinsters' or 'old maids' stimulated doubts and innuendo about their lack of sexual experience, taunts from young people and 'the amused contempt of some married neighbours'.[92] 'There used to be a lot said about women who were spinsters. Things about doubting their virginity, and thinking, "Oh, well ... she's going to die wondering", all that sort of thing. And I think very often it was quite wrong, and just for the sake of talking about it.'[93] Robert Roberts reflected that the very word lodger 'stood, so to speak, pregnant with meaning' offering scope for scandal which malicious tongues made the most of.[94] Religious bigotry had similarly strong roots in gossip and sexual prurience:

> Well, first of all everyone was very conscious that, when new people came to live in the road as they fairly often did, you know, and the first bit of gossip was, have you found out where they go? Meaning which Church they went to ... oh ... goes to St. Joseph's. And the Protestants were very conscious of this and there was this inbuilt, it was almost like ... a bit like Ireland today. It's gone now a lot, thank goodness, but in gossip, they would all, you know, take sides very, very strongly and over race too, er, you know, there were certain handed down 'cockeyed' notions actually, but handed down as gospel. And I remember one occasion where I was playing out and someone came and said, hey, there's a Jew come, and they're down at that shop, that new shop down on the main road. So we all left everything, we had to go to gaze at this Jew and I was very disappointed, he didn't look very much different from other people, you know, but it was an event ...[95]

A woman who described herself as having been brought up on 'Methodist superstition' in the Collyhurst area of north Manchester described how it had always been 'Protestant gossip ... that the priest was sleeping with the Children of Mary'. She knew a man whose house over-looked a small Catholic cemetery attached to a nursing home, 'and he rein-forced the popular belief that the bodies of babies that nuns had had were buried there. Now that was a very common belief, very common.'[96]

Besides focusing on more vulnerable members of the community and helping ensure neighbourhood hegemony, such talk was also important in excluding undesirable newcomers to a locality. Louie Stride's memoirs, recalling her bleak childhood as the illegitimate daughter of a prostitute mother in Bath during the 1900s, give an important insight into life at the social and economic margins and painfully reveal the devastating effect which talk could have upon a woman's status.

> In the year 1907 when I was born there was not any welfare State bounties, or societies for unmarried mothers etc., if one had been 'unfortunate' as did sometimes happen such as in my mother's case, one was often turned out of the family home owing to the disgrace and resultant gossip in poor neighbourhoods.[97]

Stride describes what she remembers as one of the most humiliating days of her life when, on moving into a new neighbourhood, all the women in the surrounding cottages verbally attacked her mother, calling her a 'Scarlet Woman', and throwing her goods out in the yard; 'coming to live amongst a lot of decent people with a Bastard, they weren't going to tolerate that and they didn't'. It was this kind of persecution which ultimately made her mother turn to prostitution 'in a quiet sort of way'. Being with a man would have made her far less of a sexual threat, and Stride does in fact describe the considerable difference it made when her mother married, reiterating what Francie Nichol highlights.[98]

Nevertheless, for those who conformed to the pattern of neighbourhood behaviour, gossip had an accepted place in local life.

> If you got a place like Colne Lane and Waterside where they are all higgledy piggledy back-to-back houses, everybody knows everybody's business more or less; but it's not vicious. Well, some were, but generally speaking it weren't vicious gossip. It were more like wanting to know for curiosity, an' women helped if ye needed it. Nobody had much, but what they had, they'd share.[99]

Similarly, a Lancashire respondent implicitly recognized the informative value of gossip. Lilian Douglas, grew up on a poor street in Bristol where 'neighbours were in and out of each others homes ... and you knew almost as much of your neighbours business as you did your own and vice versa. Of course, there were bad neighbours and since gossip was practically the only form of entertainment, some of it was malicious, but not much.'[100]

Such examples suggest how gossip oiled the mechanism by which women in the poorest neighbourhoods were integrated into a supportive grapevine which provided mutual aid in times of hardship. As the sociologist Elizabeth Bott wrote in her work *Family and Social Network*:

> Being gossiped about is as much a sign of belonging to the neighbourly network as being gossiped with. If one refuses contact with neighbours one is thought odd and eventually one will be left alone; no gossip, no companionship![101]

Remaining aloof meant missing out on 'having a laugh' and the reassurance of knowing that other women shared the same troubles. 'If someone else says, well, I'm the same, we're all the same, you feel a lot better.'[102] Participation involved a necessary sacrifice of privacy because, 'If one wants to reap the rewards of companionship and small acts of mutual aid, one must conform to local standards, and one must expect to be included in the gossip.'[103] Yet this sense of shared experience had undoubtedly negative connotations for those women who aspired to a more privatized version of respectability, and for whom feeling separate and different held the promise of higher social status. Thus, despite its apparent attractions, not all participated in this gregarious culture, since participation in the gossip network meant not only gossiping about others, but also being a subject of gossip.

The mutual dependence and conformity with neighbourhood norms of behaviour which such activities implied were also restraints from which some were quite happy to escape (particularly if they had a degree of freedom from financial pressures). Florence Bell, in her study of the Edwardian iron-working community in Middlesbrough, described the hostility and suspicion with which those who considered themselves 'superior' regarded their more extrovert neighbours, 'There is an implied praise of the contrary attitude, a consciousness of virtue in the woman who says "I make no neighbours", or "I keep myself to myself", which constitutes, no doubt, an indictment against the general influence of the talk at the street door.'[104] Such feelings were likely to be reciprocated since refusal to gossip tended to be viewed as 'stand-offish' or 'snooty', as it so obviously rejected the values which helped cement the local community.

Aspiring to be 'respectable' could consequently be a considerable block to communication between women (and children) in such situations. Even friends skirted around certain more intimate details of their lives. 'Where I lived two of the girls that I was friendly with didn't have a dad. I would imagine they were divorced. Then you didn't ask questions.'[105] Similar sentiments were expressed by Angela Rodaway, who grew up in working-class Islington in the inter-war years. Her family had known better days, and belonged to what she described as the 'deserving' poor. She recalled overhearing the whispered conversation of some older girls when she was about nine years old:

> They were talking about the 'lady' who, I suppose, was the relieving officer. I had a feeling that my mother would not approve of my listening nor even of my knowing about it. My family were 'superior'. That was a good thing to be, but if you wanted to remain in that state, you had to be very careful; ignorance of some parts was part of it.[106]

Rodaway's observation about the 'deserving' poor was reiterated by Ann Bailey, whose family frowned on credit. Asked whether she ever saw

people pawn, she replied: 'Yes, I saw that when I was going to school –
opposite the school gates there was always a row of women, and most
used to have shawl on, and there'd be bundles on the floor. I used to
wonder about those ladies. If you asked your mother she would say "get
on with your dinner" or something like that. I didn't tumble to it till years
after. It was something you didn't talk about.'[107] Ivy Corrigan didn't even
realize her family was poor since 'they never discussed anything in front of
us'. Her father was a labourer who only worked irregularly. The family
were active church goers, and never bought anything on hire purchase
because they were afraid of being unable to pay for it if her father lost his
job.[108] Talk about financial circumstances was another aspect of this same
taboo: 'You never discussed money at all – that was your own private
affair.'[109] As another woman explained: 'I always used to say well I've paid
me rent and if I've got nothing, nobody'll know. It was your pride.'[110]
Respectability implied a distinct set of values which were impressed upon
children from an early age. Mrs Hopwood's parents emphasized the virtues
of hard work, and the fact that 'You mustn't listen to anything'.[111] For
others it was: 'Honesty, yes, always stressed honesty. And, of course, cleanliness etcetera – very, very strict. And never to borrow, never to borrow, or
gossip. She didn't like you to start talking about people, and she said,
always, she always said, "If anybody tells you, tells you anything, and it's
to do with gossip, you should say yes, aye, no".' It was a technique which
was designed not to cause offence, allowing them to listen, but ensuring
that they did not add anything to what was being told.[112] Ada Hunt's
mother 'always brought us up to be good neighbours. That was part of her
religion.' However, neighbouring to her did not represent the kind of 'toing
and froing' which could so easily become a 'nuisance', so that while she was
always willing to give a helping hand, she did not go to gossip.[113]

   'Respectable' withdrawal into domestic privacy was also removal from
potential trouble, as manifested in quarrels and street fights. Maurice
Broady, writing of communities in the Mersey ward of post-war
Birkenhead, stated that 'jangling ' or gossiping about other people behind
their backs was considered to be a characteristic of 'rough' families. It was
disliked because it unsettled social relationships and caused trouble due to
loss of temper and fights. 'Indeed, the rough ones were sometimes generi-
cally defined as "people you have to be careful what you say to," for they
were often characterised as being prepared to resort to fighting as a means
of settling differences of opinion.'[114] Harry Watkin's mother and grannie
regarded the people who lived in the smaller streets off theirs as a little
lower on the social scale, since 'doorstep rows were common. Women – it
was always women – cursed and blackguarded each other from the security of their own door steps. Barefoot children played around and fought
and now and again gangs of older boys battled with each other.'[115] This

fear of disturbance, particularly as expressed in drinking, dirtiness and quick loss of temper, reflected the ever present social tensions which were engendered by acute poverty. The Birmingham midwife mentioned earlier observed how, 'the toilet was always leading to terrible fights in these yards, because when twelve families were depending on one toilet, if it broke down and the landlord wasn't speedy in getting it repaired then they went to the next one, and that caused problems'.[116]

Under these circumstances, conformity with neighbourhood mores not only implied a belief in the importance of shared experience, but also reflected a desire to control or at least stabilize the uncertainties of daily life. Gossip's own identification with poverty and vulgarity was rather how the more respectable came to regard the wearing of curlers in public – an intrusion of what should have been private into public space. Gossip's interest in private doings threatened to nudge intimacy into scandal, and as such had a considerable capacity to deflate those with social aspirations. Nevertheless, holding aloof from the local gossip exacerbated a conspiratorial, evil-minded interpretation of its function, since those women who kept themselves apart from street conversations made themselves more susceptible to damaging myths about the poor and their apparently feckless behaviour, which effectively hid the importance of reciprocity and supportiveness. Cultivated ignorance of those aspects of life which could otherwise stain a family's reputation and identify it with 'roughness' can, in a sense, be seen as a deliberate removal from what has been called the 'knowable community', that common stock of knowledge about local people and circumstances which gave strength and cohesion to community life.[117] The 'housewife', whom Walter Greenwood interviewed in his collection of essays *How The Other Man Lives* during the 1930s, had little patience with such time wasting as gossip in her highly organized day, which left not a moment to spare until noon: 'I can't be civil to friends who come gossiping of a morning. I've had to arrange my household work systematically and I resent any interruptions. Anyway, they usually come from people who're irresponsible.' She had been 'born in a slum', but had moved with her husband to a semi-detached house which they were buying on a mortgage. She had a small baby, and found it took all her energy to attend to the house.[118]

By the inter-war years, a growing stress upon the housewife's function and the need for women to pay 'proper' attention to domestic tasks possibly made such women increasingly sensitive to the more invasive aspects of street and neighbourhood talk. Shoddy housing and cramped living conditions had, of course, always left the poor with little privacy: 'We could escape to the lavatory in the backyard, but even then it would not be long before someone would shout, "How long are you going to sit out there? I'm waiting to come on there!"' (In Kathleen Dayus's yard, ten households shared five dry privies.)[119] There was often no escape even within family, for the public nature of life in poor working-class areas easily led to a running commentary on activities by fellow family members – 'Where have you been? ... Where are you going? ... What are you doing? ...', which had an intrusive quality from which the younger generation, experiencing a gradual broadening of experiences, were happy to escape.[120] Set in this context it is possible to see how 'gossip' could readily become something of a codeword for dislike of the past and an apparently outdated way of living. Gossiping was something associated with the poor, the elderly and ill-educated whose fluid sense of time was at odds with the discipline and efficiency of 'modern' life.[121] Elizabeth Roberts, for example, describes how, in the inter-war years, there was, among the more aspiring of her respondents in three Lancashire towns (Barrow, Preston and Lancaster), 'a growing fear of being too open with neighbours in case one became the object of gossip'.[122] Such tendencies may have been reinforced by the growing number of new public health professionals who promoted an 'ideology of motherhood' among working-class women. They gradually infiltrated the networks which had traditionally sustained such communities, undermining the authority of older women and denigrating 'traditional methods of childcare – in particular care by anyone except the mother: neighbours, grandmothers, and older children looking after babies were automatically assumed to be dirty, incompetent and irresponsible'.[123] Margaret Loane, writing in the 1900s, maintained from her experience as a district nurse, that the working-class women she knew in London were generally grateful for the attendance of a visiting nurse, 'more especially if of a class so distinct from their own that they have no fear of her gossiping about their affairs'.[124] That is not to say that the matrifocal emphasis of many working-class communities in which the maternal grandmother dominated disappeared, but that channels of communication to and from a much broader society became stronger, promoting an external and more individualized solution to domestic problems. As a result, gossip started to lose the bonding function it had performed in enclosed and largely sexually segregated working-class communities where few such outlets and external influences had previously existed. While it undoubtedly manifested itself in many other spheres of life, gossip's localized, neighbourly role was gradually to decline in many urban areas.

The physical deprivation of their homes forced a frequently uneasy public life upon the poor, in which exhaustion, stress and depression easily triggered quarrels and street fights. Gossip helped mediate this tension between the public and private, particularly in terms of its monitoring of street behaviour and neighbourhood standards. Concern for such issues was one of the ways that working-class communities struggled to assert their self-respect, although poverty and patriarchal forces narrowed the focus of such preoccupations to personal behaviour and the domestic scene. With few other channels through which to express themselves, some women preserved their self-esteem by elevating the value of domestic chores, while the weekly pattern of household activities itself contributed an important collective rhythm to life which helped give women the psychological momentum to keep up their daily struggles. Older women, from whom the burdens of childcare had receded, tended to be particularly concerned with monitoring local standards, deriving considerable status from the power which their judgments generated. Their identity was largely defined by their maternal function, since they were often at the centre of a web of kinship relations. However, the strength and creativity to which this communal and familial influence testified should be treated with care, and it is to this issue that we turn in the following chapter.

Notes

1. White 1890, 2.
2. R. Roberts 1971: 1974, 43,
3. Social Welfare History Archives, University of Minnesota, Helen Hall papers, Box 108L, Folder S. Helen Hall, head resident of Henry Street Settlement, New York, visited Britain in 1947 to interview a range of housewives about rationing schemes. My thanks to Mike Rose for this reference.
4. MSTC, Tape 604.
5. Hooley 1981, 6–7.
6. Turner 1988, 2.
7. MSTC, Tape 795.
8. Tebbutt 1983, 58–60.
9. Select Committee on Infant Life Protection, 1871, Q. 4527–4563. Quoted in Rose 1986.
10. Haythorne 1986, 8–10; Oral History Archive, Lancaster University, Mrs. H 8P, born 1903, Preston.
11. R. Roberts 1971: 1974, 43.
12. Hoggart 1958: 1962, 61.
13. R. Roberts 1970: 1978, 71; Forrester 1974: 1981, 99–100.
14. *Porcupine*, 21 May 1864.
15. OLHG, EB.
16. *Porcupine*, 4 June 1864, 76.
17. Westwood 1984, 138 ff. Describes the importance of gossip in the Indian Community of 'Stitchtown', a post-war British city, whose industry is based on hosiery and knitting.
18. Dennis, Henriques and Slaughter 1956.
19. Dayus 1985: 1986, 5, 43, 73, 75.
20. E. Roberts 1984: 1986, 193.
21. Oral History Archive, Lancaster University, Mr B7.
22. Chinn 1988, 43–44; see also Bourke 1994, 74–81, Ross 1993, 84–85, 250.
23. R. Roberts 1971: 1974, 44, 85; R. Roberts 1970: 1978, 82, 83.
24. Lancaster Oral History Archive. Mrs H 8P.

25. Robinson 1975.
26. Taped conversation with Mary Turner, describing the recollections of a student in one of her local history classes.
27. MSTC. Tape 163.
28. Chinn 1988, 42.
29. Chinn 1988, 145.
30. Widdowson 1976, 38.
31. Wakefield 1980: 1988, 62–64.
32. Gillis 1985, 235, referring to the period 1850–1914.
33. Widdowson 1976, 38. Even during the 1970s the grandmother of a lower-middle-class family in Sheffield still invariably used 'the word "brazen", with strong pejorative connotations, when referring to such a woman, and her comments and intonation indicate her scorn of such behaviour, and stigmatise it as socially unacceptable'.
34. Chinn 1988, 31.
35. Williamson 1982, 149.
36. Foundling Hospital Petition, 1870/11, cited in Gillis 1985, 256.
37. Dayus 1982: 1987, 164, 166.
38. Miscellaneous tapes, Miss Badby.
39. *Ibid.*
40. Burnett 1982, 218.
41. 'John O'London', 'Manchester: An Impression', in *T.P.'s Weekly*, 3 March 1905, 265. My thanks to Terry Wyke for this reference.
42. Linton 1982, 52.
43. Cf. Ardener 1993, 82.
44. *T.P.'s Weekly*, 3 March 1905, 265.
45. Conway 1983, 2.
46. Oral History Archive, Lancaster University. Mr B. Born 1927 in Preston, 'in a fairly typical street of terraced houses but superior, or at least the people in the street thought so'; 'we were poor but respectable'. Father was a waiter. Mother had wanted to be a teacher, but had to leave school at 13 to work in the mill. BOHP, Tape 32a.
47. MSTC, Tape 544.
48. Davies 1985, 13. Fred Davies was born in 1908. His mother had ten children. Other writers have also observed how lack of paid employment for women led them to elevate the status of domestic work by adding ritual to it. Crook 1982, 43; Gittins 1977, 84–100.
49. Harris (undated).
50. MSTC, Tape 493; BOHP, Tape 18.
51. MSTC, Tape 506.
52. Slater 1984, 24–25. This practice has been described as an old Lancashire custom which was supposed to ward off evil, although its magical meaning had long since been replaced by a more pragmatic one.
53. Blair 1985, 67.
54. MSTC, Tape 803; BOHP, Tape 23c; McCrindle and Rowbotham 1977: 1979, 126–27.
55. Tildsley, 1985, 12; Hoggart 1958: 1962, 3. Peter Donnelly expressed similar views on the volatile nature of much local gossip: 'there was jealousy that sometimes became an obsession'. Donnelly 1950, 111.
56. OLHG, L.
57. OLHG, AM.

58. Miscellaneous interviews, May Thompson; McCrindle and Rowbotham 1977: 1979, 221.
59. Stride (undated); James Stewart and Sons Ltd, *Retail Credit Drapers' Training Guide*, Manchester, Undated.
60. Williamson 1982, 125.
61. Davies, C.S. 1963, 156.
62. Conway 1983, 24.
63. Dayus 1982: 1987, introduction, x–xi, xvi, 19. Dayus was born in 1903. Her family was poor, but not as badly off as others in the area; despite three dependent younger children, three older offspring were earning a wage while her father was irregularly employed in a casting shop and her mother went charring.
    The imposed intimacy of court life also had its more formal side. Dayus's mother does not appear to have been on first name terms with any of her neighbours, all of whom were referred to as Mrs.
64. OLHG, DM. The respondent's shifting or encompassing use of 'you' is also an interesting illustration of such proximity. My thanks to Anna Davin for many useful comments on this chapter.
65. Dayus 1982: 1987, 64–65.
66. Robinson 1975, 95.
67. Miscellaneous tapes, May Thompson
68. Pettigrew 1989, 28.
69. OLHG, E.B.
70. Robinson 1975, 133–34.
71. Glasgow Women's Studies Group 1983, 126–27.
72. Chamberlain 1975: 1977, 32.
73. OLHG, DM.
74. MSTC, Tape 964.
75. MSTC, Tape 964.
76. Lewis 1980, 221.
77. Davies 1915: 1978, 38, 89.
78. Quoted in Lewis 1980, 20.
79. Roberts 1971:1974, 183.
80. Northampton tapes, Mrs Roberts.
81. Hinson 1984, 8. Edith Hinson was born in 1910 in a four roomed terraced house in Newbridge Lane, Stockport.
82. R. Roberts 1970: 1978, 56, 106; Hooley 1981, 36.
83. Oral History Archive, Lancaster University. Mr F1P. Born 1906 near Whitehaven in Cumberland, moved to Preston in 1917. Father a miner who was injured in a pit accident and subsequently worked as a poultry dresser in Preston. Mother a cook in domestic service before marriage; after marriage, took in washing.
84. Oral History Archive, Lancaster University, Mr G1P.
85. Jackson 1990, 8. Jack Jackson was born in 1922. His father was a dustman.
86. Roberts 1970: 1978, 57, 106; Haworth 1986, 35–36.
87. *Comment*, Lancaster University Magazine, *c.* 1979–80, Childhood in the 1930s, Hilda Scattergood. Mrs Lyons also wrote describing the pleasures, talk and laughs of making rag rugs with two very good neighbours. Letter to Norma Watkins (undated), 1988.
88. Williamson 1982, 122, 126.

89. Linton 1982, life in Hoxton, London, about the time of the First World War, 53.
90. Heaton 1982, 2.
91. Furniss 1979, 12.
92. R. Roberts 1970: 1978, 81.
93. Miscellaneous tapes, May Thompson
94. R. Roberts 1970: 1978, 82–83.
95. MSTC, Tape 803.
96. Miscellaneous tapes, May Thompson
97. Stride (undated), 6.
98. Stride (undated), 6–7; Robinson 1975.
99. MSTC, Tape 628.
100. Lilian Douglas was born in 1910. Her father was a carpenter who ill-treated his wife. Murray 1986, 35–36.
101. Bott 1957:1968, 67. As Oscar Wilde observed in a rather different context, 'There is only one thing in the world worse than being talked about, and that is not being talked about.' *The World of Dorian Gray*, 1891.
102. Glasgow Women's Studies Group 1983, 126.
103. Bott 1957:1968, 67.
104. Stride (undated), 6.
105. OLHG, AB.
106. Rodaway, 1960: 1985, 4, 6–8, 32.
107. OLHG, AB.
108. OLHG, IC.
109. OLHG, L.
110. OLHG, AM.
111. MSTC. Tape 42.
112. MSTC, Tape 36.
113. MSTC, Tape 39.
114. Broady 1956, 225. My thanks to Pat Ayers for drawing attention to this article.
115. Watkin 1985, 10.
116. MSTC, Tape 964.
117. My thanks to Dermot Healy for drawing attention to this point.
118. Greenwood 1939, 122–3.
119. Turner 1988, 1–2. Describes the wash-house in Levenshulme, Manchester, during the period 1968–76. Dayus 1982: 1987, xii, 19, 25.
120. Interview notes, August 1987. Davies 1915: 1978, 190.
121. Lewis 1980, 221.
122. E. Roberts 1984: 1986.
123. Davin 1978, 12.
124. Loane 1909, 238.

CHAPTER FOUR

Blood thicker than water?
Family and street tensions

> Hillgate always comprised of families, they all lived close by, do you
> understand what I mean? The daughter would get married and live
> close by, the son would get married and live close by. There was clans,
> if you understand me, and we all lived close by. When I say we, I
> mean my aunts and uncles, and the grandmother was the queen of the
> clan, do you understand? And there was all that. That's why there was
> always a lot of fights on Hillgate, because if you touched one, you
> touched that clan, and this clan and that clan would fight, like in
> Kentucky, you know, the, and this is what used to happen. That's
> why it got a bad name, Hillgate, because of the fighting that took
> place.[1]

Many women shared a collectivity of interests with men in the eighteenth
and early nineteenth centuries when they played a public and vigorous part
in such communal actions as agitation during food riots, opposition
against the enclosures and fights with bailiffs and other figures of authority. However, this kind of collective involvement was diluted during the
course of the nineteenth century as the social, cultural and economic focus
gradually shifted to more privatized and formal expressions of political
life. More institutional forms of political expression developed which
modelled themselves on male experience and took no account of women's
domestic and family responsibilities. At the same time suspicions of female
power declined as the time-honoured forms of communal politics in which
women had traditionally participated were gradually marginalized. Yet
despite the tendency of such trends to push women's experiences to the
edges of formal political experience, working-class women sustained a way
of living which continued to maintain values deeply rooted in the collective moral code of 'traditional' life. Mutual aid and neighbourliness
became the bedrock upon which working-class women managed to establish whatever self-esteem and confidence were possible under the trying
conditions which beset their daily lives. The complex mesh of neighbourhood and kinship networks which underpinned poor urban communities
was largely their responsibility, and the political response of many
working-class women became more tied to questions of survival and the
perpetuation of this collective morality than allegiance to a specific political group or party.[2]

The working-class mother

The extent to which mothers moulded and influenced life in working-class communities has been increasingly recognized in recent years, although such observations, in their desire to redress the imbalance of traditional emphases, can also extend a rather unhelpful stereotype of women's lives. Their stress on the 'self-sacrifice' of motherhood and the 'devotion' this generated among their children, particularly males, is couched in the language of sanctification, whose sometimes reverent overtones threaten to place women back on another pedestal. Not only does this language over-simplify the reality of women's lives, it fails to acknowledge the tensions which were inherent in such relationships. The mother and son bond, for example, had particular implications for the relationship with daughters-in-law, and while the common cultural stereotype is of the dominant mother-in-law viewed from the son-in-law's point of view, less has been written from the daughter-in-law's perspective. A man frequently disliked the influence which his wife's mother exerted since it undermined his assumptions about a man's 'right' to be master of his own household. The regard in which he held his own mother, however, established a standard of perfection against which his wife was judged and frequently found wanting.

Ellen Ross has pointed out how working-class London mothers kept 'each of their sons close to them for almost two decades', and suggests that one of the 'major projects for young men given how emotionally close and how long working-class mothers "kept" their sons, was to distinguish their future wife from their mother'.[3] There was consequently an important contest to be waged in the early period of marriage as a husband attempted to pattern his wife's behaviour on that of his mother while establishing dominance over her. Joyce Storey wondered why 'mothers and aunties' spoilt the lads so, as she described how her mother-in-law pandered to her son's needs. Finding her 'dear boy' without cigarettes at breakfast, his mother

> extracted a fresh pack of fags and beamed with pleasure when her beloved Bertie threw his arms about her neck and kissed her. The black cloud vanished and the sun came out. When his gaze travelled over to me sitting there watching this little domestic scene, it seemed that the look conveyed a clear message.
> 'This is the sort of thing my mother does for me, and because I like it I want you to do the same.'[4]

Despite the strong links which working-class women frequently retained with their own mothers on marriage, powerful mothers-in-law could have decided views on the obligations of their daughters-in-law and were not averse to implying that loyalties elsewhere were a betrayal of husband and adopted kin. Mrs Perkins, a Northampton woman, for example, recalled how her mother-in-law criticized her for spending some time at Christmas with her own relatives, asserting that, 'After all, you're a member of this family now.'[5] A.S. Jasper's elder brother 'picked up' with a local girl who caused some unspecified rift between him and the rest of his family. They eventually got married, but none of Jasper's family attended. 'He was just not one of us. My mother never got over his desertion of the family and in future years would not have his name mentioned.'[6] Daughters-in-law who did not fit into the family's familiar pattern of behaviour in some way could find life rather difficult. Mrs Hill, from a very quiet working-class street of skilled workers and men in clerical jobs, married into a less well-off family of largely unskilled workers. She recalled the little humiliations which her mother-in-law tended to inflict on her:

> she used to wait to embarrass me in front of everybody ... She used to know I used to blush ever so easily ... I know when we went to a social ... and they were doing something, and I didn't know how to do it, so I thought, well, I'd wait, some dance or something, so I said, 'Ooh, I'll do it in a minute.' So his mum said, 'You can't come here', in a loud voice, 'You can't come here and not join in, you know'. She said, 'You have to join in, you'll have to learn to join in.' I thought, 'You sod!' And that's the kind of thing she used to say.

This particular mother-in-law was well known in her street for helping out neighbours, but was also kept at arm's length by some for her argumentativeness and fierce defence of her family's interests if anyone took advantage or offended them. 'She'd got a real good tongue, she could pull people to bits.' Her daughter-in-law's reticence was suspected and interpreted as snobbishness. After being very ill in hospital with her first baby, she was discharged and went outside with a nurse and baby to wait for her taxi, which her husband had failed to order.

> 'Mother said you didn't need a taxi, you could walk.' And the midwife went mad. She said, 'She's not walking!' I'd been in a month, I'd been ever so ill. And when we got to his mother's, she said 'You got a taxi? I told him you didn't need one. Our Viv next door walks up with hers!' I said, 'I don't give a damn what your Viv does, she's nothing to do with me, I don't know the girl!'[7]

As was the case with this working-class mother, the mutual dependence and bonding which took place when they had their own children reinforced a tight allegiance which made many women willing to enter the fray on their children's behalf, regardless of the rights and wrongs of the quarrel and the need for peaceful coexistence with neighbours.[8] 'I think very often they were quite powerful figures in the community, and very often big, strong women that you'd hesitate to tangle with. I've known one in particular, nobody locally dare say anything about her kids in her hearing. And you didn't say anything about her either.'[9] Mrs York's mother-in-law told her

> that when the children were small they had an old lady living next door. Apparently the boys annoyed her, and she complained. Gran said she wasn't having that and apparently caused some big rows. In the end, the old lady got fed up, saw a solicitor who sent a letter warning gran that if there was more trouble she would take it to court, as it was making her ill. Gran said she wasn't bothered, but Granddad was so angry at the shame of it, that she stopped the boys from upsetting the old lady, and quietened down herself.[10]

The tribal image established by the Stockport man quoted at the beginning of this chapter was reinforced in the poorest areas by the size of local families, and there was an extent to which fecundity remained the measure of women's power in such districts, especially as their children grew older, when some women took (or attempted to take) a controlling influence in their children's lives long after they had reached maturity.

It is pertinent to raise these issues and to examine the role of the working-class mother in relation to gossip because interest in and sensitivity to the nuances of individual behaviour which were expressed in such talk owed much to the experiences and expectations of family life. They stemmed from the 'servicing' function assumed of women, which was demonstrated in frequent self-sacrifice and responsiveness to family needs. Such women remained attentive to street talk, filtering and drawing upon it as an important survival tool. However, their family focus often made them unduly aware of slights directed at their children and family, and contributed to an ambivalence about gossip because of its role as potent source of quarrels and disagreements.

Information gleaned from gossip was often pooled and tested out within the family circle, and contributed to the working-class mother's reputation as a powerful, wise and knowledgeable protector holding her family together. The power derived from an awareness of other people's 'secrets' added, as we have seen, to the influence and authority of older working-class women, and helped sustain the mother's image as someone who always knew best.

Gossip in communities where larger families were common could have a significant family dimension, since a large number of relatives maximized the sources of neighbourhood talk. Large families gave plenty of opportunity for the discussion, dissection and dissemination of local gossip, and often helped establish family consensus against the outside world. The harsh effects of street talk became less threatening under such circumstances, since family members could unite against negative stories and occasionally perpetrate their own rumours. Mrs Pearson, for example, took against her son's fiancée when she found that he had made over his army family allotment to her while serving overseas during the Second World War. She started 'keeping tabs' on the young woman, and before long a close neighbour reported that she had seen her having a drink in a local pub with the man she worked with.

> It was what she had been waiting for. She told me that she wasn't having her son two timed, although Mary was quite honest about it and said they had just been discussing work. She said she didn't believe a word of it and she told her daughter to write to Sam to tell him about it. Pat didn't want to, she said, but she made her. There was a dreadful row, and when Sam came back, he didn't want to break the engagement, but eventually did. As far as Mary's own neighbours were concerned, and there were a lot of them, Mrs Pearson's name was mud, because they all said that what she had said about Mary carrying on was totally untrue.[11]

Extensive family connections eased the gathering and distribution of local talk, and the extent to which this information was relayed back to the older woman who was frequently at their centre helped reinforce the working-class mother's perception of her own power and strong sense of identity. Gossip in this context contributed to the mythical aspects of working-class motherhood, since its dynamic was often to maintain the servicing, protective values of maternity and a narrow sexual morality. Yet the supportiveness of family links should not be exaggerated, since members were also aware of the need to fence off access to what they considered their own private business. Mrs Atkin's sister, for example, married one of her mother-in-law's nephews, Neville Baker. 'When his mum heard that Ivy was marrying Neville, she said she had told Joyce (her daughter) that she thought it was great pity because "now the Bakers will get to know all our business".'[12]

In some respects contraception intensified divisions within working-class culture, since demographic distinctions became increasingly apparent even to children in the inter-war years when some members of the working-class were at last able to limit the size of their families. Children born into the smaller families which became more common during the inter-war years were not unaware of the economic implications of a less crowded family life, and could feel themselves different from, even slightly superior to, the larger families of more impoverished streets. Joan Green, for example, who grew up in a two-up, two-down in Ashton-under-Lyne recalled a very poor street a short distance from where she lived which had big families.

> I thought we were posh because there were only two children in our family ... Not posh but, what's the other word ... I felt because we hadn't got a very big family, I felt, I suppose, a bit snobbish, really, that we'd er ... you know, you could tell all these children, came from the same families and, I used to dread going down that street.

Q. Why?

A. I don't know. I think it was the poverty.[13]

Yet even smaller and more medium-sized families often provided a community in themselves via extended links with relatives. Discussions about neighbouring which dwell on the supportiveness of the old working-class communities often reveal a considerable difference between the social relationships of the street and who was allowed over the threshold into the house. Given the importance of extended family relationships in poor urban areas, there was an inevitable tension between street gossip and family gossip of which men were often particularly aware. It was not unusual for men to be a privatizing, individualistic influence in this sphere, resenting street intrusions into their home life and setting down narrow boundaries of neighbourliness which women were only likely to cross when they were not around. Mrs West, for example, observed of her Northampton childhood that although some neighbours didn't mind people entering without knocking, that was not the case in her house since,

> our dad was very strict that way ... He didn't, it was your house and our dad wouldn't have people in and out, we never did have people in and out our house, because our dad didn't ... No he didn't like neighbours. Mind you, my dad was a man, he wouldn't stand and gossip in the streets. He'd, always polite, and always touched his cap and everything like that, but he'd never stand and have a lot of, never, you know, have like a conversation or anything.[14]

Mrs West's comments suggest an important distinction in awareness of neighbourliness and the life of the street. Although aware of the dangers of over-involvement in street life, women tended to have a better understanding of the rules and obligations played out there, and were more capable of controlling its intrusions. Poverty forced women to take the initiative and gave them a role and influence which was often denied women in less straitened circumstances. Sociability was, in this context, a survival strategy, which inevitably meant more to women than to men. Mrs West's mother, for example, was well known on her street for helping out whenever anyone was in trouble. Neighbours frequently touched her for the odd shilling when they were hard up, or in need of bedspreads and sheets for a confinement, and her generosity often came into conflict with her husband's more reserved manner:

> even in streets, you got people that they knew, who were kind hearted or good natured, and you could, you knew, 'Ooh, if I go to Mrs So-and-So I know she'll help me out'. Well, you see, they got to know them in the street that they, you see, they used to come to our old mum. And, of course, that used to annoy our dad sometimes! (laughing) ... He hadn't used to like that really, but that was our mother's nature, you see, you can't change a person, can you?[15]

Street relationships were bonded by the 'reciprocal exchanges of favours and goods' which helped create an expectation of collective responsibility. As this example suggests, women who demonstrated skills or talents in any sphere likely to be useful to local people and who had a reputation for being capable were consequently assumed to be at the general service of the neighbourhood, with their abilities harnessed for the good of the street in which they lived. Although a sense of obligation to the people amongst whom they lived meant most acceded to these neighbourly requests for help, such assistance was not always given without resentment, as was apparent from the remarks of the mother of a Preston woman who was frequently sent for whenever anyone was ill, had a baby or died. 'She said the next time she came on this earth she was going to be a mopus. That means she wouldn't be able to do anything. So as they wouldn't ask her to go.'[16] The same levelling sense of obligation meant there was often distrust of those who took an active, directive part in the neighbourhood, since leadership within such communities remained subject to strong democratizing tendencies. Gossip was consequently used 'to maintain a sense of equality by checking any unprecedented rise in the prestige of others'.[17] Thus, while it was usual for streets and courts to have a woman who was generally recognized as the boss or organizer of local ritual and activities, any woman who endeavoured to set herself up above her neighbours in some way, particularly through domineering behaviour, was likely to be 'put in her place'.[18]

> Any outward sign of a claim to be different, particularly a claim to be in any way superior, was looked down upon and would invite gossip and adverse comment. Phrases like 'she's got a nose above her mouth' and 'she's getting above herself' or derogatory words like 'posh', 'la-di-da' and the like could be savagely applied, bringing in their tow the social isolation which would make life impossible in a community which depended so much on mutual co-operation.[19]

Similarly, neighbours who attempted to take on an organizing role were likely to be criticized for 'getting above' themselves, in other words, setting themselves up as better than others.[20] As these remarks suggest, respect within such communities had to be earned rather than assumed.

Gossip was the medium through which these mores were monitored and regulated, this mediation being strongly based on particular expectations of female behaviour. The values which women were assumed to uphold were based on 'generalised reciprocity, generosity, self-sacrifice and devotion' , and were epitomized in their mothering function, which also had a wider application in reciprocal relationships outside the home.[21] These values were not unproblematic, as the 'mopus' example suggests, and could themselves generate much tension. Kathleen Dayus, for example, who was forced through widowhood and poverty to let her children go into a Home, is acutely sensitive in all her books to the effects of gossip, since her actions went in the face of neighbourhood values which maintained that children should stay with their family at whatever cost. The fact that Dayus's mother was still alive and, despite her dissolute behaviour, in a position to help merely compounded the unacceptability of her daughter's actions. The background to Dayus's decision, which had taken place after much heartsearching, was that Dayus's mother drank, and took half of her daughter's pay to look after her grandchildren, whom she nevertheless neglected to go on binges. Returning unexpectedly one afternoon from work, Kathleen Dayus found her youngest baby in a disgraceful state, 'still lying in her cot, with her nappy caked hard to her bottom'. Furious, she decided to offer a neighbour payment to be the childminder instead, but was turned down:

> It ain't the money Kate – God knows I could do with it! But yer know what yer mum's like, she'd 'ave the 'ole street up in arms, sayin' I took 'er job off 'er, an' them bein' 'er grandchildren an' all.[22]

The strain of trying to maintain one's self-esteem in communities which allowed few things to go unobserved put particular pressure on the women who held such neighbourhoods together, and, although impossible to quantify, the various forms of mental strain which frequently distorted their lives should not be neglected. It was common for Northampton women reaching the end of their tether, for example, to issue dire warnings to unruly offspring that their behaviour would send their mother to Berrywood, the local psychiatric hospital. Mary Chamberlain's grandmother and mother used a similar phrase in controlling their children, 'You'll drive me to Bedlam.'[23] Such sayings give some insight into how women perceived the pressures and tensions of domestic life. The inevitable stresses of life in large families were compounded for many women by fear of indebtedness and the constant worry of making ends meet, while women's role as the emotional pivot of family life made anxiety about their children an inevitable offshoot of this investment, prompting the observation by Susan Harding that 'Worry about well-being is distinctly on the women's side of the division of labour.'[24] Indeed, the very process of channelling much of their energy into home life could create a disturbingly hermetic atmosphere in which unnaturally strong dependency thrived. Anna Martin, for example, described in 1911 the working-class women she knew, each of whom 'knows perfectly well that the strength of her position in the home lies in the physical dependence of her husband and children upon her and she is suspicious of anything that would tend to undermine this. The feeling that she is the indispensable centre of her small world is, indeed, the joy and consolation of her life.'[25] It was these sentiments which fuelled the dark side of maternal influence within the family, which at its extreme was expressed in emotional black-mail and exaggerated expectations of loyalty.

The control which mothers exerted over their neighbourhoods, particularly as they entered their middle years, has been well documented in both contemporary accounts and more recent studies.[26] Younger women could be almost overwhelmed by the practical exigencies of day-to-day life, as Lady Bell indicated, while it was not uncommon for women in their forties to experience pre-menopausal health problems and the fear of unwanted pregnancy.[27] The passage through middle age, however, could lead to something which was very much the reverse of a downward slide. Maria Goddard, for example, remembered her Manchester mother being much happier in her fifties after having experienced very bad health in her late thirties and forties, and older women often found themselves with the freedom to become more self-important, bossy and selfish once the menopause had passed and their family had reached maturity. Women could retain compassion while diluting the nurturing role which was customarily expected of them, although some used gossip to extend their views on local tradition and behaviour into the whole community. Public perceptions of propriety were particularly important in the socialization of younger women by older women, which was largely promoted through gossip. The determination that they should not stray from an 'acceptable' standard of female behaviour could be cruel, and in this sense often had an extremely divisive effect upon relationships between women. Carl Chinn, for example, cited a woman who grew up in Studley Street, Birmingham, during the 1940s. She remembered that 'for her, the street's clique of older women always seemed to find something wrong with everyone else'.[28] The influence these older women exerted could be extremely irksome to a younger generation anxious to pursue their lives away from the prying eyes of the neighbours. Mrs Flower, for example, recalled how when one young woman's mother died in the 1930s 'the old ones started whispering and that, about how late her boyfriend stayed ... They'd be in their fifties. I think fifties are the worst, (laughing). I suppose they've nothing better to do. Their families have gone, you know, and they've more time on their hands.'[29]

Motherhood was a powerful motif within working-class communities. Working-class autobiographies, popular songs and even plastic and pictorial representations of maternal devotion in the form of fair and sea-side trinkets and tattoos all extol the virtues of the working-class mother in contradistinction to the critical observations of many middle-class observers. However, the frequently maudlin qualities of such expression not only reflected popular working-class feeling but also pandered to a narrow conception of female behaviour, since significantly it was less usual for the virtues of the working-class wife to be extolled. Motherhood itself

had usually to be sanctified by age, with the all too apparent struggles of
the younger mother being largely ignored. Richard Hoggart's model of the
'morally good' family with mother at its centre, while acknowledging
women's influence, failed to address the multifaceted nature of their
experience in working-class communities, where maternity was but one
manifestation of the many roles they were expected to play. It was a one-
dimensional focus since motherhood itself embodied a range of expressions, as even the music hall cliché appreciated when it proclaimed that
mother was also a 'pal'. She was also friend and confidant to her neighbours, family chancellor, worker (both paid and unpaid) – even oppressor,
in terms of the negative influence which could be exerted in family and
community. Yet these identities remained largely subsumed beneath a
sentimental concept of Motherhood, a concept readily commercialized by
producers of novelties and knick-knacks for the sea-side visitor. The senti-
mentalization of mothers as they moved towards the menopause and old
age powerfully contributed to a sense that women's only response to
events and experiences outside home life (such as paid work) derived from
their primary identity with home and family.

The responsibilities which working-class women shouldered for family
life inevitably coloured perceptions of their self-sacrifice, and there was
perhaps an undercurrent of discomfort, even guilt, among some more self-
conscious writers as to its extent. It became part of the mythology of
working-class experience, depictions of such women at the fulcrum of
working-class life typically failing to expose the more ambiguous qualities
of their drudgery in the domestic workplace. In a rather different context,
Orwell similarly failed to discern the qualitative difference in experience of
working-class men and women, which was apparent in his cosy conjuring
of the working-class family 'on winter evenings after tea, when the fire
glows in the open range and dances mirrored in the steel fender, when
Father, in shirt-sleeves, sits in the rocking chair at one side of the fire
reading the racing finals, and Mother sits on the other with her sewing.'[30]
While the father's relaxation takes an escapist route into the betting news,
Orwell indicates that the mother, even when 'at rest', remains diligent with
her domestic tasks. It is significant that while his diary accounts of mining
life dwell upon the daily degradation and exhaustion experienced by
working-class women, Orwell's fictional rendition of the same experiences
presents an heroic image of male labour, or the humiliation of men forced
to take on domestic tasks.[31] Orwell identifies work with male strength and
the physical 'nobility' of the miner, so that his fictional romanticization
consequently negates the value of women's own labour although it is more
than apparent in his factual writing. As with Hoggart, when the value of
women's work is expressed, it retains the soft qualities of sentimentality
promoted in popular culture.

This sentimentalizing of the working-class 'mum' in popular mythology provides a pertinent insight into the nature of women's confinement in such communities, not least because the devotion of sons to their mothers had distinct limits which tended not to be translated into a comparable understanding of the hardships endured by their own wives. It was safe to eulogize the older mother, who represented a standard by which younger women could be measured. (There is an important distinction to be made here in perceptions of mother and mother-in-law. The mother-in-law, another staple of music hall humour, was usually seen as interfering and as undermining male influence within the family.) Carl Chinn has observed how 'Sons were generally more doted on by their mothers than were daughters, who had to fend for themselves, and this "spoiling of the lads", the treating of them as lords, increased as they became wage-earners.'[32] This emotional investment by sons in the mother was consequently qualitatively different from that experienced by their more pragmatically regarded sisters. Carolyn Steedman, for example, has described the 'shocked' amazement with which she encountered Kathleen Woodward's book *Jipping Street*, for her mother of the 1890s was the one Steedman recognized in the 1950s:

> mothers were people who told you how long they were in labour with you, how much you hurt, how hard it was to have you ('twenty hours with you,' my mother frequently reminded me) and who told you to accept the impossible contradiction of being both desired and being a burden, and not to complain. This ungiving endurance is admired by working-class boys who grow up to write about their mother's flinty courage. But the daughter's silence on this matter is a measure of the price you have to pay for survival.[33]

Working-class women were heroic in the way they struggled to ensure the survival of their families, and frequently deserved the approbation of their offspring, but these differences in perception among an educated generation commenting on their own family experiences are testament to the qualitatively different bonding process to which women were subject. The ambivalent quality of relationships between older and younger women was reflected in that which apparently existed between many mothers and daughters. It was likely to be particularly acute when the daughter had aspirations beyond the limited horizons of her parent, and as such, may have become more pronounced in the inter-war years when working-class fatalism and respect for tradition, although still deeply entrenched, was being eroded in certain areas of behaviour. (Elizabeth Roberts, for example, has described the gradual change in women's attitudes towards their own health and bodies which took place in the inter-war period.[34]) The relationship between mothers and children was frequently more stark than the romanticized image of many male working-class autobiographies (epitomized in the work of D.H. Lawrence). Poor health, chronic physical discomfort, large family size and the sheer monotony and grimness of impoverished living conditions easily produced a stunted emotional relationship between a woman and her children, which could be particularly marked between mothers and daughters. John Burnett, for example, has remarked that unhappy relations with the mother were more frequently recorded by daughters 'often because they were burdened by excessive housework and seemingly treated without love and affection'.[35] Kathleen Woodward, writing of life in south-east London before the First World War, observed that although her mother sweated and laboured for her children, she was 'utterly oblivious to any need we might cherish for sympathy in our little sorrows, support in our strivings. She simply was not aware of anything beyond the needs of our bodies.'[36] Jean McCrindle and Sheila Rowbotham, in describing the bitterness with which many of the older women they interviewed regarded their mothers, were surprised by this hostility, until they realized

> that teaching a daughter her role as a future housewife can all too easily develop a sadistic quality when the mother herself is tired, over-worked and oppressed by her own existence.[37]

Annie Jaeger, who grew up in Stockport during the last years of the nineteenth century, described how her mother gradually became harder and harder because of 'overwork and strain'.[38] Angela Rodaway remembered how as children she and her siblings were usually punished 'not in proportion to the crime we had committed but according to the amount of strain my mother was undergoing at the time'. There had, for example, never been a cane in the house until her twin sisters were born and the pressures of a baby-bound existence immeasurably increased.[39] Hannah Mitchell similarly observed how her mother's temper grew with the advent of each child. 'She would fall into violent passions about the merest trifles and drive us all out of the house for hours.'[40] Alice Linton, who was raised in Hoxton during the period around the First World War, thought it strange that looking back on her childhood she could not remember that she loved her mother very much. 'I always seemed to be a little afraid of her I suppose. I was a nervous type of child, and can only think that mother must have always been worried and anxious about money, and rather tired and impatient. Whenever I fell and hurt myself, or broke my glasses mother always spanked me first and then asked what happened.'[41] Woodward described her own mother's frequent violent anger, when blows were aimed 'without feeling or restraint', and which erupted whenever 'she touched that extreme verge of tiredness in mind and body'.[42] Burnett, from his great survey of working-class autobiographies, has highlighted how 'mothers are frequently represented as over-burdened with work, irritable, nagging and demanding', and the strains of everyday living were often etched in the faces of these hard-pressed women.[43] The 'chief characteristic' of Rodaway's mother was 'an unremitting, lifeless energy. She had a thin mouth and tired eyes, like dents in a tin', while Woodward was similarly graphic when she described her mother as 'flinty, enduring, strong and proud ... the suffering had bitten in until it was itself impotent against the granite it laid bare'.[44] As Margery Spring-Rice observed of the working-class women in her 1930s study, only the strongest could possibly be well since hard work and 'entirely inadequate funds' made it impossible for them to lead healthy lives.[45]

Women such as these, locked away in themselves, seem almost to have lost the capacity for talking in any positive or creative sense. Emotionless, unexpressive, they lacked a language through which their frustrations could be articulated. Gossip involved too great a risk to allow the degree of self-revelation which was required, and was in any case a narrowly defined convention which tended to exclude other forms of talk. Tom Wakefield, writing of his childhood in a Midlands mining family during the 1940s, recollects disliking his mother, who frequently 'sulked, withdrew or nagged' at her family, after two major operations for ulcers had left her 'drained and in a chronic state of nervous exhaustion', although she was well-liked by other women in their row of houses because she never gossiped. After a fierce quarrel over her refusal to accompany him to the VE-Day festivities, the confrontation culminated in her thrusting some newspapers containing concentration camp photographs at him:

> 'They were just like us; that's what the Nazis have done to them. It's not only soldiers who have gone under in this bloody war yer know.' She buried her head in her hands. I wanted to put my arms around her. Comfort her, kiss her neck or lick her ear. But she had never shown me physical affection and would not have appreciated me expressing any towards her. She didn't like to be touched by me. Yet I wanted to touch her. I couldn't reach her suffering but I had glimpsed some of the depths of it – thanks to the horrible photographs. It dawned then, it entered my head then, that my mother was clever, she thought about things but had no one to talk to about them. Her injuries were buried within her. I had discovered a nest with eggs in.[46]

The mistake of equating women's apparent passivity with acquiescence in their cheerless lot is apparent in the autobiography of Angela Rodaway. Rodaway was a scholarship girl with ambitions quite at odds with her mother's outlook, which she described as being that of a 'typical housewife, rather dull and content to be what she was'. However, these rather disdainful perceptions were abruptly shattered when her mother's smouldering resentments suddenly erupted one day when she stormed out of the house, 'saying that she was sick of it all and was going to get out of it'.

Her rage soon dissipated, and after wandering through the local streets for a time she had returned home in silence and 'glumly got ready for bed'. Nevertheless, the experience brought home to Rodaway the nature of her mother's own disappointments, and the opportunities she had lost when she abandoned her own 'routine clerical world of business' on marriage.

> We heard a lot, in those days, about 'frustrated spinsters' but ever after this, the word 'frustration' did not call to my mind the unmarried, working woman; it made me think of my mother. She did, in the end, get back where she wanted to be, but it needed a war to put her there and, in nineteen thirty-five, we did not seriously think of it.[47]

Cosy depictions of evenings by the fireside appear rather differently in the light of such despairing manifestations as these. While Rodaway's mother was not necessarily typical, her example does indicate how deceptive appearances might be. Other women also had recourse to occasional outbursts which acted as safety valves in otherwise intolerable conditions. Maria Goddard's aunt, who had nine children, was married to a violent husband who used to 'knock her about something awful'. About once a year she would break out, 'as if she was fed up, you know'. She would spend up all the housekeeping, 'such as it was', have a few drinks and stay overnight with her sister, where she would stay awake all night, singing. The following day she would return home, to another certain beating. This woman did eventually leave her violent husband, although not until her children were grown up and away from home.[48]

Oral history interviews and autobiographies have given few insights into the more intimate aspects of parental/child relationships, possibly because so much was often left unspoken. Indeed, such revelations are painful and often difficult to expose to an outsider, while the true meaning of childhood incidents often do not become apparent until much later in life. Maria Goddard, for example, grew up in Manchester during the inter-war years. She described how her mother would occasionally go into the parlour to play the piano in the dark, 'And it was so sad, that. And I think she was ... fed up, you know.' It was not until Maria's mother was in her fifties, and her husband dead, that she admitted to her daughter that she felt that she had never done anything, 'never done what she would liked to have done'. She said 'she always had a rage inside her'.[49]

Gossip at work

These glimpses into the interior life of working-class women are occasionally revealed in attitudes to paid work outside the home, which could be valued not only for its vital financial contribution but also for intrinsic job satisfaction and the opportunities provided for socializing.[50] Mary

Bertenshaw's mother, for example, worked from financial necessity in a laundry because of her husband's disability and frequent unemployment, yet her daughter specifically noted how much she liked her job as 'fancy ironer'. Another woman, Jessie Jenkins, was born in 1912 in Warrington. Her mother married young and had nine children, seven of whom survived. They lived in a cramped two-up, two-down in 'a very slummish area' of town. Her mother gave up paid work when she married a fore-hand furnaceman. She told Jessie that the happiest years of her life were when her husband was in the War and she returned to work, as a fustian cutter, although she gave up her job again as soon as he returned.[51] Alice Linton's mother, like Mary Bertenshaw's, also worked in a laundry, and the psychological value of her employment was discernible on pay day, since it provided the opportunity to dawdle on the way home, as she stopped off in a pub or two with her sister-in-law. In her daughter's words, 'Poor mother, she wasn't really fond of pubs but I suppose she was putting off having to go home to an irritable husband.'[52] Paid work was a means to partial freedom, as Clementina Black recognized in 1915 when she described the women of what she called Class B, those who were forced to seek paid work because the family income was inadequate due to low pay, irregularity, sickness, drink, idleness or desertion. They were, in her words, the most overworked, hard-pressed and probably unhappiest of working women. Yet harassed and overburdened as they were, these women valued more than money in their work, being touched and inspired by that 'wave of desire for a personal working life which forms so marked an element in the general development of modern women. They liked having money of their own, and the woman who said: "A shilling of your own is worth two that he gives you" spoke the mind of many of her sisters.'[53] Her comments were echoed in the observations of a woman who was billeted in Nottingham during the Second World War. She remembered the advice her landlady had given her that even though her own husband was 'one of the best', she should make sure she always kept her 'own little bit of money' when she got married. 'She told me, now you remember what I say, you keep your independence if you have a little bit of your own, that you can draw on. She said her mother told her that.'[54]

Domestic friction

Money was, of course, a major source of domestic discord, and the quarrels and 'nagging' which commonly resulted from male intransigence over money were also indicative of deep dissatisfactions which ran counter to the stereotype of female acquiescence and fatalism. Although attempts to confront mean behaviour often met with little success, many women remained doggedly persistent in the face of overwhelming odds which often ended in beatings and ill-treatment. (Brian Harrison noted how 'drunken husbands were often stung by the wife's silent or open reproach into the wife-beating for which Englishmen were notorious abroad'.)[55] Money – or lack of it – was a major source of such confrontations in working-class homes. A Salford woman described how being on the dole in the 1930s made little financial difference to her family:

> it was just the same as when he was working because I'd very rarely get any money off him. I more or less kept the family on my money. When he give it me, it was about a couple of quid, but he generally only give it me if we had a fight. No, if he came home, I'd be alright, but if he went for a drink, I'd had it.[56]

The usual distribution of resources, which meant that the male wage earner frequently kept back a portion of his income for spending on alcohol, tobacco or entertainment, allowed little argument in terms of fairness and sorely tried women's verbal skills.

> Did I talk about money problems with him? I just shouted all the time about money. Took him all his time to give you his money. If men drank, the women used to shout at them – try to show them up in the pub – but they just ignored you.[57]

Edith Burwin talked about money problems with her husband, 'but you had to argue over it – it wasn't done voluntarily.[58] As this woman suggests, discussion over money more frequently took the form of a row than rational debate.

> I argued over it with my husband and I never got enough. 'Cos I just threw it at him one night and I said, 'here, you manage on it'. He said, 'Right, I will but I'm not paying any bills, I'm not paying any insurances'. I said, 'Well, if I didn't have to pay them I'd be well off. I could manage'. You see, they thought that when they gave you their money that was them finished. They didn't realise all the money you had to pay out. I paid rent, insurances, electric, everything – food, clothes, kids' dinner money. I used to have to get 'em on tick, but I still paid them.'[59]

Women were used to maintaining secrets and keeping up appearances through a variety of different roles, and their perceptions of home differed significantly from those of men. Home was their workplace, where role-playing persisted even after the front door had closed on the outside world. For men, however, it was somewhere where they expected to be able to drop the mask which helped maintain friendly social relations among their workmates; it was a place in which to relax, away from the unwarranted intrusions of visitors, especially women.[60] While a man might drop his public persona once he had returned home, women had to remain vigilant, and were frequently the protective partner in the sense of keeping men in ignorance of the struggles needed to ensure the family's survival. The accepted stereotypes applied to male and female behaviour are very misleading in this context, since it was the man who not only became the more 'privatized' partner, but was also the passive recipient of bed and board, awaiting service rather than actively initiating events. The sociability which the worker displayed amongst his workmates similarly contrasted with the isolated existence he often led within the street community, as Harry Watkins portrayed in his description of men sneaking in and out of their homes.[61]

Public attitudes could, of course, differ greatly from what went on in private in all sorts of ways, even among those men who were more supportive of their wives, as a Salford woman observed, 'Me dad would do nothing outside but he'd help me mum inside.'[62] Both Robert Roberts and the oral evidence collected by Carl Chinn suggests 'that many men helped their wives in the house, so long as it was behind closed doors and workmates and drinking partners remained unaware of such assistance'.[63] Although even those who (often due to unemployment) helped around the house clung on to established perceptions of a man's status. 'Oh yes, he thought he was boss. Till I started! He was to a certain extent. Even though Annie kept everything going: everything in the house was his – my house, my this, my the other. Made no difference him being out of work.'[64]

One woman described her husband as being 'very good natured', although significantly this good humour did not extend to members of his own family:

> not to his own. He didn't bring it home. But he was very good natured outside. Everybody liked him. It used to make me mad. I could kill him. You never heard anybody say a word against him. Very good natured. He'd take his shoes and give them to you. That was his fault. Sometimes I moaned about him. But you didn't really let anyone know your business. You more or less kept it to yourself. I mean they used to hear the shouting and they used to think it was me, you see. He was so nice outside![65]

Another woman, speaking of her sociable, philandering father made a similar tacit comparison with his domestic behaviour: 'He was a hail-fellow-well-met was my dad with anybody else but in the house, I don't know.'[66] Both observations complement the sociologist Ferdynand Zweig's description of the 'model worker', who had always to be ready to do his mates a good turn and whose main characteristics were friendliness, generosity and a readiness to 'live and let live'. As Zweig put it, 'He must be happy, that is, he must keep himself happy and make others happy.'[67] Unfortunately, this sociable impulse could have hidden costs within his own domestic circle, where the pressures of poverty and close proximity could feed resentment and turn the 'model worker' into a morose and somewhat detached figure. Indeed, the obverse of the image of the violent male who was roused to fury by his partner's caustic tongue was that of the long-suffering refugee from a termagant wife, who sought asylum in the pub, pigeon loft, allotment or sometimes domestic silence.[68] Here, again, we find a more passive representation of male experience. Women were often perceived as a source of noise and turmoil, making it socially acceptable for men to seek peace and quiet in their own social space, away from the demands of family life. Within the house itself some retreated into their own private world. A Rochdale woman, recalling the friction which had characterized the family life of her childhood, could not remember her father speaking very much:

> I have a feeling he got fed up because of my mother, him and mother always quarrelled and he got fed up with quarrels so he just shut up, clammed up, but I think he was to blame for the quarrels because of the shortage of money.[69]

Although gossip could put a brake on more overt forms of domestic violence, there was also an element of street collusion over what happened in the 'privacy' of the home. Responding to the question of whether men beat their wives, a Salford woman observed: 'There was one or two in the street who did, but it was all hush hush. You lived in such a close environment, you knew what was going on, but it wasn't discussed. Even if you saw your neighbour with a black eye and bruises, you didn't say to her, "has he hit you again?" You kept your mouth closed.'[70] Keeping a closed mouth with the beaten individual did not, of course, preclude gossip with neighbours about the treatment she received, although this distrust of getting involved in what were seen as private family matters was deeply embedded and helped protect the neighbourhood from disruptive public conflicts. Consequently, attitudes towards male violence could be both ambivalent and disturbingly accepting, as this woman suggests, responding to a question on what she thought about men hitting their wives. 'Well, you didn't think much about it really. And you never got the full story – you didn't know whether the wife had deserved it, or not.' Women tended not to leave their husbands (even violent ones). 'They had to put up with them. If you had children, you had to consider that.'[71] 'They had nowhere to go. And they had no money to keep them with. Now – if we'd been like they are now – we'd've been off. We'd've been one parent families. But we had nowhere to go. We had to stick it. I mean more or less you stuck it for your children. Because you did love your children.'[72]

Neighbourliness and nosiness

A frequently harsh discipline and conformity helped deaden women to the lack of choice in their lives, and made children the key to self-esteem and influence as they grew older. Collective support had both a family and neighbourhood dimension which often sat uneasily together, for the tight-knit, matriarchal focus of much street life had many contradictions in which family and broader collective pressures were frequently at odds. Indeed, while it was not unusual for the strongly rooted, democratic impulses expressed in communal activities to be countered by the negative, more individualistic pull of family loyalties, there were also occasions when relatives could be much less supportive than neighbours, particularly when behaviour threatened the reputation of other family members. One woman, whose mother suffered a psychiatric illness during the 1920s, described the disgrace she felt as a child when her mother was sent away to hospital.

> You didn't know what to think, didn't know what'd hit us. Dad didn't know. You're bewildered, 'cause it was something as ... And it all 'ad to be swept under the carpet, you see, them days, it was such a ... ohh, it was dreadful, it was, it was a sin, it was a crime.
> Q. But she hadn't done anything?
> A. Doesn't matter. They looked down on you, they did ... ohh, what? And relatives were worst.[73]

The values which underlay neighbourhood life itself were understandably complex, and elderly people reminiscing about the past often express contradictory judgments about the part which supportiveness played. One woman, for example, explained how:

> Everybody helped one another, and everyone was sympathetic to one another's needs. Every street was like one big family. You got the odd one who didn't bother with the rest, but on the whole it was a nice friendly atmosphere to live in. Women didn't have mental breakdowns like they have today because there was always an older woman to confide in. The older women would counsel the young ones, if you sought the help of an elderly neighbour, you always came away much wiser.[74]

Yet this 'community spirit' was hardly comprehensive. It could even exclude those who lauded and felt part of it. This woman's father, for example, was a Muslim seaman, and the family lived in an area where there were no other mixed race families. Despite her description of the neighbourhood's friendliness, she refers elsewhere to her own family being regarded as different, foreign and not entirely accepted. Similar selectivity frequently informs recollections of neighbourly relations during the Second World War, when, despite comforting myths to the contrary, insecurity generated suspicious and even hostile attitudes. Dorothy Tildsley, for example, while nostalgic for the 'strange sense of community' which attended life in local air raid shelters, also reveals the mean-mindedness to which the war period gave rise. Her father occasionally received sweets and fruit from American troops at an air base, but her family had to keep that knowledge to themselves for fear of being reported to the police by neighbours. 'They watched for people having more than them, and immediately thought they were getting it through the black market channels which were rife then.'[75]

Sensitivity to the surveillance aspects of gossip had been similarly heightened during the Depression years, when the 'means test' tapped deep into the petty jealousies and resentments which characterized the insecurities of close-knit, impoverished districts. It was not unusual for the casual asides of neighbourhood gossip to find a damaging, institutional outlet in anonymous declarations to the public assistance officer, whose knowledge about some claimants could seem quite exhaustive. Mindful of their humiliating insights, a Rhondda miner wrote how insidiously the notion of being spied on 'seemed to creep into the minds of the men' who were unemployed.[76]

Even under less strained circumstances, status and self-esteem were uncertain factors in poor communities, and women remained very aware of the fine line to be drawn between neighbourliness and nosiness, which could easily lead to intrusive gossip. Kathleen Dayus, for example, struck up a close friendship with a woman called Sal Briggs, who confided in her the details of her deprived childhood which she had never told anyone else, not even her own children, 'you're the first one I've felt like talkin' to. I ain't ever spoke about me life before, not even ter me sons an' daughters'.[77] Yet later, when Kathleen Dayus had herself started to reciprocate with insights into her own background, she felt she was breaking one of her own rules for self-preservation:

> I noticed Sal was becoming too inquisitive. It was then that I realised my tongue had run away with me ... No doubt when I had gone she would find time to gossip with her other neighbour, Mrs Freer. I had nothing to hide or be ashamed of, yet I didn't like neighbours' gossip, and I don't know why I should have talked as I did. Therefore when she did ask questions, I would say, 'When we have more time' until she got tired of asking.[78]

Dayus's relationship with Sal epitomizes the perennial tensions which undermined daily life among the poor, for even the apparent openness of this friendship was marred by Dayus's sense of being taken advantage of in the little favours which she never refused Sal. Her remarks echo an observation on Geoffrey Gorer's survey into post-war attitudes, that 'Taking England as a whole, the poorer the group of informants, the more often they complained about their neighbours' gossip and tendency to borrow things.'[79]

Gorer's findings were based on a questionnaire published in a popular Sunday newspaper, which was answered by over 10,000 people. Although his statistical methods were criticized and it is often difficult to identify regional and social differences from the published data, his book, *Exploring English Character*, published in 1955, gives a suggestive insight into attitudes towards gossip. Thirteen per cent of his respondents complained of the neighbours' inquisitiveness, those most likely to think they were being spied on and to resent it being those under 24, 'the unmarried (followed by the divorced and separated), the people of medium income living in smaller communities and who consider themselves lower middle or lower working class'.[80] Thirteen per cent also objected to gossip.

> It is not altogether the same group who object to gossip as object to inquisitiveness, though again it is specially stressed by the young and single. It is a complaint made somewhat more often by women than by men, and its incidence increases steadily as income declines. The regions where this complaint bulks highest are the South-West and North-East and North; it is relatively low in the Midlands. It is mentioned somewhat less often by people living in the metropolises. As far as length of residence is concerned, it only starts to become important as a source of annoyance after people have spent four years in the same house; it never dies down.[81]

Familiarity with neighbours varied, of course, from area to area, and within neighbourhoods there were frequent differences between individuals. Nevertheless, mutual support and more individualistic pressures were not exclusive in working-class communities, and emphasis on the matriarchal nature of many close-knit working-class neighbourhoods as in parts of Liverpool and the East End of London can exalt community consensus at the expense of considering the divisive qualities suggested here, for the self-enclosed nature of many poor communities encouraged a hot-house atmosphere in which rumour and exaggeration often flourished. As Jeremy Seabrook has observed, the working-class community had 'developed extraordinary skill in detecting irregularities of conduct, especially if these were sexual'.[82] An important aspect of survival was the maintenance of certain myths to outsiders, and gossip frequently threatened to penetrate and expose such pretence, although gossip itself could be used to maintain certain illusions, as was the case with Margaret Grant's family. Her father was a steel erector who worked all over the country. He failed to return from one of these jobs after going off to live with another woman, which gave rise to much talk among the neighbours that he was in prison, a rumour that Mrs Grant's mother let them believe, rather than admit that he'd left her.[83]

Despite gossip's many positive aspects in a neighbourhood context, its undoubted capacity to prey on vulnerability means an examination of its role cannot afford to ignore the negative effects of malice, and the fact that an embittered or frustrated minority did use invention and envy to manip-

ulative effect. Gossip's occasionally malign qualities were a reminder of the
need for care and circumspection in personal behaviour, although refusal
to gossip did not necessarily reflect a defensive desire to protect aspirations
to higher social status. Remaining aloof from street talk, or certain aspects
of it, could also have a moral dimension, and some women undoubtedly
tried to put brakes on their neighbours' talk. Maria Goddard described a
childless neighbour who was known as a gossip, and regularly tried to pass
on snippets about local people.

> Q. But how would your mother respond when she was tittle-tattling
> these bits and pieces?
> A. I think she, many a time I've heard her saying to me dad, you
> know, 'I wish she wouldn't say these kind of things, I had to repri-
> mand her'. She sort of seemed to get very shocked if people, or, talk
> about the worst in people, you know, p'raps some girl or some boy,
> and some family, and me mother used to say, you know, 'If she had
> some of her own, she wouldn't talk like that'.[84]

Despite her dislike of such talk, Maria Goddard's mother did not try to cut
herself off from her judgmental neighbour, towards whom she felt a
certain sympathy, telling her daughter many years later that she thought
she did it because she was lonely.

Other women adopted a far more direct approach when faced with
unnecessary speculation. Mrs Flarty, the nosy neighbour whom Walter
Greenwood describes in his autobiography, started to gossip about a new
family called the Seeleys who had moved into the area.

> Mr Seeley was said to be a widower but Mrs Flarty asserted that Mrs
> Seeley had 'run off' with another man. For this uncharitableness she
> had come in for a public ticking off from Mrs Boarder.
> 'You're at it agen, you back-bitin' old besom.'
> 'The truth's the truth, isn't it?'
> 'It's a long time since that was on your tongue. Another thing, I'd
> like to see the feller that'd want to run off wi' thee, you faggot. An' if
> you spent more time inside with that brush o' yours your house'd be
> a sight cleaner.'[85]

Mrs Boarder's put-down was a characteristic attack upon her neighbour's
own claims to be regarded as an efficient housekeeper.

Gorer's suggestion that the poor complained most about gossip
reflects the extent to which the cramped circumstances of their poverty
allowed such talk to intrude into their lives. There is an implication that
better-off communities were less susceptible to its influence, and discussion
of 'respectable' working-class communities often implies a clarity of division between the classes when the boundaries could in reality be rather
more blurred, particularly in neighbourhoods where families were sliding
down the social scale as well as hoping to move up it. Working-class experience was diverse in expression, and while many 'respectable' families

undoubtedly held themselves apart from local gossip, this aloofness did not necessarily imply a complete divorce from the life of the street, particularly if the neighbourhood was stable and had a fairly static population. Individuals might claim that they did not gossip, but could still be connected into the local grapevine via the involvement of relatives. Ostensibly quiet families could engage in very rich talk behind the closed doors and net curtains that set them apart from their neighbours, and for this reason it is useful to move in closer to look at the sensitivities and insecurities apparent in a street on the cusp of the upper-working and lower-middle-class between the 1930s and 1950s. This more specific examination enables us to explore in some detail the relationship between family life and street talk.

Family myth and street mythology

Lawson Road was a terraced street in Northampton, which in the interwar and immediate post-war years was 'a market and factory town surrounded by countryside'.[86] It was on the borders of the upper-working-class and lower-middle-class, near other streets lower down in the social scale. The houses comprised a hall, front room, parlour, kitchen, outside toilet, three bedrooms (one the size of a boxroom) and a back garden. The largest local employers were the railway, which had built several local streets for its workers, and two shoe factories. Lawson Road was at the edge of the town, however, and nudged up against the countryside, being exposed at one end to open fields, which helped to maintain a semi-rural feel. It was built in the early 1900s. It does not appear on the 1901 Ordnance Survey Map, but is mentioned in the 1906 street directory for Northampton, which refers to 20 houses.[87] These had risen to 27 by 1914 and to 31 by the late 1930s. The directories obviously provide only the most rudimentary of outlines to street life, but do confirm the recollections of inhabitants as to the names and house numbers of their neighbours, and the changes in residence that took place there.[88] One woman, for example, born in 1922, accurately remembered all the names of residents from the inter-war years, and only faltered slightly in the numbering of three houses that were at the far end of the street where she lived. The cursory character of the street directories largely sweep women aside, unless they happen to be unmarried or widows, and fail to enlighten about the family relationships which even access to the census enumerators' records would be unlikely to reveal, given the difficulties of identifying nieces, nephews, uncles, aunts and cousins in the surrounding area once women relinquish their paternal surname. Nevertheless, they are useful in underlining the essential stability of the area. Of the 27 households mentioned in 1914, for example, 12 were still present in 1936, and six still lived there in 1952. Unfortunately, no street directories exist for the late 1900s and early 1920s, when several families appear to have moved in with the aftermath of the Great War. However, if we move to 1928, of the 28 households mentioned then, 15 were still present in 1952.[89] Of 31 households mentioned in the 1936 directory, 20 (64.5 per cent) were still resident in 1952.

Several Lawson Road residents had a sense of being slightly superior to the inhabitants of the surrounding streets, which partly reflected the small size of the average family and the lack of married women in paid work.[90] Of 23 women with children, 13 had only one child, six had two children and three had three children. The largest family on the road was one with four children. This woman, Mrs Baxter, was a widow who not only looked after her own immediate family, but also cared for a disabled brother and another brother, Tom Franklin, who lodged with them. The men were largely skilled workers with a scattering of white-collar employees. Of those males who were in work and had an identifiable occupation, four were skilled shoe factory workers, five worked in transport, on the railway or as bus drivers, two were fitter-welders, two worked in the building trade, as a plumber and a painter and decorator, two were clerks and one was a nurseryman. There were also a police sergeant and shoe factory foreman, both of whom moved from Lawson Road on receiving promotion. Of the seven households with a retired resident, one contained a former bank manager and another a retired station master.

The handful of married women in paid work included a woman who worked in a transport cafe and another who worked in the closing room of a local shoe factory. This woman's situation was rather unusual since she was married with a young son yet lived at home with her parents while her husband lived across the street with his relatives. The mystery of these domestic arrangements, which intrigued the respondent as a child, was revealed when she was older. The woman had become pregnant in her late teens by Tom Franklin. 'Her family detested him, but when they found out that she was expecting insisted (like his family) on a sort of "shotgun" wedding to protect the baby, but forbade Kathleen to live with him as his wife. The Franklins being a very respectable family themselves, agreed with them and turned him out. That was why he was living with his widowed sister.' He went over once a week to visit his wife and child and occasionally took her out for a drink, but they never lived together and always went on separate holidays. The child was thus legitimized in the eyes of the world, while the family signalled its continuing disapproval of illicit sexual relations by severely restricting the relationship.[91]

The other women in employment were rather less exceptional, and included three young single women who also worked in the local closing rooms and a handful of widows who worked in various part-time jobs such as cleaning and waitressing.

There were also three elderly single women on Lawson Road. Miss Ruff, who lived alone, was 'a quiet, elderly spinster, very pleasant but reserved', who always wore a cotton mob cap when doing chores. Miss Andrews, a lodger, was described in similarly respectable terms. 'She was tall, thin, refined in her manner and looks, and always dressed in black like Grandma.' Miss Clarke lived with her married sister's family. 'I often thought that she may have lost her sweet-heart in the trenches. There were scores of girls left spinsters because of the 1914–18 war.'[92] Their physical description, with its echoes of the late Victorian and Edwardian periods, suggests the continuation of earlier fashion trends long after time had apparently moved on.

The presence of these rather genteel older women who testified to an older set of values and style of living helped fix Lawson Road's reputation for difference in the minds of some of its inhabitants. This reputation included notions of respectability promoted, as we shall see, by a significant chapel influence and a sense of having come down in the world that reinforced the need to preserve front before outsiders. Not all residents fitted into (or necessarily accepted) this image, yet there were sufficient numbers for a myth of refinement and social superiority to develop which was moulded and enhanced by gossip. Families also maintained myths about their own origins which were only dimly perceived by or were even unknown to neighbours, although such stories enhanced their self-esteem and interconnected with street talk in many complex ways. One means of exploring these links is to look at the experiences of two Lawson Road families, the Jordans and the Dixons, who were related, albeit uneasily.

The Jordans were a family of some weight within the Lawson Road area. They were active in the chapel, and Frank Jordan (followed by his son, Ernest) was landlord of a 'respectable' pub and owner of several local houses. All the Jordan children were privately educated, and seem to have kept their distance from other families in the district. One of the daughters, Hannah, became a teacher and married John Dixon, a young farmer she met while working away from home. They moved to Lawson Road at the outbreak of the First World War so that Hannah could be nearer her parents after John had volunteered for the army, leaving the family farm to be run by relatives. They rented a house from Hannah's brother, Ernest, never intending to remain there permanently since they hoped to emigrate to Canada. However, these hopes were unfulfilled. The Dixons' farm was split up and sold after a family argument, and John returned from the forces to find that Hannah had changed her mind about emigration under pressure from her mother and sisters. Her Mother, Alice Jordan, had already 'lost' one daughter to Australia and was very reluctant to see another go overseas. The decision had significant repercussions for the family's broader reputation within the neighbourhood, for although John Dixon established a successful smallholding and could eventually have afforded to move somewhere more in keeping with his wife's background and her family's aspirations, he determined to stay where he was, knowing how much it irked his in-laws to see their daughter living where she did. Hannah Dixon's sisters were regular visitors to Lawson Road, much to her husband's dislike, since he regarded them as troublemakers. His daughter, Celia, remembered him saying once that he wouldn't have them in the house. 'He said, "Your sisters have caused more trouble for us than anybody I know, and I'm not having any more of their evil tittle tattle again".' They continued to visit, although he never really forgave his wife's family for interfering with his and his wife's emigration plans, and this was the main source of her parents' disagreements as a child.

> My mother was always urging him to move (that was the only time they quarrelled), but he always said that if her relatives hadn't interfered, she wouldn't be there. He could have bought a new house or bungalow any time he chose, but he knew that it annoyed and embarrassed the Jordans to have them living in that house, and it was the only way he could retaliate. The only trouble was, it was my mother who suffered, not them! He loathed the aunts and uncles – he said they were nothing but a pack of nosy, gossiping troublemakers, and if they came to see my mother, would mumble, 'hello', and then bury himself in his paper.[93]

John Dixon's dislike of his relatives was reciprocated by the more snobbish among them, such as his sister-in-law, Hilda, who insisted on referring to him as a 'jobbing gardener'. Such slights encouraged the Dixons' daughter, Celia, to champion what she described as her father's 'gentleman farmer' ancestry over the lower-middle-class pretensions of her aunts and uncles, particularly as her own parents did not share their airs and graces. For although a reserved family, the Dixons did not remain aloof from what went on around them. They seem to have been well liked, and quietly helped out other neighbours in distress during the bleak inter-war period. Whenever Hannah Dixon got to hear of a neighbour in difficulty, she would ask her husband to put together a basket of garden produce and groceries for them, although it was not until years later, through talking to elderly neighbours, that Celia became aware of exactly how much support her parents had given. 'There was a dreadful lot of poverty around in the 30s in families who were too proud to complain, but all help was given secretly and tactfully – friend to friend and no thanks expected or required. I have always been proud and thankful that I had parents like that.'

Hannah was also prepared to call in favours if it would help out a friend in need. When, for example, her next-door neighbours got heavily into debt and flitted, leaving the woman's father (who owned the house) to pay up, he was so angry that he began throwing out all the couples' valuables. Seeing what he had done, Hannah rescued everything and returned them when he had calmed down. 'He was so grateful, he said if he could ever do her a favour he would. She reminded him of this a little while later, as a friend of our family, Annie Bunting, was desperately looking for a house. He said on her recommendation he would let her have it, (a "good turn" which Annie Bunting repaid a thousand times over)'.[94]

Neighbours' perceptions of the Dixons were coloured by what they knew of the Jordans, since John Dixon's family had no local connections and this combined with a general sensitivity about their background made the Dixon children very aware of street talk. On the one hand, neighbours' ignorance of or indifference to Mr Dixon's slide down the social scale and relatives' sneers about his situation reinforced counter myths about the family's origins, as in the case of Celia's pride in her father's well-bred farming background. On the other, the Dixons' relationship to the superior Jordans was experienced outside the family as both an asset and a handicap. Celia felt, for example, there was some jealousy among two or three of the neighbours,

> although they liked and respected my parents. Mrs Green wanted to know why I had passed the scholarship exam and her Lily and Dora Adderley hadn't – she said there 'must have been some influence some-where', otherwise I wouldn't have. I told her I was as puzzled as she was … and my mum and dad just laughed. Apparently it was the Jordans generally that they were jealous about, because as Auntie Ellen said, they *did* have that air of superiority and refinement. She said they must have good blood in them somewhere, even if as in the case of her own family, it was on the wrong side of the blanket … I was very interested, so she told me that her great grandmother had eloped with her father's groom, and had been 'cast off and cut off without a shilling', which I thought very romantic.

Aunt Ellen was married to Harry Jordan, one of Hannah's brothers. They lived across the road to the Dixons and John got on with them better than with any other members of his wife's family. Ellen, too, suffered from Jordan snubs, as was apparent in her need to assert the colourful aspects of her own background. Such stories exemplify the sense of dispossession and myths of lost status that influenced the attitudes of these and other families on Lawson Road. The Dixons, for example, were also friends with the Gilberts, another family that had also experienced some decline in their family fortunes. Mr Gilbert was a foreman in a local shoe works but his wife's father was a professional man who lived outside Northampton in a large house set in its own grounds and she had other relatives who owned shops in the town. A certain mystery surrounded her relations with her family, with whom she had little contact, but despite few revelations about her family origins, there were enough to form the basis of a romantic fancy as the Dixons wondered whether they had approved of her marriage. Such conjecture and myth, not unusual in family histories, were important in establishing a 'second identity' that helped set families apart and enhanced their self-esteem via a 'glamorous alternative' to the more mundane present.[95]

There was little hard evidence for the casual speculations of Jordan family gossip. Neither Frank nor Alice Jordan had particularly illustrious origins, coming from small villages outside Northampton where the fathers of both had been carpenters. Frank Jordan had moved away from village life to become a foreman in charge of the coopering at one of Northampton's many breweries. He only became a publican after an accident blinded him in one eye and forced him to abandon the trade. He was fortunate that his employers had known his family since village days and were sympathetic, giving him compensation and helping him to set up as a licensee. Perhaps more significant was Alice Jordan's employment before her marriage, as lady's companion with a well-to-do family from her village. This may have been responsible for the 'airs and graces' that were so apparent in some of her offspring, as irritated neighbours were not averse to pointing out to the Jordans' granddaughter, Celia Dixon. Mrs Adderley, for example, remarked how she had known the Jordans when she was little, but

> that they were far too good and high and mighty to play with ordinary children 'like us'. Their mother would not let them! As Grandma had a large family and they had plenty of room to play together, it must have been less trouble to let them do so ... Whenever there were catty remarks made about my mother's family, I just laughed and ignored them because as far as Uncle Ernest's lot were concerned, they were true![96]

The latter observation reflects Celia's own ambivalent relationship with some of her more pretentious relatives, who looked down on their taciturn brother-in-law. (When Celia married a skilled manual worker, her aunt Hilda refused to buy the cut-glass bowl that a cousin thought she would like as a wedding present, saying it was hardly suitable for the life she'd lead. She selected an iron as being far more appropriate.)

Gossip within the family was as important as that outside it. John Dixon particularly disliked his sister-in-law, Minnie, whom he described as a natural born gossip, because she had caused so much trouble when the family had been planning to emigrate to Canada. 'They just loathed each other.' Being the eldest girl of the eight Jordan children, Minnie had been expected to stay at home with her mother as nursemaid to her younger brothers and sisters. The experience left her very bitter, not least because her parents refused to let her go away and train as a nurse. She described an occasion when one of her mother's friends had come visiting when she was 18. The friend had remarked how useful the experience of looking after the younger ones would be once Minnie got married and had a family of her own. Minnie shocked everyone present by retorting that if she did get married, she would never have any children. Talk about her behaviour only reinforced her determination to be (almost) true to her word, since at 21 she married a man disapproved of by her parents and subsequently had only one child. Jim Barclay came from a respectable family but her father had been warned against him through talk at the chapel since he was known to be too fond of drink. Nevertheless, she insisted on getting engaged, and as soon as she reached her majority, married, despite her family's opposition. 'She said, "I wouldn't have married him, but they tried to stop me, and I wanted to get away". She told me herself that she was fed up with being kept at home.' Minnie remained resentful that she was the only one of the girls denied a career because of the need to help her mother. Hannah trained as a teacher, Hilda became a buyer in the mantle department of a large drapery firm, and another sister was apprenticed as a dressmaker.

Minnie and Jim Barclay owned and lived above a hardware shop a short distance away from Lawson Road. As we have seen, shops were good trading areas for neighbourhood talk, but could be very exposed places if there was scandal in the family. Jim's drinking was difficult to hide, and the marriage eventually disintegrated in the 1930s. Minnie returned home to live with her parents and the humiliation of being proved wrong to both them and her sisters, who frequently threw her mistake back at her. 'She told me, they all kept saying, "We told you so"!' Her own lack of career left her with plenty of time to take an interest in her younger sister's affairs, as her niece ruefully acknowledged: 'I loved Auntie Minnie, but she did make mischief ... She was jealous. She loved my mother, and she was jealous of anybody else. She was the eldest, ten years older if not eleven. And my mother always used to go to her, and I think she was jealous of dad, you know.'[97]

Gossip about the break-up of her marriage reinforced Minnie's vulnerability, but rather than cutting herself off from innuendo and street chatter, she regained influence by both passing on talk within the family and by transgressing the convention of silence that was designed to protect the family's reputation from outside talk, much to their irritation. As a sister-in-law remarked, 'I can't understand your Auntie Minnie, we don't say anything, but they've only to ask her and it all comes out!'

Although Minnie returned to nurse her husband in his final illness, his death threw her back upon her family's goodwill since he had drunk the profits of his small business, leaving her nothing but a small pension. She continued to stay with her parents, but when they died, in her sixties, she

was left without a home, since the family house where she was living was
sold. She was forced into lodgings (a cramped middle bedroom) on
Lawson Road since her son's family had no room, and although several
brothers and sisters could have accommodated her none were willing to
take her in. They even refused to let her take any of her mother's things
because she lacked storage space for them. There was a great deal of
sympathy for her among the neighbours, and the injustice of her treatment
combined with resentment of the family's arrogance to produce a potent
brew of condemnation. 'Ooh, it was a scandal. The gossip was shocking
about the Jordan family.' Eventually the 'talk got so bad' that Hilda, the
most sanctimonious of her chapel-going sisters was pressurized by the rest
of the family and 'out of decency and charity' took her in, 'and let her
know that it was charity as well'.[98]

Minnie's experiences well illustrate how gossip in various guises
moulded and influenced women's behaviour. She rebelled against the
rumour concerning her fiancé, yet remained a subject of gossip because of
the trials of her subsequent marriage. Placed in a position of having to
negotiate gossip on a regular basis in her husband's shop, she skilfully
displaced attention from the vulnerability of her own position by trading
information about her family. Despite the lack of economic independence
which forced her back to live with her parents on separating from her
husband, she maintained her investment in street talk. This paid its divi-
dend when her parents died and gossip forced her relatives to accept their
responsibility for her.

Minnie adapted gossip as a weapon in her own defence, her sensitivity
to its uses possibly being reinforced by her upbringing in chapel, which
was an important cultural influence among many families on Lawson
Road.[99] Chapel membership encouraged frequent moral scrutiny of other
peoples' behaviour, while intensifying anxiety about losing face. It
promoted codes of behaviour that were so internalized that some could not
face the shame of their contravention, regardless of how excusable were
their actions or how sympathetic the rest of the congregation. There was
sometimes a debilitating sense of other peoples' talk and opinion.
Embarrassment at becoming an object of public discussion could deal a
fatal blow to the self-esteem of a family moulded by the judgmental attitudes of chapel membership, as was exemplified in the experiences of a
woman member in her fifties who was arrested for taking a nailfile from
Woolworths in the 1950s. She suffered a nervous breakdown as a result of
the disgrace, and was hospitalized for psychiatric treatment. She was obviously ill, and the minister and several of the family's closest friends tried
to give her and her husband support, but they both shut themselves away
from everyone, including family and friends. 'They were afraid of gossip.'
Her husband resigned from both the choir and the bowling club, despite

being one of their oldest members. Another woman in her fifties committed suicide the day she was due to appear in court, after receiving a summons for shoplifting a similar small item from Woolworths. 'She was so scared, she hadn't told anybody. Not her daughters or anybody, what had happened. And she was so frightened, of all the gossip and all the rest of it, she killed herself ... She thought she had disgraced her family, and couldn't face that ... The neighbours were really upset, they said, if she'd have told one of them ... but she didn't.'[100]

The power of these stories partly derives from the myths they perpetuated about middle-aged, menopausal women being overemotional and neurotic. They hung in the memory as a frightening lesson on the dangers of isolation from neighbours and friends. Middle age was a vulnerable time for women. As we have seen, it could lead to new powers and influence, although this tantalizing prospect could sometimes be rudely postponed. Two women on Lawson Road, for example, were reputed to have been very annoyed at conceiving unexpectedly in their forties. There was an 18-year gap between the two children in one family, and the unwilling mother regarded her pregnancy with 'disbelief and horror'. Both her doctor and husband insisted that her suspicions could not be true until a few weeks before she went into labour, 'which made her madder than ever. Her worst fears were realised, as the last plagued the life out of her as she grew older.' The other woman who had two late babies already had a daughter, and 'was angry when the first turned up when she was 41 (the result of a boozy Christmas). But when another turned up two years later, she was so mad, we expected her to commit murder!'[101]

There is an element of humour in the language this respondent employs to describe her neighbour's situation that suggests how gossip could be used to belittle and transform experiences that might otherwise be too close or threatening for comfort. Gossip's narrative capacity easily turned its subjects into characters, giving recollections of gossip a certain caricatured quality that, incidentally, made it such a rich source of material for comedians who focused on working-class domestic life.

The embarrassment that some women experienced at having a late pregnancy, knowing it would cause much talk, was reinforced by the uncomfortable juxtaposition of age and sex in the minds of the respectable. Mr Hughes, a widower in his fifties, started to court a widow in her early forties, and shocked the chapel to which they belonged by having to get married. Celia Dixon's Aunt Ellen, a staunch chapel member, thought their behaviour was disgraceful, but Celia, then in her early twenties, thought 'it was so unbelievable (and funny) that I just stared at her and laughed. She got mad and said it was no laughing matter, it was disgusting at their age, especially his. "Ooh", she said, "It's the shame. His family will never forgive him. Of course, his daughter will have nothing to do with him."

Yet they'd been gossiping about her when she was at home, because they'd said how sluttish she was as far as the house was concerned. But it all changed when she [the widow] came along.'

Lawson Road experienced an influx of new families in the late 1930s when a row of 18 semi-detached houses was built there. One woman was able to remember 11 of these 18 households. Of those she remembered (which included one retired couple), three contained married women who worked outside the home. These included a full-time clerical worker, a full-time teacher and a woman who worked part-time. Six of the men were skilled workers in the shoe trade, two worked in engineering, one was a draughtsman and one was a college instructor. Many of those who moved in already had some connection with the surrounding district, but were mostly younger than established families on the street, and the behaviour of several was sufficiently different to presage changes that were to accelerate in the post-war years. Lawson Road neighbours had greater freedom to comment on the new residents since they were largely removed from the nexus of talk and ties that characterized the longer established residents. More scandal seemed to attach to these families than to others and largely centred on their sexual mores, which were kept under scrutiny by the Row's resident gossip, an older woman named Mrs Russell, 'a holier than thou woman', of whom it was said, 'if she didn't know about "it", no-one else did!'. Her judgmental attitudes were given plenty of encouragement by the activities of her more sophisticated neighbours. Mrs Moore, for example, was 20 years younger than her husband, who was in his early sixties. She was 'slightly common', and had a 'flighty' reputation, 'a lot of make-up and smart clothes'. Mr Moore disliked socializing, so his wife started going out drinking alone in the mid-1930s. 'Every night we would see her, made up to kill, prancing down the road in her high heels!' (Again, the language used in this description gives the sense of a challenge being laid down to the neighbours.) 'I remember Mrs Russell, the Row's old gossip, remarking to Mrs Bunting, "She's off gadding again, dressed to the nines as usual, there will be trouble there, mark my words" – There was!' Before long, talk started that she was having an affair, the rumours being fuelled by her own lack of discretion since she said goodnight to her 'fancy man' in the jitty at the top of the road. The relationship was well known in the factory where he worked, as one woman was informed by her fiancé, 'You know what men are, they're worse than women.' Mrs Moore eventually received what was considered her come-uppance for abandoning her wifely role, since she returned home late one night to find her suitcases in the porch and all the door locks changed.[102]

Both of the women who worked full-time attracted similar moral disapproval. One was part of a 'quite sophisticated couple' in their mid-thirties who had two children aged five and eight. The husband was a draughts-man, and, to neighbours accustomed to assessing success on a basis of material comfort, they seemed to have everything. Appearances were deceptive and one day in the late 1930s early 1940s, she stopped the neighbour and told her that she was 'bored to tears' staying at home and intended getting a job. She went back to work as a secretary, but childcare was difficult and as both parents had to leave for work by 8 o'clock in the morning the older child had to get his sister's breakfast and take her to school. This led to 'dreadful gossip' over her behaviour as a full-time working mother among the largely nonemployed women of Lawson Road who thought 'she was no better than she should be, and they were proved right', because despite being married to a 'lovely husband', she left her family to go off with a married man, while her husband kept the children and moved away to another area.

As this example suggests, the gossips in such accounts have the air of a Greek chorus whose prognoses are usually, with hindsight, proved uncannily correct. By dwelling on the women's soothsaying abilities, the language used to describe them subtly perpetuates an image of matriarchal wisdom. Their retelling of such incidents reinforced prejudice against women who worked outside the home. It also provides an insight into the morality of the interviewees themselves, as the elderly gossips are disparaged at the same time as their views are tacitly condoned. 'I remember one wedding, all the old biddies ..."Only nineteen, she's too young, she's too young and too flighty", they said, they were going on like that. "He's silly, he should have waited." Well, she did, she hopped it about four years later! Left a little girl, her grandma brought her up.'

Although women moved in and out of this chorus, closer examination reveals that the number of those with a real reputation for ferreting out gossip was small. There was, for example, Mrs Russell in the Row, and Mrs Bailey in Lawson Road itself, who was deliberately kept in the dark about many things. 'I don't think she meant any harm, but she would poke her nose into other folk's business, which did put the back up of most people ... When Mrs Thompson, a great friend of ours, was taken ill, we knew through Auntie Minnie about it and so did her close neighbours but no-one told Mrs Bailey. When the ambulance came, Mrs Bailey was seen hovering on her doorstep, dying to know what was going on. At last, curiosity got the better of her, and just as they were lifting the stretcher inside, she, to the utter amazement of everyone, dashed across and asked the ambulance men exactly what was wrong and apparently was told politely to huff off! When I had my second bad miscarriage, she stopped my sister and asked why the Queen's Nurses were visiting our house twice a day. Eva had to think quickly, and told her I had a bad cold and had to stay in bed!'[103] Such directness was viewed as rather eccentric, and Mrs

Bailey was tolerated despite her intrusiveness perhaps because there was some sympathy for her given that her only daughter had died of TB when she was 18. At another level, however, one could argue that these gossipy 'characters' were an important myth in street life. Their willingness to engage in the extremes of speculation articulated what others might be thinking, yet absolved other women of guilt at being the first to say it themselves. They were a sounding board against which various views and prejudices could be tested.

The other married woman in the Row who worked full-time, Mrs Nichols, had no children of her own, but was responsible for her young orphaned sister aged 11 who lived with her. Both she and her husband were active in the Labour party and in the chapel, so were frequently out in the evenings as well as during the day. These activities kept Mrs Nichols largely apart from other women in the street, which reinforced her perception of them as troublemakers. She consequently dismissed rumours passed on to her about her sister, who, although supposedly in by the mid-evening, was sneaking out to meet soldiers at the local park. 'People tried to tell them, that she'd been seen with some soldiers, because it was war-time, and her sister wouldn't take any notice. She said they were just a pack of malicious gossipers, and that Rosa wouldn't do that because she was fast asleep in bed when they came home.' She was consequently astounded when a school medical revealed that her sister was pregnant. Local gossip went far beyond the usual disapproval. 'The shock and horror in Lawson Road was terrible, so was the anger', not against the child, but against her sister and husband. 'Ordinary, reticent women like Mrs Bampton and Mrs Hepworth rounded on her and told her exactly what they thought of her and her neglect … I think, as well, it was the awful thought of a tiny girl of twelve having to go through childbirth, that hit most of the married women'. (Neither the Bamptons nor the Hepworths were usually known to gossip.)[104] Others more used to commenting on their neighbours' behaviour were quick to reinforce another moral message, blaming the older sister's politics for her dereliction of domestic duty. 'I remember Mrs Russell saying, "If she'd have spent more time with Rosa than with politics and trying to convert us, it would have been a lot better!"' The girl was taken into care, and this couple also moved away a few months later.[105]

Another unmarried young woman became pregnant in the 1950s in Lawson Road Row under very different circumstances. In this case, an attempt to enhance the family's reputation in an extravagant public show rebounded in an equally public humiliation. Dora Appleton was an only child whose mother and grandmother were so elated when she became engaged that they used the gossip network to great effect by spreading the news around the district that she would have the best and biggest wedding that anyone had seen.[106] Neighbours started to become suspicious, however, when the young woman 'boasted' to a contemporary on her birthday about the expensive presents she had received from both her fiancé and another boy-friend. Soon after, her mother, 'without my asking, informed me that she had gone away on a secretarial course for a few months and promptly burst into tears and hurried away. I thought it was because she was missing her!' No-one would have noticed if her grandma hadn't insisted on informing everyone who would listen that she had gone to be a nurse. Clues began to be pieced together and matters came to a head at the local post office when her fiancé's mother publicly denounced the stories that were circulating about her son's behaviour, 'if that dirty little beast thinks she is going to put the blame on my son, she is making a big mistake, plenty of people have seen her carrying on ... She was broadcasting it, and of course, the Post Office was full, and she was shouting at the top of her voice.' There was little sympathy for the two-timing young woman, who moved away to live with relatives, although there was a good deal for her parents, especially her father, because 'he looked like an old man' after he found out what had been happening, 'he went all quiet and he never spoke to anybody. He looked so ill, because of course, he doted on her ... it smashed him.'[107]

Such accounts offer up a different kind of street myth, in which it is men who appear as remote, idealized figures, reserved and intensely private, almost victims of their womenfolk's 'misdemeanours', while women take the active role, whether kicking against the assumptions made of them or subverting the reputation of other women. It is sometimes hard to avoid what seems to be satisfaction at the misfortune of those who had been bumptious to their neighbours. Men tend to emerge as largely bystanders in this world, where women often reserved their most critical judgments for female rather than male behaviour. It should not be assumed that this was because women considered themselves more worthy of blame. There was a sense in which men were not really players at all, but waited in the wings, the real equality of emotion, however debased or distorted, being shared with other women.

One way the experience of women on streets such as Lawson Road differed from that of those in poorer areas was the tendency for neighbours' feelings to simmer largely beneath the surface rather than exploding in the manner depicted by Jim Hooley at the beginning of this chapter. As a consequence, those who were more extreme stood out vividly from the life of the street. Celia Dixon, for example, recalled a neighbour called Mrs Green who moved into the house next door from the East End of London. She was very quarrelsome and relations got so bad between her and her next-door neighbour, Mrs Adderley, that in desperation Mrs Adderley saw a solicitor, who sent Mrs Green a formal letter threatening legal action if she didn't behave herself. Celia described another occasion when her mother heard Mrs Green screaming at her younger daughter who was playing in the garden:

> 'You stick your bleeding fingers through the fence again, you little bugger, I'll cut your bleeding hand off!' My mother was so appalled that she just said, 'If you have a complaint, will you kindly come to me and *not* use foul language in front of my children.' Whereupon Daisy picked up a big brick and raised her arm to hurl it at my mother's face. Just then a stentorian voice bellowed, 'Put that Brick Down!!' Which Daisy as taken aback as we were, promptly did, and scuttled away. Looking round, we saw that it was Mrs Warwick who (as she said afterwards, by God's Grace) happened to be cleaning her back bedroom windows. She came over to see if my mother was alright, because as she said, if the brick had been thrown, my mother could have been blinded or killed. We then heard a terrible noise from next door – screaming and laughing – and Mrs Add, who had heard the commotion (as had quite a few more) came along to say that "that woman must have gone round the bend'. She was sitting on the back doorstep and tearing her hair and drumming her heels in a fit of violent hysterics.[108]

Mrs Green's confrontational approach sat uneasily in Lawson Road, as is apparent in this episode's revealing clash of temperament and class. Other neighbours tended to leave her alone since 'it was a very respectable street as a rule, and they didn't know how to deal with her ... she could be friendly one minute and spiteful the next. You had to be careful what you said to her, in case she turned on you.' Possibly because of this deliberate distancing, Mrs Green had a reputation for being rather 'pushy' at finding out what was going on, her only close friend in Lawson Road being Mrs Bailey, with whom she was said to share a common nosiness.[109]

As suggested in earlier chapters, there was an important distinction between initiators of gossip and more passive participants in the process. The active gossip performed an important signposting role, since neighbours knew where to listen in for the latest news, which could be mulled over in peace within the safer confines of the family. 'Respectability' tended to transform gossip into something which other people did, yet the very vividness with which these respondents recall the street scandals of over 50 years ago testifies to the part it played in the life of even such apparently 'privatized' streets such as Lawson Road. While concentration on the scandals of the time can give a misleading impression of what was, in reality, a far broader and more complex process, it does illustrate the powerful dynamics that established and reinforced moral values at a street level. The exposition of such gossip and of one family's experience also suggests how perceptions of other people, mediated through gossip, were woven into the invention and transference of family myth and into the broader mythology of the street. It illustrates how even the most respectable families dipped in and out of local gossip and the extent to which gossip was manipulated by those who would probably never have recognized themselves as skilled practitioners of the art. For although life on streets like this was less public than in poorer areas, the importance of avoiding public humiliation made gossip a particularly powerful medium there.

The Dixons' uncertain social position aggravated their sensitivity to gossip, although this did not prevent them from sharing in the talk that went on. They were too well embedded into the local network of family and social relationships to be able to opt out. Participation could, in any case, be a way of getting back at superior relations, as was apparent from Minnie Barclay's experience. Anxiety about the harmful potential of local gossip was defused in the way it tended to acquire a comic flavour in the retelling, although this itself reinforced the prohibition against even minor transgressions or any nonconformity that would make the family into a 'laughing stock'.

Relatively static neighbourhoods carried the burden of overfamiliarity that irked many who felt themselves to be victims of neighbourhood judgments and misconceptions. Celia Dixon, for example, moved completely out of the area on marriage, to the other side of the town, adamant that she would not have wanted to get a house near where she grew up since 'They knew too much of your business, because they'd known my mother's family, you know, they'd lived down there for donkey's years. They knew too much.'[110]

Her removal to a new estate in the early 1950s was symptomatic of the desire for a different way of life which was made possible by the housing developments of the inter-war and immediate post-war years. Gossip with neighbours and acquaintances remained important in the lives of many women on these estates, although it began to lose some of the easy familiarity which had characterized it in the closer-knit traditional working-class areas. There was not the same shared mental landscape which helped draw inhabitants of the older areas into conversation, despite their misgivings. There was not the same variety of locations in which to talk. There were fewer opportunities to sit on the doorstep and catch the eye of the passer-by. Indeed, there were often few passers-by until the children started to come home from school. Daytime rhythms were just as likely to be punctuated by Mrs Dale's Diary or The Archers as by casual conversation with neighbours. The external street rituals like donkeystoning, which had affirmed local values and united neighbours in an unconscious collective undertaking, gradually diminished, partly perhaps because of their very association with life in poorer housing areas.

Greater prosperity undermined the need for the reciprocal, informative, supportive aspects of gossip and reinforced its inquisitive, excluding tendencies, fear of nosiness being exacerbated by greater opportunities to worry about its consequences. New networks developed among frequenters of coffee mornings and groups gathered at the school gate, but their powerful controlling tendencies excluded women who failed their 'critical scrutiny' and encouraged others to deliberately distance themselves.[111] Removal to a new housing estate implied a fresh start, which inevitably made people more cautious in the relationships they established with neighbours. Their insecurities also increased sensitivity to the malicious, judgmental side of gossip, which was particularly important in establishing status and reputation in such a new environment. Women like Celia Dixon were likely to find that their new problems were less to do with those who knew too much as with those whose judgments were based on too little.

Notes

1. MSTC, Tape 604.
2. Prochaska 1980, 15.
3. Ross 1993, 66, 152–53.
4. Storey 1990: 1992, 94–95.
5. Northampton interviews, Mrs Perkins. Although in tightly knit, geographically distinct neighbourhoods such as the 'Island', a small group of five streets in Hackney, East London, men from outside the area who married a local girl were known by her surname. Centerprise 1979, 41.
6. Jasper 1969, 88.
7. Northampton interviews, Mrs Hill.
8. Northampton interviews, Mrs West.
9. Miscellaneous interviews, May Thompson.
10. Northampton interviews, Mrs York.
11. Northampton interviews, Mrs King.
12. Northampton interviews, Mrs Atkins.
13. Miscellaneous interviews, Joan Green.
14. Northampton interviews, Mrs West.
15. Northampton interviews, Mrs West.
16. Oral History Archive, Lancaster University. Mrs C2P.
17. Almirol 1981, 296, 298.
18. Chinn 1988, 42.
19. Williamson 1982, 124.
20. Broady 1956. My thanks to Pat Ayers for drawing attention to this article.
21. Caplan, 185.
22. Dayus 1991, 52–53.
23. Chamberlain 1989, 5.
24. Harding 1975, 291–92, 295.
25. Martin 1911, 29-30; Lewis, 39.
26. See, for example, Chinn 1988 and Ross 1993.
27. Klein 1965: 1970, 187.
28. Chinn 1988, 44.

29. Northampton interviews, Mrs Flower.
30. Orwell 1937: 1974, 104–05.
31. For a more detailed exploration of this theme, see Swindells and Jardine 1990, 1–23.
32. Chinn 1988, 14.
33. Steedman 1985, 113.
34. E. Roberts 1984: 1986, 108–09.
35. Burnett 1982, 232–33.
36. Woodward 1928: 1983, 19.
37. McCrindle and Rowbotham 1977: 1979, 4.
38. Jaeger 1968, 12–13. Annie Jaeger was born in 1875.
39. Rodaway 1960: 1985.
40. Mitchell 1968: 1977, 40.
41. Linton 1982, 3–4.
42. Woodward 1928: 1983, 19.
43. Burnett 1982, 235.
44. Rodaway 1960:1985 23; Woodward 1928: 1983, 6–7.
45. Spring-Rice 1939: 1981, 92.
46. Wakefield 1980: 1988, 77, 78–81, 158–59.
47. Rodaway 1960: 1985, 141–42.
48. Miscellaneous interviews, Maria Goddard.
49. Miscellaneous interviews, Maria Goddard.
50. Bertenshaw 1980, 12.
51. MSTC, Tape 582.
52. Linton 1982. 46–47.
53. Black 1915: 1983, 1–4.
54. Northampton interviews, Mrs Gee.
55. Harrison 1971.
56. OLHG, AMD. Woman worked on piecework in rubber shop of local factory, so wage varied from week to week. Her husband was a hawker.
57. OLHG, AMD.
58. OLHG, EB.
59. OLHG, AM.
60. Klein 1965: 1970, 139. Mogey's observations on the strictness with which men segregated 'outside the home' and inside the home have been observed in an earlier chapter.
61. Watkin 1985, 13.
62. Transcript, OLHG. L born 1914, Broughton, 10.
63. Chinn 1988, 16.
64. OLHG, AMD.
65. OLHG, AMD.
66. Oral History Archive, Lancaster University, Mrs H8P.
67. Zweig, in Klein 1965: 1970, 133.
68. Allotments and gardens were spaces where male gossip was shared. By the 1900s the allotment was a male domain into which women only ventured as onlookers. Gardening did not begin to attract great female involvement until the Second World War. Bourke 1994, 88–89, 227.
69. MSTC, Tape 251.
70. OLHG, EO.
71. OLHG, L and M.
72. OLHG, AMD.

73. Miscellaneous interviews, Mrs Palmerston.
74. OLHG, EO.
75. Tildsley 1985, 21.
76. Beales and Lambert 1934: 1973, 103, 143–44; Vincent 1991, 86, 107–08.
77. Dayus 1991, 112, 118.
78. Dayus 1991, 129.
79. Klein 1965: 1970, 135.
80. Gorer 1955, 59–60.
81. Gorer 1955, 60–01.
82. Seabrook 1992, 21.
83. Northampton interviews, Mrs Grant.
84. Miscellaneous interviews, Maria Goddard.
85. Greenwood 1967, 72–73.
86. Gosling 1980, 17. Lawson Road was a real street whose name has been changed.
87. The sequence of these street directories is unfortunately rather erratic and there are considerable gaps. Those available before the First World War are as follows: 1900–01; 1906; 1907; 1910; 1912; 1914.
88. There is a gap of 14 years after the 1914 directory which makes the detail of the early 1920s difficult to verify from written sources. Directories for the inter-war period are as follows: 1928; 1929; 1936.
89. 1952 is the first Northampton street directory available after 1936.
90. Northampton interviews, Mr Edmund.
91. Northampton interviews, Mrs Roberts.
92. Northampton interviews, Celia Dixon, (c).
93. Dixon 1989.
94. Dixon 1989. Annie Bunting's husband was a fitter-welder. She was a great support to the Dixon family when Hannah subsequently suffered a long illness.
95. Samuel and Thompson 1990, 8.
96. Northampton interviews, Celia Dixon. Mr Green was a tramdriver. Mrs Adderley was a widow who worked part-time as a cleaner.
97. Northampton interviews, Celia Dixon, (f).
98. Northampton interviews, Celia Dixon, (d, f, g).
99. Religious affiliation is known for just under half the adult inhabitants of Lawson Road, of whom one was a Catholic, three were Baptists, nine were Church of England and 18 were Congregationalists.
100. Northampton interviews, Mrs Flower.
101. Dixon 1989, Northampton interviews, Mrs Roberts.
102. Northampton interviews, Celia Dixon(b), Mr Billingham.
103. Northampton interviews, Celia Dixon. Mr Thompson was a retired bank manager.
104. The husbands of both women were shoe operatives.
105. Northampton interviews, Celia Dixon, Mrs Knott.
106. Mr Appleton was a shoe operative. His in-laws kept a pub.
107. Northampton interviews, Mrs Roberts, Mrs Flower.
108. Dixon 1989.
109. Northampton interviews, Mrs Thorpe.
110. Northampton interviews, Celia Dixon, (a).
111. For a more contemporary analysis of this phenomenon, see Erica Wimbush, 'Mothers Meeting', in Wimbush and Talbot 1988, 65–66.

CHAPTER FIVE

No coats hanging on the door: neighbourhood networks in decline

> The slums at any rate have their gossip and common life, but with the advance in the social scale, family life becomes more private and the women, left alone in the house while their husbands are out at work often become mere hopeless drudges.[1]

Neighbourliness was a major source of support for working-class women and gave rise to the many complex networks on which their survival frequently depended, although this neighbourliness – made visible in the sociability of gossip – tended to be misinterpreted by men, who disliked its intrusiveness and tendency to clash with privatized notions of family life and expectations within the household. The close proximity of life in working-class neighbourhoods and the public tensions of poverty, associated with over involvement with other people's lives and frequent arguments, all served to accentuate the apparent invasiveness of female society which neighbourliness expressed.

We have become used to a model of collective working-class behaviour and privatized middle-class conduct. The reality has, of course, always been far more complex. The communal life of the poor was defined to a great extent by its impoverished material circumstances, forcing many working-class people to assume a public life which could be extremely stressful. Personal and territorial space are important human needs and the infringement of either of these is known to drive up arousal and annoyance levels, although levels of such 'need' are culturally variable, and close proximity could sometimes be a source of great comfort to the urban poor. Nevertheless, crowded working-class neighbourhoods were consequently very susceptible to the tensions of spatial encroachment, which led to great value being placed on the personal and family privacy that was so difficult to maintain. Bill Mitchell 'once saw a woman advance on her neighbour with a carving knife, only to pass by and cut down a clothes line. It was a small matter of territory – a trivial matter transformed by temper into something big.'[2] There were frequently disturbing undercurrents to street life which meant that even those who were outwardly integrated adopted various strategies to maintain a private space and territory against its intrusions, whether adorning the outside of the house through donkeystoning or by laying aside a 'best' room for special occasions. Standards were important in working-class communities not only as an expression of a family's status but for self-respect, credit, job opportunities and collective identity. Their manifestation was defined by poverty and the details of respectability varied, so that what was 'ordinary' behaviour in one area could be defined as 'stand-offish' or 'rough' in another. Neither were the conventions of neighbouring as straightforward as a general dropping by of any neighbour who happened to be passing. Close examination reveals that even where 'popping-in' for a chat was acceptable, it was often restricted to extended family members and close acquaintances with more general gossip and socializing being conducted across the defining boundary of the front doorstep.

The pressures of overcrowding were contradictory, and privatizing, self-protective impulses often vied with a persistent curiosity about neighbours' activities, producing an inevitable tension in social relationships.[3] For the public arena in which the poor lived was an insecure place in which the revelations of a private confidence could be exposed to vicious public scrutiny if neighbours fell out with each other. Vocal arguments, insults and quarrels were an important way of externalizing pressure and frustration in poor, overcrowded communities, although it was the physically dominant and those afforded the protection of extended family connections who could most afford to release their tensions in such a manner. Others who lacked these advantages had to take a more circumspect approach to social relationships, women made vulnerable to public exposure by lack of relatives, local support or their social aspirations being likely to view overfriendliness and intimacy as 'rough' and perilous behaviour.

The tensions of sociability and privacy: questions of time and space

Space was a luxury among the urban poor, and inevitably imposed a public dimension on much which would have more comfortably remained private. Analytic categories of a male dimension of public affairs and female domain of private domestic life fit uneasily into the lives of many working-class women, whose complex spatial experience contrasted with the more proscriptively home-based lives of middle-class women, marginalized in the distant suburbs.[4] Cramped housing conditions often spilled their domestic life over into the public realm of the street, while many women had some form of paid employment which took them away from the home and into a public sphere of social and economic activity. Poorer districts tended to have a large number of places in which to meet and converse, and despite their lack of participation in formal collective activities, working-class women, as we have seen, often filled the rare gaps in their busy lives with talk or gossip in the public spheres of street, shop or

wash-house. Women of the urban poor were unapologetic in their possession of the public sphere, and their uninhibited behaviour could shock even
those who lived amongst them:

> my eyes used to boggle and I was only a kid, I don't know why I used
> to, and, and, it always stood out in my memory, big, fat women, they
> didn't bother wearing corsets and bras, they couldn't afford them ...
> and some people, some women were very fat and they had big fami-
> lies and they used to sit on the step, feeding the babies with the breast
> and men walking past, no shame.[5]

The large families that were most common in such neighbourhoods gave
local women a particular investment in street activities, since involvement
there enabled them to keep an eye on their children's behaviour, while
allowing them occasionally to escape the confinement of their crowded
homes. The close attention paid to outer show, whether sweeping down
the yard, putting out washing, cleaning the windows or donkeystoning the
doorstep, also provided a useful (public) opportunity to keep a watchful
eye on street 'doings'. Women played an assertive role in street life, and
Harry Watkin's recollections of growing up in inter-war Hulme highlighted the nature of their daily witness. Weather permitting, most front
doors were kept open all day.

> Women stood on their front doorsteps watching passers-by and
> hoping for a neighbourly gossip, sometimes shouting to each other but
> generally carried on by groups of two or three at a door with arms
> folded underneath their turned up aprons. One saw very little of the
> men, who sneaked in and out of their homes as though it was inde-
> cent to be seen in their own street.[6]

Referring to his Edwardian childhood in Salford, Robert Roberts
suggested that local street talk had been, on the whole, a single sex affair,
and in support of his contention described a singular feature of the conversation which greeted the outbreak of the First World War, when 'Little
groups, men and women together (unusual, this), stood talking earnestly in
the shop or at the street corner, stunned a little by the enormity of events.'[7]

Some men, like Watkin's own father, hated being 'confined to the
house'. He repaired the family's boots only after much persuasion from his
wife. 'As soon as he had finished off, off he would hurry to Jimmy Allen's
beerhouse to refresh himself.' Watkin felt the men of his neighbourhood
regarded homes as 'unmanly places', which reflected their own territorial
discomfort. He presents an image of the privatized working-class male,
who preferred to remain indoors when not at work or at leisure, in
contrast to the public visibility of mothers who 'usually occupied their
front doorsteps as often and as long as possible, gossiping ("gassing" we
called it) or just watching passers-by'.[8] Even within the house, a man's
space was usually well defined and formalized, as in the privileged

comfortable chair by the fireplace, which symbolized both dominance and marginalization, a sense of not really belonging to the domestic world. In Alice Linton's inter-war household no-one ever dared sit in her dad's old wooden armchair, 'which held the place of honour in front of the fireplace, since it was sacred to father alone'.[9] Mary Bentley remembering the largely hard furniture of her childhood in Clayton, Manchester, described how as soon as there was a little more money in the family, 'a really comfortable chair' was bought for her father.[10] With the softening of domestic relations in post-war Oxford, Mogey's description of working-class life transformed the man into something approaching a respected household pet.

> At certain times he appears for food, and food is placed before him, a chair is reserved for his leisure, and he is kept in, and himself accepts, a place just outside the more intense mother–children relations.

Mogey observed the strictness with which men kept 'outside the home' and inside the home as separate domains. 'Coming in from the outside world the symbols operative there are removed: off comes the jacket, off come the collar and tie, off come the boots or shoes.'[11] Once he came home, this private space by the fire became male terrain.

If working-class women had symbolic possession of the doorstep, there were other rituals within the home which men tended to appropriate. A woman's time, for example, was marked and accounted for by the waged labour of her husband, a lack of ownership reflected in the way that the mechanical marking of time and ritual of locking up were frequently claimed by men. Many employers consciously manipulated time within the early factory system, altering the factory clock at will to suit their own purposes, but as clock time became generally established, working-class men asserted their own rights over it by purchasing watches or clocks which became tokens of status, respectability and authority, as is apparent in the clock-winding rituals common to many working-class homes. Maria Goddard observed of her father during the inter-war years, for example, that 'Only he touched the clocks, and he locked the doors ... They don't think women can do it ... You know, how they do, methodically.'[12] Les Billingham's father was the same, 'Dad used to wind the clocks up, and used to always religiously lock all the doors, front door, the back door and everything.'[13] In some households, where the time-piece was a family heir-loom or had some considerable money invested in it, the clock-winding custom acquired an even greater significance and almost sexual connotations. That owned by Bill Williamson's collier grandfather was his prized possession, and

> Sunday morning was a regular time for a very serious ritual. This was when the grandfather clock was wound up and set, a task for my grandfather alone. No one else dared touch the clock. He used to give

the mechanism a brush with a cockerel feather and carefully wind up the clock. His private name for it – and this was something of a family joke – was Hannah. The Sunday ritual with Hannah often prompted my grandmother to exclaim, 'You think more of that clock than you do of me'. And she told him more than once that she 'would have his coffin made from it'.[14]

Locking up and clock winding attested to a right of possession in the same way that carving the Sunday joint affirmed the man's role as head of the household. Edward Ezard's father, like other men in his neighbourhood, prided himself on his carving, since in his area (and many others) it was said that whoever did the carving wore the trousers.[15] Such domestic rituals of masculinity presented an image of competence and control which in some respects reinforced the man's position as outsider within the domestic sphere, reflecting as they did a need to control the routines and rhythms within the home which were largely regulated by women.

The methodical, almost obsessive qualities of the clock-winding and locking-up observances expressed a particular kind of working-class masculinity, with its overemphasis on procedures, rules and regulations. As the examples cited earlier suggest, such practices were often deeply irritating to women and drew on an assumption of male competence which could be extremely misleading. The inner mechanism of clocks (and wireless sets), for example, often held a strange compulsion for men, who were not infrequently described as taking them apart for recreation.[16] Although Jean Pearson's father had 'no idea of the workings' of the family clock, when he was bored he would often decide to 'mend' it, 'even when it was ticking away normally on the sideboard'.[17] Accounts of ill-advised attempts to 'repair' the family time-piece are not unusual in the oral record, where women also express exasperation at the procrastinating perfectionism of their menfolk. Maria Goddard's mother, for example, 'was a bit impatient. She wanted things done quickly, and my husband was a bit like this, a perfectionist, me dad was like that. He'd put a piece of paper up, then look at it ... And I think it irritated me mother, so she used to say, "I'll do it!"'[18]

Technology, time, talk – none were considered appropriate to women. The disciplined dictates of industrial employment had a knock-on effect upon women's domestic life, whose routines had to be developed around the requirements of male working patterns, and were perhaps most starkly expressed in the expectations of men in the mining communities. Yet the move to clock time was neither 'unilinear or uniform', and the less educated and unskilled remained attuned to a 'non-compartmentalised' sense of time. Many households among the urban poor of late Victorian and Edwardian London, for example, possessed neither clocks nor watches, and although regular domestic routines became common in many working-class homes, the extent to which women followed them varied and reflected distinct periods in their own life cycle, the demands of babies and toddlers undermining a clock based sense of time and more closely approaching the 'conventions of "pre-industrial" society"'.[19] The impact of the Puritan work ethic upon attitudes towards women's gossip was suggested in Chapter One, and could be seen as part of a broader attack upon pre-industrial patterns of socializing and recreation whose 'task-oriented' sense of time blurred the distinction between work and passing the time of day. (While women were criticized for the indolence of gossip, men were berated for the excesses of Saint Monday.)[20] As the new time discipline was imposed with varying degrees of success in the eighteenth and nineteenth centuries, women's experiences at particular stages of the life cycle continued to manifest the patterns of an earlier pre-industrial experience, ensuring that the talk which was associated with these periods was dismissed or condemned for its failure to be marked by any useful, quantifiable activity. These more disciplined attitudes reinforced a sense of unease about gossip as a wasteful activity, which were reflected in attitudes towards domestic tasks and talk in the street and on the front doorstep, gossip being increasingly confined to certain periods of the day in communities where there was a strong sense of clock time.[21]

Spatial divisions within the home

Spatial definitions within the household also had more than a purely physical significance. The best room or parlour which better-off working-class families managed to keep was a token of the kind of order it was usually impossible to achieve in a busy working-class household, and mantelpiece mottos such as 'What is a Home Without a Mother?' helped reinforce awareness that such a space was only possible through the budgetary surplus she had prudently garnered.[22] The parlour's symbolic qualities were apparent in the fact that it was seldom used, apart from special occasions or Sundays, and that entry to it tended to be carefully regulated. William Atherton, for example, described his family's parlour as 'a sanctuary', while in Walter Southgate's London household the mantelshelf was nicknamed 'mother's alterpiece' because it harboured his mother's wedding ornaments.[23] Bill Mitchell's mill town front room 'had the best furniture, the cleanest wallpaper, the smartest lace curtains and an all-pervading chapelish tang of damp books and furniture polish. Most front rooms were little used and in winter achieved the coldness of a tomb.'[24] The maintenance of a best room was in some respects a useful strategy against being caught unawares, part of the pretence involved in keeping up appearances which was another aspect of survival, for deception too could become 'a form of resistance, a form of protection for the family when intrusions from outside could all too easily disrupt the equilibrium'.[25] Yet the reverential overtones which often colour depictions are a reminder of its role as imaginative space, as a cypher of celebratory occasions – games, parties, Sunday dinner, memories of which signified hope. In this sense it was in many respects more of a woman's room than a man's, a special space which testified to her dreams of something better.[26]

The front parlour sustained an ideal of life as it should have been, although outsiders did not always recognize its significance. Loane, for example, felt the working-classes displayed a lamentable lack of discipline in their choice of furniture, even many of the 'most worthy' buying goods for which they could afford to pay but certainly could not afford to use, 'The blinds must not be drawn up because the carpet will fade; the gas must not be lighted because it will blacken the ceiling; the window must not be opened, because the air will tarnish the frame of the looking glass ...'[27] However, the care taken to protect such purchases could in other contexts be seen as an astonishing sense of discipline which expressed a proper sense of the cost and value of things only purchased with great difficulty. Such solemn criticisms also belie the fact that families were not immune to the comic implications of striving to maintain the parlour's 'sacred' status. A Salford woman, for example, laughingly described how many families endeavoured over several years to acquire a sofa for their best room, and took so long to buy one that by the time it was fitted up as they wanted the children were old enough to be courting and were using it themselves. In another variation on the same theme, a couple saved up all their lives with the aim that:

> when they was so old they'd have this parlour and he would be sitting reading his Sunday paper, and she'd be making the dinner and so on. And they'd have a nice carpet and er, when they got it she called out what ever they called him, Jim or Jack, you know, 'Where are ye?'
> 'I'm in the parlour'.
> 'Not on that new settee!'
> 'No, no, I'm on the carpet?'
> 'On the carpet?'
> 'No, I've rolled it up.'
> And the idea was that when they got it, they were so afraid of using it, you see.[28]

Such jokes played on the essential hollowness of such aspirations, which by deferring gratification to a distant future, were at variance with the more immediate preoccupations that frequently coloured working-class attitudes. Nevertheless, such care was not unusual. A woman recalled how the 'average' home in Rochdale during the 1930s had two kinds of carpet: a good one for use during the weekend and an older one which served during the week. 'On a Monday morning, the best carpet was rolled up and put under the sideboard. There it would remain till week-end.'[29]

The dilution of matriarchal authority

Insecurity of employment and susceptibility to the hazards of ill-health meant that working-class families often lived a precarious life balanced between coping and bare survival, which made sensitivity to many minor signs of status and awareness of subtle distinctions in social space very important. Indeed, as has been suggested, the closeness of life in over-crowded neighbourhoods placed many restraints upon social behaviour. Not only the amount of space available within individual houses but linear street plans, back-to-back housing, alleys, courts and tenements all affected the quality and extent of personal contact in working-class communities, as did the proximity of relatives, who were often neighbours. The complex mapping of other people's lives which was possible in close, fairly static communities was both supportive and inhibiting. Changes in the physical pattern of working-class housing and neighbourhoods and the technical and sanitary advances which slowly (and unevenly) improved the material circumstances of women introduced a frequently welcome sense of space and distance, which owed little to wider ideological forces promoting 'acceptable domestic behaviour'.[30] The greater ability to limit family size also helped weaken the links of communal living and opened up greater opportunities for a more personal expression of individuality. Domestic standards and childrearing practices had risen considerably in working-class communities by the inter-war years, when working-class women were described as being more 'refined', desiring 'better homes, better clothes for themselves and their children', and 'far more self-respecting and less humble than their predecessors'.[31] Yet higher standards introduced differ-ent tensions and new pressures in the mental struggle to juggle resources and maintain the level of material respectability which was now required. Gossip could appear more threatening under these circumstances, under-mining women's new aspirations and encouraging a tendency for some to withdraw from its neighbourhood expression. At the same time, as younger women began to acquire greater freedom in work and social activ-ities during the inter-war years, so their perceptions of gossip as a mali-cious medium with which to undermine character and family reputation were heightened.[32] Maria Goddard recalled how, as a 17 year old, she had been given a lift back from an evening out in a car owned by the elder brother of a friend. She dare not let him drop her off at her door, for fear of what her mother would say, and got out a couple of streets away. She did not go unnoticed, and one of the neighbours who had seen her told her mother, who was 'infuriated, she was horror stricken, what were you doing in a car? Whose car was it? Oh, it was terrible. You were no good if you went in a car.' Her mother's anger and fears were understandable given the contemporary connotations of accepting such a lift, but Mary's resentment stemmed from the manner in which she had been given away since the neighbour had made

> a beeline for her ... she couldn't wait to tell me mother ... She was a nosy one out of June Street where Joan lived ... She called me and Joan goody goodies ... Afterwards me mother said it was all jealousy really. It was awful that. I couldn't go out for a week ... I think perhaps me mother must have told her off for something, you know. She was quite outspoken, me mother. Not rude, she wasn't a rude person, but she could be outspoken, you know. She might have said something about somebody, and me mother would tell her.[33]

The working-class street was an extremely moral arena in which women were custodians of family morality and 'decent' moral behaviour. The struggle of younger women to move beyond its restrictions was bound to lend a coating of resentment and regret to relations with an older genera-tion of women, as Jerry White suggested happened between mothers and daughters in Campbell Bunk, a notorious London slum, during the early 1920s, under the lingering influence of pre-First World War behaviour.[34] The impact of broad social forces gradually loosened this tension, although it remained a persistent theme in mother–daughter relations.

The access of young working-class women to new forms of recreation in the inter-war years far surpassed that which had been available to their mothers and grandmothers. Technical advances introduced fashionable materials which allowed greater scope for the development of a more sexual persona, particularly as there were greater opportunities to develop a social life away from the street.[35] Not surprisingly this often clashed with the Puritan attitudes of the older generation and the desire of fathers to control the behaviour of their daughters, encouraging secrecy and decep-tion among the young. Edith Hinson, for example, described life as a teenager in Stockport during the 1920s when she did not dare show her mam the Rudolph Valentino hat she had bought out of her own money (it was black and shiny like a matador's) because her mother's morals were so strict. (The hat ended up on the fire, as 'unsuitable' finery for girls so frequently did.) Edith was 'mad' about dancing, and had to go to elabo-rate lengths to creep out of the house without Mam seeing her 'wanton' daughter.[36] A Bolton woman dare not tell her father she went dancing, 'Oh, he wouldn't let me. He wouldn't let me put no lipstick on. If I went near the mirror, he'd say, "You're vain enough, off!" But I put it on when I went outside but I had to wipe it off before I come home.'[37] Forbidden make-up, whether used by older or younger girls, was applied secretly out of sight of parents, although as an Oldham woman observed, 'nothing so brash as a lipstick was used ...' In the twenties even the little booklets of 'Poudre Papiers', those little pages of powdery papers which were dusted on the face, had to be kept hidden in a 'clutch bag'.[38] The father of another Bolton woman used to take his daughters' handbags off them if he was around when they were about to go out. 'If there was any make-up he used to throw it on the fire and say my girls don't need make-up ...'[39] A growing self-consciousness among the young about personal appearance intensified dissatisfaction with the scrutiny of their elders, particularly as it accentuated the questions of reputation which were so often a subject of street talk and innuendo. The ever present eyes of street life could be extremely off-putting to young people, particularly when they started courting. 'My friend and I lived up Newhall Lane and we were courting and married two sisters and we used to come down together and there were that many people stood at the doors that we used to wonder which street to go down, hoping there would be less people out. You always seemed to do something silly. If you were walking down the street and all these people were stood, you knew for a fact that they had nothing else to do but just watch you walk down. You could tumble over any little thing.'[40] At one level such sensitivity on the part of the young was nothing new, but it had become perhaps more intense than in the past as the growing influence of broader social and cultural forces encouraged a greater dissatisfaction with the more stifling aspects of street life. The advent of mass circulation periodicals, cinemas and radio all served to offer new images of female dress and behaviour which accentuated inter-generational differences. At the same time, young women's greater access to jobs in factories, shops and offices brought them into contact with new ideas and information which frequently challenged hitherto accepted wisdom about such matters as pregnancy, childcare and personal behaviour. Child related issues which had once been the exclusive preserve of women were increasingly coopted by the state and medical professionals. The spread of child welfare and social service agencies encroached upon the influence which women had exerted in these areas, helping to substitute the self-sufficient family unit for the social networks and groups of community life. These changes all helped undermine the influence of those older women who wielded neighbourhood power and authority and who were the archetype of the 'gossipmonger'.

While many 'traditional' working-class areas retained their strong informal support networks and dependence on gossip, young women who had worked and been exposed to ideas emanating from outside the neighbourhood became more likely upon marriage to step back from the 'old-fashioned' intrusions of community life into a more self-contained form of domestic experience, which seemed to hold the promise of greater autonomy and freedom from outside interference. This trend, which Diana Gittins suggests was more apparent among the wives of skilled workers, was likely to be encouraged by husbands who viewed their homes as a private haven to which the outside world had no entry.[41] Different expectations and attitudes reinforced a negative re-interpretation of the behaviour (and gossip) of an older generation of relatives and neighbours as hypocritical, nosy and unforgiving, the expression of an ignorant 'slum culture'. This old-fashioned, restricting image of street life held little appeal for many young women, who were the most likely targets of its attentions, and ironically it was sometimes men who had the greatest nostalgia about the old communities which women had done so much to support and nurture. Jerry White, for example, suggested that return visits by former residents to Campbell Bunk in the immediate post-war years were 'probably more common among men than women'.[42] This was not surprising given the leisure-based nature of young men's involvement with street life, through sport, gambling, drinking and membership of local gangs. By the same token, this overt culture of masculinity could itself be an incentive for some women to move away from its influence.

New housing estates: common characteristics

The broader processes of centralization and privatization in family life which started during the inter-war years, although apparent in varying degrees throughout the country, appear to have been more pronounced in the south-east than in the rest of the country, where greater suburbanization and mobility fragmented social networks and communities and generated a more privatized family life. Women like those in post-war coal mining communities such as 'Ashton', remained part of a close-knit neighbourhood and regularly gathered together over cups of tea for what they called 'having five' (that is, five minutes) – a nominal description, which while capable of being 'stretched indefinitely' underlined the continuing guilty need to set a limit upon the amount of time allocated to such distracting talk.[43] However, by the 1950s a resident of a working-class district in Oxford could observe that 'we never go in to each other's houses, because once you go inside, people begin to chatter', implying a degree of intimacy and idleness which was no longer acceptable.[44] The increasing home centredness of the 1930s and 1940s found physical expression on housing estates, both private and municipal. More prosperous working-class families were particularly affected by the housing boom of the 1930s, while local authorities re-housed over a million people as part of slum clearance programmes.[45] This housing, although more spacious, lacked the intimacy of the old 'slum' communities and removed women from the networks and relationships based on such institutions as the corner shop. A woman recalling life on the Wythenshawe estate on the edge of Manchester during the 1930s, observed that 'a lot of people ... eventually went back to what we used to call the "corner shop". You see, they didn't like the atmosphere here, because it was a bit lonely, and you know this idea of the corner shop not being here.'[46] Others were more sanguine about their new way of life, for the move to an estate undermined links with kin and old acquaintances, and those who made a conscious decision to stay found themselves with a kind of freedom to establish a different way of life. The ability to get on with neighbours was not as essential as it had been when life was poorer. There was a greater possibility of choosing friends on a basis of like and common outlook rather than need, and given the uncertainty of gossip about standards in these new milieus some women expressed a preference for just one close friend or neighbour rather than the generic sociability which had been common in more 'traditional' working-class areas. Ray Gosling, who grew up in a modern semi built in 1938 on a private estate at the edge of Northampton, described how neither of his parents liked to get involved.

> We didn't have social callers. There was enough to do. 'I haven't got time to gossip all day,' they both said, often. There were no neighbours popping in, though they were always civil – 'Nice day!' – over the garden fence. Everyone had high fences, the builder built them to enclose the gardens.[47]

Hodges and Smith similarly observed of a Sheffield council estate in the early 1950s that the degree of contact between neighbours was 'probably rather less permitted' than it had been in the past. (It had been built in the late 1920s.)[48]

Any desire for greater personal autonomy was powerfully reinforced by much broader pressures upon women to keep themselves to themselves. Reformers had, since the nineteenth century, seen the home and family-based housing as an important means of promoting individualism and political conservatism at the expense of class antagonism. This construction assumed a self-enclosed family unit whose respectability was based on self-sufficiency; family welfare agencies in the inter-war years also promoted the self-sufficient family unit. A competent mother was expected to cope alone and to keep herself to herself, reciprocal exchange arrangements from outside the family (especially to do with children) being identified with irresponsible and inadequate mothering.[49] The planning and architecture of most inter-war and post-war housing, whether public or private, quite consciously turned women away from a collective life outside the home and from the public and disruptive sociability of working-class neighbourhoods which had been so frequently criticized. (Some builders of council housing in Hertfordshire during the 1940s and

1950s constructed what were described as 'anti-gossip' walls to discourage the kind of intimacy associated with 'slum' life.)[50]

These estates were, above all, housing developments, which in their emphasis on the individual family unit inevitably neglected the broader mix of services and activity which were apparent in older neighbourhoods. Common characteristics were a lack of facilities such as shops, transport and meeting places other than a local clinic. (A frequent complaint which Leo Kuper's post-war survey of housing in Coventry recorded was that there was 'nowhere for women to chat, except at the Welfare Clinic'.)[51] Local shops were often concentrated in one shopping area and attracted shoppers from a wide area, so that the gossip which took place there was less intimate and detailed. The shops at Greenleigh, a housing development on the outskirts of London, did not allow the frequent dropping by which had been possible in the scattered retail outlets of the older terraced areas. They were 'grouped together into specialist centres', and customers were 'gathered from the corners of the estate' instead of being neighbours with whom they already had a point of contact.[52] Nevertheless, despite the limitations, shopping remained important for social contact. Women still shopped as much for company as for immediate need, walking to the shops together, meeting up with others when they arrived, grouping and regrouping in fluid patterns of contact. 'They used to meet up, little groups of four or five.'[53]

While women often moved to such new estates with a dream of health, space and happiness, the reality was not always what they had anticipated, especially given the inadequate facilities around which they were expected to reconstruct their lives.[54] Facilities promised on the developers' plans could take a considerable time to materialize in practice. Celia Dixon, who moved to a housing estate at the edge of Northampton in the early 1950s recalled, 'I know when I first moved in, I cried, there was no bus stop anywhere near. When we came up, we were told the buses would come up on the estate, but they never did. It was all mud, because they were still building, it was dreadful. I couldn't get round with a pushchair, to get a bus.'[55] However, new contact points for gossip did eventually become established, as among women meeting children from school. It is possible to overestimate the distancing effects of greater geographical space on post-war housing estates, particularly until the early 1960s. The estates were certainly not as sociable as pre-war terraced communities, but there was a transitional period when many were serviced by mobile retailers, who were often an important focus for the spread of local talk. By the late 1950s and early 1960s, for example, this Northampton estate was regularly frequented by a travelling butcher, greengrocer, baker, library, fishmonger and occasional door-to-door traders (although there was less time to stay around and chat under such circumstances since the shopkeeper always had to move on to the next pitch). The same was true of inadequately serviced estates elsewhere, while the bus stop also provided a recognized meeting place for many women:

> as most housewives shop in town the ride gives an opportunity to talk to people with whom contact would not otherwise be made. Such 'chance' meetings are not always random, they can be and are engineered, and if anyone wishes to avoid a meeting it is possible to do so.[56]

Although the dispersed nature of such estates discouraged the development of very close-knit relationships, it is perhaps rather too sweeping to assert that 'the social pressure exerted by the close knit network' was removed, just as the extent to which the 'women's support networks of the older communities' were 'overtly rejected' is not certain.[57] Even those women who moved with an aim of rising in the social scale often retained the social patterns of the culture which had formed them and were disinclined to join formal associations, feeling more comfortable with the informal socialization which had been a traditional pattern of survival among working-class women. Informal forms of socializing remained important, despite being diluted by the spatial drawbacks of their housing and poor facilities, so that privacy, while a dominant trend, did not go unchallenged by the efforts which women made to communicate with each other – sometimes despite themselves. Mrs King, who grew up on Wythenshawe during the 1930s, described a 'silent, unofficial "neighbourhood watch" ... composed mainly of onlookers from front windows, particularly those who had kitchens at the front of the house. We children were always aware of being observed. Whatever we got up to, it would not be long before our mothers knew all about it.'[58] As such comments suggest, the gossip network did not need to be as intensely interlinked as in the old neighbourhoods for women to be aware of what was being said, and there was possibly a tendency for some post-war surveys to underestimate the amount of informal contact which went on between women. Women remained sensitive to the power of gossip, and although the 'inveterate and malicious "gossip"' tended to be 'sealed off from the friendship groupings of the street ... Gossip in the everyday derogatory sense of the term' went on 'in spite of the taboos'. As was the case with 'keeping oneself to oneself', there was 'probably a wide divergence between ideal and actual behaviour'. The results from a pilot sample of inhabitants on a Sheffield housing estate in the early 1950s found that 'interaction' was on a much more informal level than the 'visiting' on which the relevant questions had been based, while a survey of people on a Kirkby council estate in 1961 similarly felt that use of the word 'visiting' in the interview schedule had perhaps established a more formal view of daily contacts which was not relevant to local experience:

They would necessarily exclude chatting at front and back doors and on flat landings, which was observed frequently, and which indeed the interviewers had occasionally to interrupt. Informal interaction between residents is therefore understated, the more so as visiting less often than weekly, which was reported quite often, has been excluded.[59]

The settlers

The ease with which people settled into a housing estate understandably depended on the extent to which they had wanted to leave their old neighbourhoods. Klein suggested that local housing policies tended to select 'better' families to go to the 'better' estates, leaving the less ambitious to be dispersed on a more ad-hoc basis into less up-to-date housing stock.[60] Families of skilled workers were usually making a conscious move to better themselves. Some wanted to escape the confinement of the old communities and developed a pioneering spirit on new estates such as Wythenshawe, outside Manchester. Others were moved as part of slum clearance programmes, and had little choice in the matter, although the inhabitants of the poorest areas were sometimes happy with such a transfer, as was the case with those who moved from Red Bank and Angel Meadow in Manchester.[61] Desperate living conditions could give residents little relish for the areas in which they lived, and estates which allowed the inhabitants a far greater degree of space than their old housing were likely to be welcomed with some relief, not only for the physical improvement but for the release from tensions which had caused such strain. For a resident such as Mrs Painswick, the quarrels which had characterized the 'rowdy, shouty' Bethnal Greeners had far outweighed the pleasures of their 'mateyness'. She found 'the less intense life' of the Greenleigh estate a pleasant contrast to her old neighbourhood. 'In London people had more squabbles. We haven't seen neighbours out here having words.'[62]

Although it was not uncommon for families to move back to the neighbourhoods from which they had come, those who held on persevered with a concrete reality of bricks and mortar which reinforced their self-esteem and gave some a breathing space in which to recreate themselves, albeit in a form distorted by the prevailing domestic ideology. Norah Kirk's memories of an unhappy childhood in a working-class area of Nottingham during the inter-war years impelled her to move away from the district in which she had grown up, and despite a certain regret at the lack of neighbourliness in her new home, the move away from unhappy reminders of the past provided the psychic space which she so obviously needed. 'I don't think we would have moved if it weren't for my nagging so much. I couldn't make him [her husband] understand how I felt about the house, although I was out at work, but as soon as I walked into it at night I just felt that dread about it, I felt I'd just had enough of the walls, and everything being the same. I detested the house, absolutely dreaded it.'[63]

While some women were glad to escape from the constant bickering and squabbles of 'slum' life others, as we have seen, missed the comforting sociability which was the reverse side to such intimacy. The elderly, who tended to be the least affected by gossip, particularly missed the bustle of their old neighbourhoods and often preferred the proximity of a bus route to give them something to keep a watch on.[64] Those from poor but less impoverished areas would often have preferred to settle near their old housing, and occasionally moved back because they missed the sociability of the older neighbourhoods. Others stayed, but within a few years had re-created a form of the old networks which had traditionally supported them.[65] Many women from estates established during the inter-war years subsequently re-established kinship networks, either through relatives moving nearer to them or through frequent visiting of parents and siblings in the communities they had ostensibly left behind.[66] A third of the couples sampled by Young and Willmott had relatives on the Greenleigh estate by 1955, and a similar process was noted by Hodges and Smith in their study of a Sheffield housing development. Yet even when new networks were established, they excluded many women, those such as young mothers on Greenleigh being particularly vulnerable to isolation. Young and Willmott, although unable to quantify and verify the statement, were told by the chief psychiatrist at a local hospital that 'the loneliness of the women on this and other housing estates was the immediate precipitating cause of so many of them coming to his department for treatment'.[67] Jane Lewis has pointed out that, during the 1930s, 'evidence began to suggest that depression or "suburban neurosis" among suburban women (including working-class women on the new council estates) might be as prevalent as neurasthenia and hysteria had been in the nineteenth century'.[68] By the early 1950s, Geoffrey Gorer, analysing the results of his survey into English character, was observing that the loneliest members of English society were younger married people, 'especially the wives, living in big towns on small incomes'.[69]

The post-war estates in particular tended to attract families with young children who, as they grew older, were an important thread in pulling together embryonic neighbourhoods. The age profile of women who moved to such developments was often much younger than in older, more mixed neighbourhoods. Most of those at Braydon Road in Coventry, for example, were aged between 30 and 39 (60 per cent), and more than 80 per cent of the households had children of pre-school and/or primary school age, who helped in breaking down barriers and getting to know local people. Appointments at the local clinic, and meeting children and accompanying them home from school, provided opportunities to exchange the latest news, while their play activities with other children often forced introductions between parents. One young woman there hardly knew anyone before she had her baby.

> There was nothing wrong, but I just spoke to them. I hadn't much cause to have a lot to do with them, but the baby has made a real gossip out of me. People always stop and look at her, and then we talk a bit.[70]

A collective identity with other women was still maintained through the children, who played an important part in redefining concepts of neighbourliness. New acquaintanceships were forged, with gossip more likely to settle upon the teachers and health personnel who came to occupy a significant part in the landscape of their children's experiences. A private estate built in Northampton during the early 1950s largely comprised women in their twenties and early thirties with young families. The male wage earners were largely in skilled trades or clerical workers, while very few of the women had any paid work. Competition at school, culminating in the 11-plus, subsequently became important in the jostling for status on this estate, 'it was when the kids were little, it was the jealousy between the mothers over the children that did it'. Most of the women in one road had daughters, and much attention was paid to their school careers and activities. There was a great deal of rivalry over the 11-plus, 'Oh, Lord, it was dreadful', and even over the badges which the girls obtained through the Brownies and Guides. 'It was all competition.'[71]

Older children could play a significant if sometimes ambivalent part in this gossip exchange, their eavesdropping role possibly enhanced in the vacuum left by the lack of other local structures for disseminating information. 'My daughter was down at the bus stop the other day and she heard two women talking about another woman's house – what she'd got and so on. I don't like that sort of thing.' Coventry respondents were often acutely aware of children's capacity to pass on the talk of their elders, for they were also the weak links in the security chain. Some felt gossiping in front of children undermined respect for adults, but a greater danger was the possibility of repetition. 'A child loudly announces in the cul-de-sac that "those three houses are always scruffy"; that's not child's talk: she didn't think it up for herself".'[72] Similar fears were expressed by residents on a Sheffield estate, who for that reason tried to keep family secrets from children as far as possible.[73] Children themselves were not averse to prising confidences out of each other.

> I remember the daughter of a neighbour asking me whether we were rich or poor. I must have been about eight. I knew we weren't rich, but didn't think we were poor, even though my mother was hard up most of the time. I didn't know what to say. I didn't realise there

could be a middle ground. I thought if I said we were rich she wouldn't like me. I think I said we were poor, 'cause my dad's work clothes were always mucky, and then felt bad because I'd let my mum down. I told her later that I'd been asked. I didn't tell her what I'd said – she'd've been furious! [laughing][74]

Development of new gossip networks

The success of the initial period of adjustment to life on these new estates depended on a number of different factors. These included the extent to which choice had been an element in the move; the social mix and background of settlers; physical layout, and pre-established attitudes to neighbouring and gossip. Gossip is a means by which 'people manage their social faces: keeping an eye out while limiting other people's view of oneself', and social face and status preoccupations were often particularly important on these new estates, which inevitably made gossip a more self-conscious activity because of the greater fears which attended self-revelation.[75] A woman who moved to a private housing estate in Northampton during the 1950s observed how one of her neighbours had spread it about that

> my husband was a labourer. I found out by chance what she'd said. She was on about her brother-in-law, about how he was a car fitter in Birmingham ... 'Of course', she said, 'your husband's only a labourer.' I said, 'I beg your pardon, you'd better put that right ... He's highly skilled. And if you've gone round telling everybody, you'd better well alter it.' And I said to Mrs Grimes, 'I don't know whether Bridget told you that my husband was a labourer, because if she did, it's a total lie. He's fully skilled.' 'Oh', she said, 'She did say something'. I said, 'Well, I'll tell you what I told her. And if you hear anybody else, perhaps you'll pass it round!'[76]

The establishment of relationships on these new estates was a risky business since settlers lacked the cues by which judgments were made in the old neighbourhoods. The natural wariness which attached to gossip was reinforced when the speakers were unfamiliar with each other, leading to an understandable caution. The strains of living together in 'traditional' working-class areas had been mitigated by the development of the 'conventions' described earlier, which helped cushion against the worse tensions, but many rituals gradually lost their relevance in these new communities. Socializing with neighbours required more effort because people were unfamiliar with each other and the local infrastructure was usually so poorly developed. Previous ways of living, while frequently sociable, had been based on well-established familiarity and had not demanded the initiative necessary in a 'pioneering' environment. This background and uncertainty about acceptable ways of behaviour inevitably encouraged a privatized approach to the world outside the home.

> For residents whose requirements in the way of privacy are not high,
> who find in the physical arrangements of the area sufficient protection,
> who enjoy and perhaps are accustomed to a deep interest and know-
> ledge of neighbours' affairs, privacy enters as a restraining factor, not
> so much on their own account, but because of uncertainty about the
> standards of other residents.[77]

Ironically, the very decision to withdraw from gossip tended to reinforce
fears of it, as speculation thrived on the suspicion that people were
attempting to hide something, since wherever 'privacy feeds on competition between social units, gossip that invades that privacy may be expected
to be a weapon of competition'.[78] Privacy was consequently a complex
matter. Partly defined by gender, partly by class and status, partly by
personality, it did not necessarily express just a desire for respectability, it
was also a means of maintaining space and distance when there was uncertainty or discomfort at the surrounding local culture. The myth making
qualities of gossip played an important part in such deceptions on the new
estates where the whole question of neighbouring and appearances was
particularly problematic, and provided opportunities to elaborate on one's
family and origins. One Braydon Road woman, for example, had got
'browned off' with a neighbour's stories about her family 'and the servants
her mother used to have'.[79] Another woman who had formerly lived in a
council house in Northampton moved to a private estate where she made
out that her mother-in-law was the granddaughter of a local squire, 'she
was boasting about it ... and she had got some beautiful plates and two
Chippendale chairs'. It subsequently emerged, however, that although the
grandfather had a connection with a squire, it was as his coachman, and
the chairs and plates had been bought when the squire's family had been
forced to sell up through bankruptcy.[80]

Neighbouring was an important source of comment in critiques of life
on post-war housing estates, although the subject is often presented in
rather asexual terms making it difficult to distinguish whether comments
are based on male or female experience. Sociability was an important function of gossip among Braydon Road women.

> Neighbours' affairs give something to talk about, a common interest
> over the tea cup. And some women are warmly interested in the activ-
> ities of neighbours, in a non-carping way; gossip may go no further
> than this.

A clear distinction was made between 'popping in and out', and making an
extended call as the result of an invitation. The more cautious perceived
casual visits as a continual threat to privacy as women developed a fond-
ness for their own private space which had been so difficult to maintain in

poorer, more cramped days, often preferring the control offered by a more formal invitation to stay. 'Poppers-in' introduced an unwelcome random element into their lives, especially as visitors to a large number of houses could spread the seeds of casual conversation across a wide area. Nevertheless, those women who identified themselves as 'poppers-in' were also aware of their own vulnerability to the talk which took place during an invited visit, possibly because of the contrived nature of the occasion. Mrs Cotton, presented as an example of a very sociable woman who enjoyed talking to neighbours, was wary of visiting because of the certainty of gossip, but did not mind being sociable from her doorstep and was 'not at all averse to a little gossip and "popping-in"'. These respondents disliked the formality of making a prior arrangement to visit since the commitment to a specific time took away their own freedom to terminate or prolong the talk according to how interested they were in what was being said. It also reflected the perennial sensitivity to time-wasting, since a set time for talk and socializing seemed less easy to justify than a snatched opportunity: 'I don't mind popping in for a cup of tea after going shopping together. I've no time to stop really.'[81]

Mrs Cotton had come from a small village where local conventions revolved around being familiar with and interested in other peoples' business. She was similar in outlook to a Northampton woman, Mrs Bennett, who shared the same village origins and who was described as bohemian and devil-may-care by a neighbour. The friendliness and 'rough and ready' attitudes of both women were completely misconstrued on their new estates, where they were put down as 'coarse and common'. Mrs Cotton subsequently moved away as did Mrs Bennett, who was always being talked about because of her failure to pay much attention to local opinions about housekeeping. When her husband eventually found another job out of the area, she told the neighbour how she would be thankful to get off the estate 'with that pack of back-biting gossipers, they've got nothing better to do than pick other people to pieces ... I just carried on, she said, the way I wanted to, but it really gets on your nerves'.[82] Even women who expressed the need for caution with neighbours were still aware of the need for friendly relations. One of the most reserved of Kuper's respondents, Mrs Watling, did not cut herself off entirely, defining a good neighbour as someone who kept herself to herself, but who was willing to help with the children, and despite never visiting, helped out a neighbour during her pregnancy.[83] Doctors and midwives who knew the inhabitants of the Sheffield council estate similarly remarked on their willingness to help neighbours in a confinement or bereavement, even though 'they may not have been on speaking terms for months'.[84]

Kuper recognized that gossip played a significant part in the attitudes towards neighbouring which developed among the home-bound women who were the 'main bearers of neighbour relations'.[85] He was less sure about the extent to which it was an instrument of social control, being struck by what he felt was the essential triviality of the local gossip, although he later commented on the resentment which often attended the discussion of even 'quite neutral topics'. Detached from the economic functions it performed in poorer communities, there was indeed a tendency for gossip to become more malicious, largely preoccupied with the 'oddities' of people's behaviour and material standards. This could occasionally be taken to extremes, as a woman remarked of her friend who moved to a new house on a council estate in Northampton.

> It nearly drove her potty. Mrs Taverner, next door. She'd got no children and was older than Eva. But she used to more or less force her way into Eva's, and say, 'Ooh, that's new then'. Then she'd call on Eva in the next week, 'I've got one like that!' And Eva got some curtains. She said, 'Well, she won't get any like that! They said that was the last of the line'. [laughing] Next time I went up, she said, 'The bitch has done it again! I don't know where she got 'em from'. She came in, said, 'Oh, I love your curtains, your net curtains. I'd like some like that', and she went and got them. 'We've got twin curtains now!' And she would, she'd copy everything. It didn't matter what Eva had, she'd copy.[86]

Uncertainty about the different social codes of life on such estates fuelled the tendency for frequent comparisons with other people to be made. As Young and Willmott observed, with nothing else to go by, judgments about people tended to be based more on obvious material factors and appearance than personal attributes. The desire to fit in and live up to the standards which removal to such an estate signified meant there was great competitive pressure to 'keep up with the Joneses', this competition being intensified by the uncertainty of life in this new milieu. In Greenleigh, the new arrivals were said to watch the first comers and the first comers to watch the new arrivals, each marking each other's progress. 'The fact that people are watching their neighbours and their neighbours are watching them provides the further stimulus, reinforcing the process set in motion by the new house, to conform to the norms of the estate. There is anxiety lest they do not fit.'[87]

Nevertheless, these particular observations, based as they are on male perceptions of local circumstances, relate rather simplistically to women's views of life on the new estates. Although not as comprehensively as in the older neighbourhoods, women had more opportunity than the men to assess other inhabitants in a rather deeper sense. While material factors certainly influenced their judgments, other factors were also significant issues in these discussions of behaviour, comments still revolving around house-keeping standards, children's behaviour and childcare and borrowing. A Northampton woman's next-door-neighbour told her, 'You want to watch what you hang out on your line because Mrs Watts said "I don't think she bothers to mend her husband's socks".' Another woman was much talked about because she used to put all her coloureds in with her whites when she was washing, 'She didn't mind what colour they came out.'[88] The emphasis placed upon order and housework identified 'scruffy' households with dirtiness and with other 'characteristics' of life in the older neighbourhoods, such as large families, 'rough' speech, the use of taboo words, an overreadiness to 'cuff' the children and, significantly, 'a forthright approach to personal relations', since attention focused not merely on material standards but also on what were considered inappropriate behavioural skills. A 'lack of neighbourly reticence' frequently featured in criticisms, and among Braydon Road informants there was an awareness that 'too great sociability with neighbours' might be interpreted as 'low-class'.

> You have to keep people at arm's distance, or you might get low-talking on their front doorsteps all the time – and if they've come from that sort of thing, they want to raise themselves above it.[89]

At Barton, a housing estate built between 1946 and 1950 on the outskirts of Oxford, those categorized as 'rough' or common tended to be neighbours who borrowed, failed to cultivate their gardens, dropped in uninvited, talked about their own affairs and had what was felt to be an intrusive, prying approach to their neighbours.[90] A woman from a Northampton estate described her next-door neighbour as 'typical back street ... She was an ignorant, bad-mannered woman, always leaning over the garden fence and peering into the garden, watching us. We didn't even know them.'[91]

Attention to the neighbours' activities and material possessions could, on some estates, assume an acute form, which was not mitigated by the supportive aspects of such interest in less affluent areas, for while gossip played an important part in promoting sociability among women, it also functioned as a vehicle for frustrations which had no other channel. The Wives' Group on the Northampton private estate, for example, had a 'dreadful' name for malicious gossip, one of its members having a particular reputation for spreading local scandal. Few of these women had paid jobs, either full- or part-time, so there was plenty said about one who worked full-time in a factory, 'palming her children on to other people', neighbours who looked after her children when they came home from school. This woman was also looked down on by the only other neighbour who worked full-time. (She used to say she was a cut above the factory worker because she worked in a department store.) Mrs Salter's next-door neighbour had been a childhood friend, yet this did not stop her causing a lot of trouble by the tales she spread. 'Helen made my life hell sometimes, you know ... I think she was jealous in a way, because I'd got two girls. She'd wanted a daughter.' At other times she could be very sweet. 'She used to come in and apologise sometimes, 'cos she used to come out with things.' Helen made some unfortunate remarks to her other next-door neighbour which led to them not speaking for a week, and to her husband telling her off for her gossip, but she seemed unable to stop herself. 'She said, it comes into my head, and I say it.'[92]

A woman interviewed as a part of a survey of a Liverpool housing estate during the early 1950s was identified for her uniqueness in trying to find a reason for the quarrels and 'general disharmony' which were common among the residents in her area. Her estate, which had been built in the early 1940s to provide emergency accommodation for the families of war workers, had poor amenities since it had only been built to last about ten years and was in an isolated position with inadequate transport. Her husband, a skilled worker, assigned a status explanation to the trouble-some relationships, and felt they sprang from the 'throwing together of various types', who would have been better off segregated according to occupation, general intelligence and culture. The woman, however, distinguished the dissatisfactions which lay at the heart of the neighbourly instability around her:

> they are caused because women on this estate have so little to do and suffer from sheer boredom. They talk to each other over the garden fence, become friendly for a while, tell each other all their confidences and then they quarrel that each has the other in the palm of her hand. Often they come out with everything they know about each other.[93]

Housing estates: male attitudes towards neighbouring and gossip

Men's growing colonization of the home on the new housing estates of the inter-war and immediate post-war years often placed greater pressures on women to accommodate male needs. Being at home more during evenings and at weekends made men critical of a lack of creature comforts at a time when the development of new domestic appliances added to women's labour by establishing higher standards of cleanliness.[94] The increasing tendency for male leisure time to become more home-oriented placed other burdens on women. Men imported their workshop based technical atti-tudes into the home, where space often had to be found to accommodate interests such as model railway and radio construction. The preoccupation with DIY as a leisure time activity helped reinforce the male's sense of possession in the bricks and mortar which comprised the home.[95] Being around more not only gave neighbours increased scope for observation of male activities but also increased male sensitivity to and defensiveness about neighbours' talk and suspicion of the world outside the front door.

In some respects men seem to have been less adaptable than women to life on the new estates, lacking the subtlety in relationships which women were more likely to have learnt through daily interaction with neighbours and relations. Men had fewer opportunities to put out the feelers of neighbourliness and sociability than women because they spent less time in the vicinity of the new developments on which they had settled, estates being largely the preserve of women and children between the hours of seven in the morning and six at night. Too exhausted during the week by work and travel to venture far outside the home, husbands could feel even more disconcerted by the unfamiliar expectations of their surroundings than their wives.[96] Mr Harper's father told his daughter-in-law, when the family moved to a private estate in Northampton, not to be too friendly 'with that lot up there. They're not our sort.' Mr Harper worked in heavy engineering and refused to adhere to the different standards expected, a stubbornness which maintained his self-esteem but which caused his wife considerable shame and discomfort given what she had to put up with from the neighbours:

> He used to do it deliberately, wear those old shirts ... He wouldn't let me go down to get him any more, I'd got the money to do it, he wouldn't let me. And he used to wear those old overalls. They used to think I wouldn't mend them for him, but he wouldn't let me. They all talked.[97]

Mr Adams felt like a 'foreigner' in Greenleigh, although he wasn't sure why. 'Up there you've lived for years and you knew how to deal with people there. People here are different.' As Klein observed, the man 'has to learn the finer shades of difference in behaviour which afford others the cues according to which they regulate their own conduct. He has to learn what are the socially important role discriminations here and what are the appropriate actions that go with them. He has to review behaviour that he had taken for granted since childhood.'[98] Mr Wild of Greenleigh complained about the unfriendliness of the local people, and even after four years was still hankering after the re-establishment of the pattern of his old neighbourhood.

> Coming from a turning like the one where we lived, we knew everyone. We were bred and born among them, like one big family, we were. We knew all their troubles and everything. Here they are all total strangers to each other. It's a question of time, I suppose.[99]

Such attitudes encouraged almost a siege mentality among some men. Mr Young, for example, told his wife, 'When I walk into these four walls, I always tell her, Don't make too many friends. They turn out to be enemies.'[100] A man interviewed as part of a survey into a Liverpool estate made similar comments about it being 'bad policy' to make friends locally because sooner or later they were bound to fall out and cause unpleasantness. Perhaps more significantly, he observed that making friends was bound to lead to visiting and getting 'to know things about your wife and family which would be repeated round the estate', thereby destroying any privacy which had been achieved.[101]

Such men could afford to assert their spatial needs by trying to distance the household from the neighbourhood, since they had a broader range of roles to fulfil outside the locality, be it in club, pub, work or community centre. Women who had no paid work outside the home needed that contact to help maintain their own psychological survival, while their views were also more heavily coloured by the hopes they held out for their children.[102] It was often this desire to make a better future for them which had prompted the move to an estate in the first place, and it was gossip about their children's activities which helped shape their own hopes for the future. Emphasis on household skills was often heightened on these new developments, and visitors who entered the house to talk or to gossip remained a subversive influence undermining the need for routine and regulation. Husbands who insisted on high standards of house care, and that 'the woman carry out her job as the man does his' allowed very little scope for sociability. Some men viewed neighbours' visits as a territorial invasion of their private space. Kuper observed how the men in his study of post-war housing in Coventry particularly resented the 'active invasion of privacy' represented by 'popping in and out'. 'I do think when you are home, and you've had no privacy at work, you should be able to have some privacy in your house.'[103] Similar sentiments were apparent in the remarks of a woman whom Gittins interviewed, who although friendly with her neighbours had never been in the habit of going into other peoples' houses:

> my husband said to me, 'Now listen, I don't like neighbours in the house having cups of tea and gossip and I don't like coats hanging on the door'. So I suppose really that it was a habit that I never went into other people's houses ... But with the neighbours we were always friendly, if she needed help I'd help her and when my father died she came in and helped me and it's always been like that. But I've never been in the habit of going in and sitting and listening to a lot of gossip.[104]

Kuper described the privatized family views and lack of neighbourhood sociability of men on Braydon Road in Coventry, some of whom were 'regular home men'. Women's concepts of a good neighbour were still based very much on ideas of mutual support, and of 90 women interviewed, only nine made no reference to mutual help in their definition, whereas less than half the men referred to helpfulness.[105] Men placed far greater emphasis on 'minding their own business', lack of interference and intrusions upon privacy. Local relations were expected to be short and to the point, 'passing the time of day, not half the day'. Several men interviewed on the Liverpool estate felt that a 'wife should spend some time each day visiting her parents, which they thought preferable to visiting neighbours'.[106] Men tended to have a far more restrictive attitude towards visiting than women, the tendency to gossip being a major source of their dislike.

> There's nothing wrong in being sociable, but after that I've finished; it always leads to trouble. Certainly not coming into your house. Gossiping and silly criticism. 'What do you think of so and so?'

Such observations highlight the discomfort which men could feel at discussing personal behaviour, and their lack of understanding at the rules of engagement which underlay having a good gossip. Kuper felt the 'more intimate' forms of neighbouring were regarded as 'effeminate, women's work', and there was a strong sense that neighbourhood relationships should be kept at a very superficial level, a 'hedged in sociability' which well reflected the suspicious imagery of folklore sayings.[107]

Time to dream

A refusal to enter other peoples' houses or allow neighbours to come into the home was not, of course, invariably dependent on the whim of the men in their lives. Women themselves came to value their domestic space for their own reasons, be it a need to protect external appearances or a desire to assert their independence against the world outside, although even studies of housing and redevelopment written from the women's perspective are often frustratingly elusive about what went on in the home. To be sure, women faced new pressures with larger houses and the stress on higher standards of household care, but the tasks they faced were not as physically onerous as in the past. The credo of 'scientific household management' certainly introduced new social and psychological pressures to use domestic time ever more productively and efficiently. Improvements in domestic appliances made domestic work less rigorous, and there was often considerable variation in the pattern of domestic organization. Not every women was excessively houseproud and there was at least some opportunity to grasp a space for reverie, which unrelenting domestic toil had traditionally prevented. It may have been just sitting down in the afternoon after chores were done – in a blessed space of peace and quiet before the children came home from school – to read a magazine, listen to the radio or even to daydream, something which had not been possible for previous generations of working-class women, as Mary Collier had indignantly asserted in 1739,

> Our Toil and Labour's daily so extreme,
> That we have hardly ever *Time to dream*[108]

Women who were not engaged in paid work could find comfortable opportunities to get together. Kuper noted how the need for company and 'pure sociability' among the women at Braydon Road was linked with the drinking of tea, although Catherine Hall observed of women from an inter-war housing estate in Birmingham that while, 'There was a good deal of tea drinking' not much was 'established in the way of close friendships. Closeness was reserved for the family.'[109]

Many women took pleasure in being on their own and, despite the emphasis on high domestic standards, developed more personal, individual interests.

> I like my own company. When I've done my work I like to read or listen to the wireless; it would get on my nerves to have the door bell ringing all the time ... I don't have many visitors; my sister comes up to see me once in a while, and although I like to see her, I feel fagged out when she has gone.[110]

Mogey suggested that Mrs Dale's Diary, The Archers and some of the picture papers served 'on a national scale' the same functions as the Young Wives' Club which he had described, setting 'detailed standards' by which news and gossip might be judged, within what was certainly a safer and more detached medium.[111]

However, women's experiences remained diverse, and the renewed emphasis in the 1950s upon a home-based, family centred model of behaviour was beginning to be questioned. For a minority of women, the very breakdown of more sustaining neighbourly relations and dissatisfaction with the isolation they experienced on these estates prompted them to seek paid work as an escape, attracted by opportunities which had not been available or acceptable to women in similar circumstances during the inter-war years. Several interviewed in Sheffield said they had gone out to work expressly for companionship – 'It takes you out of yourself', 'it is good for the nerves – the doctor advised it'.[112]

Post-war planners attempted to recreate the social spaces which had encouraged the cosy familiarity of the old working-class communities, but broader social forces were already undermining the family and social structures which had given it substance. While many who moved to these new estates may well have been committed to a 'concept of respectability' based on privacy, privatizing tendencies were also reinforced by uncertainties about the kind of behaviour which the new milieu demanded and the fears of being shown up to which this gave rise.[113] With greater affluence, the malicious capacity of gossip was enhanced for many families there by the consumerist pressures which increasingly acquired a domestic focus and also by the frustrations which some women experienced in the 1950s. Such insecurity could reinforce conformity, but also made some women more sensitive to the social forces which imposed on them through the press, radio and television.[114] A reduction in the number of children allowed women to focus more intensively on their interests, admittedly to a some- times counter-productive extent, but which achieved some outlet in increased educational opportunity. Children's activities had always been a focus of women's talk, but there was now a sense in which women's own identity was more strongly associated with their children, 'revolving around them to the exclusion of most other issues'.[115] It was the burden of this identification which contributed to the uncertainties and dissatisfac- tions of a new generation of women in the 1960s.

The 1950s witnessed much discussion of the decline of the 'traditional' working-class and a recognition for the first time of the part which women's gossip and socializing played in the maintenance of neighbour- hood life. The planners' preoccupation with neighbouring and neigh- bourliness reflected a sense of declining community and concern for the erosion of the 'traditional' working-class. Yet the apparent weakening of the traditional working-class community which so disconcerted male commentators, held benefits for women, whose dissatisfactions, while often unarticulated, began to seep out into the wider world. These were transitional years for women's behaviour and were, in many respects, the seedbed of changes which more dramatically began to alter women's lives in the 1960s.

Notes

1. R. Nash, 'How the Poor Live', in Investigation Papers, Women's Co- Operative Guild, 1902.
2. Mitchell 1991. 137.
3. See, for example, how the physical and social proximity of villagers in the Mexican hamlets of Zinacantan typically produced both intense scrutiny of each other's lives and a 'morbid sense of privacy'. 'In the midst of a village where everyone lives on top of everyone else, there is great manoeuvring for self-protection and isolation. The corollary is intense curiosity about other people.' Haviland 1977, 187.
4. For an examination of the separation of the two spheres in the lives of the middle class, see Davidoff and Hall, 1987.
5. MSTC. Tape 12.
6. Watkin 1985, 13, 41, 57. Father was a carter's mate.
7. Roberts 1971: 1974, 186.

8. Watkin 1985, 13, 41, 57.
9. Linton 1982, 2.
10. Bentley 1985, 4.
11. Mogey 1956, 60–61.
12. Miscellaneous tapes, Maria Goddard.
13. Northampton tapes, Mr Billingham.
14. Williamson 1982, 124.
15. Centerprise 1979, 30; Ezard 1979, 24, 26. For the significance of the Sunday dinner in the working-class household, see Ross 1993, 29, 37–39, 47, 50, 74, 80, 87, 197.
16. Radio construction became an important new hobby for many men during the inter-war years, encouraged by do-it-yourself magazines like *Amateur Wireless and Electrics* (1922), *Popular Wireless Weekly* (1922), *The Wireless Constructor* (1924) and *Practical Wireless* (1932) Constantine 1981, 399.
17. Northampton tapes, Mrs Roberts; Pearson 1988, 35–36.
18. Miscellaneous tapes, Maria Goddard.
19. Vincent 1989: 1993, 191; Ross 1993, 144; Seymour 1992, 189; Thompson 1974, 55.
20. The backbreaking routine of 'Blue Monday' or washday was, in contrast, one of the busiest times of the week for working-class women.
21. Landes 1983, 227–30, 285.
22. Bourke 1994, 66.
23. MSTC, 515. Southgate 1982, 67. Such deceptions were akin to those employed by the studio and out-door photographers of working-class family and street scenes who consciously set out to promote a happy, Sunday-best image which could be proudly and symbolically displayed on the parlour wall and in the family photograph album. Linkman and Warhurst 1982, 5.
24. Mitchell 1991, 110.
25. Chamberlain 1989, 51.
26. Ross 1983, 38, 68, 79–80, 87.
27. Loane 1910, 152.
28. MSTC, Tape 665.
29. Mitchell 1991, 140.
30. Rendall 1990, 79–98.
31. Davies 1915: 1978, 78.
32. See, for example, Andy Davies's comments on young people's leisure in *Leisure, Gender and Poverty: Working Class Culture in Salford and Manchester, 1900–39*, 1992, 82–108.
33. Miscellaneous tapes, Maria Goddard.
34. White 1986, 197, 211
35. Mowat 1955: 1978, 212.
36. Hinson 1984, 5–6.
37. BOHP, Tape 34a.
38. Hinson 1984, 22.
39. BOHP, Tape 28b.
40. Oral History Archive, Lancaster University. Mr G1P.
41. Gittins 1982, 71.
42. White 1986, 235,
43. Dennis, Henriques and Slaughter 1956, 203.
44. Mogey 1956, 94.

45. Mowat 1955:1978, 506–12. Almost four million new houses were built in England and Wales between 1919 and 1939 – approximately one-third of the country's housing stock. Constantine 1981, 395.
46. Kay 1993, 226
47. Gosling 1980, 17.
48. Hodges and Smith 1954, 110.
49. Lewis 1980, 198.
50. My thanks to contributors to the discussion which occurred after a paper given to a Women and History School held at the Department of Continuing Education, Oxford, in 1991.
51. Kuper 1953, 120.
52. Dagenham, 88–89, cited in Klein 1965: 1970, 230.
53. Pickett and Boulton 1974, 112–13. Northampton tapes, Mrs Mitford.
54. In terms of expectations, see Jerry White's observations about Campbell Bunk: White, 1986.
55. Northampton tapes, Celia Dixon, (f).
56. Hodges and Smith 1954, 115.
57. Klein 1965: 1970, 232; Hughes and Hunt 1992, 94.
58. Kay 1993, 227.
59. Hodges and Smith 1954, 129; Pickett and Boulton, 1974, 53.
60. Klein 1965: 1970, 244.
61. Hughes and Hunt 1992, 90.
62. Young and Willmott 1957: 1979, 150.
63. McCrindle and Rowbotham 1977: 1979, 213–14. Norah Kirk was born in 1926.
64. Hodges and Smith 1954, 117.
65. Klein 1965: 1970, 220.
66. Hall 1977, 80, Young and Willmott; Hodges and Smith, 1954.
67. Young and Willmott 1957: 1979, 125, 150, 158.
68. Lewis 1984: 1986, 116. Lewis cites an article by Stephen Taylor, entitled 'The Suburban Neurosis', in the *Lancet*, 26 March 1938, and PP., 'Report of the Royal Commission on the Distribution of the Industrial Population', Cmnd. 6153, 1939–40, 263, p. 49.
69. Gorer 1955, 66.
70. Kuper 1953, 30, 137.
71. Northampton tapes, Celia Dixon, (h).
    Hodges and Smith, in their investigation of a Sheffield estate during the 1950s, observed how much the housewives there were 'very much creatures of their immediate environment, and as the majority of those who do not go to work live their social life within a comparatively small circle of neighbours and relatives, their choice of acquaintances is restricted'. 'The street is indeed a most important point for social activity.' Hodges and Smith 1954, 105.
72. Kuper 1953, 51, 76.
73. Hodges and Smith 1954, 116.
74. Northampton tapes, Sally Chambers.
75. Haviland 1977, 191.
76. Northampton tapes, Mrs Hampson.
77. Kuper 1953, 48.
78. Haviland 1977, 188, 191.
79. Kuper 1953, 98.

80. Northampton tapes, Mrs Waddell. Such tendencies were not, of course, confined to life on the new housing estates. Bill Mitchell, who grew up in a northern mill town during the inter-war years, recalled how 'Ma told us that Grannie had come from a well-to-do family at Melton Mowbray in Leicestershire. Most families made this sort of claim, to imply they had experienced better days.' Mitchell 1991, 109.
81. Kuper 1953, 51, 56–57.
82. Northampton tapes, Mrs Salter.
83. Kuper 1953, 55; Kay 1993, 227.
84. Hodges and Smith 1954, 105.
85. Kuper 1953, 43, 45.
86. Northampton tapes, Mrs Thorpe.
87. Young and Willmott 1957: 1979, 148, 159–64.
88. Northampton tapes, Mrs Mitford.
89. Kuper 1953, 65, 79.
90. Klein 1965:1970, 261. One of Elizabeth Roberts's respondents 'spoke of men in the neighbourhood being shamed by gossip in the pub into keeping their gardens tidy'. E. Roberts 1993, 43.
91. Northampton tapes, Mrs Knott.
92. Northampton tapes, Mrs Salter.
93. Mitchell and Lupton 1954, 18–19, 55.
94. See, for example, Ruth Schwarz Cowan 1989.
95. Constantine 1981, 399.
     Elizabeth Roberts uses the example of Mr Trickett, one of her interviewees, to generally typify the problems which 'many inhabitants had in their neighbourhood relationships in the immediate postwar period'. However, his attitudes also seem to exemplify the particular difficulties which men often experienced with neighbours. Mr Trickett returned as a married man in the 1950s to buy a small terraced house on the street where he had grown up. He explained how much he had objected as a young working man just after the war to one of the neighbours coming in every dinner-time while he was eating. She was one of his mother's friends, but he described her as a 'nosey bitch' and eventually told her to keep away, much to his mother's annoyance. The experience was used to illustrate just how particular he was about inviting people into his home. 'At work fellas would tell you. "You'll never get into Trickett's place." This is mine. I haven't got a lot but by Christ it's ours.' Again, the shifting use of 'I' and 'ours' gives an interesting hint of where real ownership was thought to lie. E. Roberts 1993, 41–42.
96. Kay 1993, 223, 225.
97. Northampton tapes, Mrs Harper.
98. Klein 1965: 1970, 234.
99. Klein 1965: 1970, 240, citing Young and Willmott 1957: 1979.
100. Young and Willmott 1957: 1979, 148.
101. Mitchell and Lupton 1954, 70.
102. See, for example, Bill Williamson's 1982 account of his mother's dislike of pit-work, compared with his father's assumptions that mining would be a good trade for his sons.
103. Kuper 1953, 47, 61–62.
104. Gittins 1982, 140.
105. Kuper 1953, 53, 60.

106. Mitchell and Lupton 1954, 74.
107. Kuper 1953, 59–60.
108. Mary Collier, *The Woman's Labour: an Epistle to Mr. Stephen Duck; in Answer to his late Poem, called The Thresher's Labour* (London, 1739), 10–11, cited in Flinn and Smout 1974, 75.
109. Kuper 1953, 44; Hall 1977, 78, 80.
110. Kuper 1953, 100.
111. Mogey 1956, 128. Mrs Dale's Diary began in 1949 and The Archers was first broadcast in 1951. By 1952 The Archers was attracting eight million listeners a night. Painting 1975: 1976, 13, 40.
112. Hodges and Smith 1954, 108, 113, 116, 119.
113. Davies and Fielding 1992, 88.
114. See, for example, comment on popular literature during this period, Radford 1986.
115. Cf. Williamson 1982; Kay 1993, 238.

Conclusion: Women of the washtub

What about those who were left at the washtub, or who acted without belonging to formal organisations, or joined everything and evaded the spot light, who dreamed, thought, met, picketed, marched, tub-thumped, plotted, died without trace or echo.[1]

The new housing estates self-consciously endeavoured to draw the working-class away from the public and disreputable sociability of 'traditional' neighbourhoods. Their construction was based upon a self-sufficient concept of respectability whose privatized, domestic focus drew women away from the forms of communication which had supported them in more impoverished times and implied a denial of relationships with other women. Greater affluence permitted the inhabitants of such estates more space and privacy than ever before, and with the material need for neighbourly relationships being less pressing, the interest in other peoples' lives and behaviour – the substance of gossip – could now be fed by a diverse range of influences, from popular novels, magazines, newspapers and radio to the cinema. Yet the growth of these forms, which often exploited the greater isolation of many women, could themselves provide new topics of conversation and were not necessarily a substitute for neighbourly relationships. The informal links which sustained many women survived, albeit in a sometimes subterranean form unnoticed by outsiders, for women tended to maintain sophisticated communication skills, being far more likely than their menfolk to strike up conversation in local shops or with neighbours in the street.[2] Gossip, in the close physical layout of traditional working-class districts, had a powerful cohesive effect in the maintenance of neighbourhood networks and so-called community life. Although this closeness was reduced on the new estates, gossip survived with all its complexity and ambivalence, becoming in some respects even more narrowly defined by gender, while perceptions of its role, where acknowledged, often became caught up in broader considerations about the need for and appropriateness of community life, as was the case in the 1950s.

Stereotypes of working-class women

The gossiping working-class woman became commonplace in a number of popular genres during the twentieth century, ranging from the comic

sketch to the cartoon, the song to the soap opera.[3] All drew on the judgmental, scandalmongering aspects which were responsible for enforcing
domestic morality and a traditional moral code, and often depicted
'paralinguistic responses' ('the raised eyebrows, the pursed lips, the sigh or
the silence') which are so difficult to identify in historical sources but
which played an important part in women's communication.[4] The inter-
war comedian Frank Randle, for example, was known for his gossipy
sketches over the garden wall, 'he'd lift his artificial bust up and say "I'm
not one as talks, you know, I don't believe in talking about other people,
but ...", and then go on with it.'[5]

Norman Evans was also famous for his pre- and post-war comic
sketches dressed as Fanny Fairbottom, 'mop-capped harridan', gossiping
over a back street wall.[6] Les Dawson, exemplar of the mother-in-law gag,
was Evans's successor, as, made up in drag as 'Ada', she chatted to her
best friend, Cissie, played by Roy Barraclough. Al Read made a similar
name in the 1950s with, among other themes, dramatic monologues as a
nosy and talkative housewife. Such women, with plenty of time to talk and
slander, tended to draw on northern experience of working-class life and
were a variation on the 'woman as slut' whom Walter Greenwood immor-
talized in *Love on the Dole*.

> Slatternly women, dirty shawls over their heads and shoulders, hair in
> wisps about their faces, stood in groups congregated on the pavements
> in the shafts of light thrown from the open doors of the public-house.
> Now and then they laughed raucously, heedless of the tugs at their
> skirts from their wailing, weary children.[7]

The gossipy women who dominated in television soaps like Coronation
Street moved this image on to a rather more positive representation, yet
remained anchored within a similarly static view of working-class culture.

While these images of working-class women dominated in popular representations of the working-class, the emphasis was rather different in the
literary and academic spheres. Both male nostalgia for the disappearing
working-class community and misogyny were stoked by working-class experience of higher education and greater material prosperity in the 1950s and
1960s, and influenced the literary and sociological works which produced the
working-class hero of the same period. Women's experiences were ignored
or marginalized in such texts, the 'images of femininity' expressed in works
like *Lucky Jim* and *Room at the Top* often revealing 'a bleak and brutal
misogyny'.[8] In contrast to this masculine emphasis, Coronation Street manifested the strengths of working-class women by self-consciously appealing to
a largely female audience. Gossip, which had been one of the few recreational outlets available to working-class women was thus transformed via
the 'traditional' British soap opera into a distinct cultural form.

It is perhaps significant that Coronation Street, which preserved the archetypal image of the gossip and the old working-class community, was based on northern precedent, since the break-up of the extended family was far less advanced in the north and Midlands of England than in the south by the 1950s.[9] First shown in 1960, Coronation Street's origins owed much to the matriarchal emphasis of Richard Hoggart's *Uses of Literacy*.[10] It cast a long shadow over subsequent depictions of working-class life and ensured that Manchester and Salford had an important impact upon popular perceptions of the urban working-class. Its focus upon women's sustaining role in the home and community became a model for other British soaps, expressed most recently in EastEnders. This, just as significantly, idealized the East End in the 1980s as it came under its greatest threat from the developers.[11]

The mother has become a central figure of these 'traditional' British soaps, selflessly assuming the emotional and economic responsibilities which were women's usual burdens in 'traditional' working-class communities. The heroine is the 'young to middle-aged mother' who is both loyal and fiercely protective of her children and family. She is the moral rock upon which the family is anchored, although her role extends to the whole community in its assertion of neighbourhood values and morality. Her counterpoint is the more ambiguous elderly grandmother figure who is freed from the selfless expectations of the younger woman. Characters like Ena Sharples, Annie Walker and Lou Beale are independent, self-centred, hard-headed and acid tongued, yet redeemed by 'a core of compassion and wisdom' which is expressed in their espousal of neighbourly values.

Soap opera women are tough, strong-minded and often domineering, with the driving qualities frequently lacking in their menfolk (as in the strong woman/weak man pairings of Hilda and Stan Ogden, Ivy and Bert Tilsley, Vera and Jack Duckworth). They sustain an ideal of community which 'only functions if women are in control ... they organise its rituals; they transmit its values and spin the web of gossip through which it is continually renewed'.[12] Such matriarchs are a bridge between the community and the family, supporting individuals who are not related by blood or marriage, reinforcing the family's position as refuge for both blood relatives and outsiders and, incidentally, ensuring that gossip is presented as a way of life rather than something which fills the occasional gaps in a working-class woman's existence.[13]

The figure of the gossip, who is nearly always female, has become a classic stereotype of British soap opera, often exposing the fragility and ambivalence of the neighbourly values which the matriarch upholds. Her musings and nosy interventions engage the viewer and propel the narrative forward. She is in some respects a mistrusted figure since everyone who participates in community life is her potential victim. Her elderly, garrulous, nosy characteristics perpetuate an unflattering stereotype of the post-menopausal woman which is very common in popular culture.[14] She is not so much subversive as comic, her post-menopausal frustration and dissatisfaction being displaced into a frequently prurient interest in other people's activities, itself a variation on the age-old stereotype of female curiosity.

Despite its self-conscious avowal of gritty, northern realism, Coronation Street nevertheless reinforced negative stereotypes of the working-class by subordinating women's socializing traditions to the broader political aim of asserting the values of a disappearing way of life. In recognizing the significance of gossip and using it to dramatic effect, it reinforced a narrow interpretation of women's lives and a largely static view of working-class culture at a time when their experiences were fragmenting and changing. A Northampton woman who had moved to a housing estate from a working-class neighbourhood, was initially not very taken by the programme 'because we're Midland and they're Lancashire'. However, she later came to like its 'sort of homely' atmosphere 'because it seemed things up there hadn't changed, not down like where we were'.[15]

Coronation Street's strong female characters were a vehicle for an ideal of community. They were the signifiers of a disappearing world rather than an instrument of challenge and change, and there was consequently little dynamic sense of women's lives. Younger women were expected eventually to assume a matriarchal role, and little attention was paid to women's desire for another life beyond motherhood. Neighbourhood values were associated with the views of elderly women whose conservatism and lack of broader political awareness helped reinforce a reactionary concept of community, their gossip becoming in a sense a vehicle for the home centred emphasis of the 1950s. Women's words were thus used to bypass the real question of patriarchal oppression, since nostalgia for the old working-class communities gave little consideration to the confining, restrictive effect such a way of life had upon the working-class women who were the main upholders of community values.

The disempowerment of women's words

Although the word 'gossip' originally possessed all the familiar connotations of friendship – affection, kindliness, intimacy – the change which occurred in its meaning, to a negative pursuit, reflected a deliberate disempowerment of 'women's words': women's words were trivialized, in a desire to drain gossip of its power. Given gossip's important socializing function, criticism of women's speech can be seen as much as an attack upon women's support networks as an attack upon language. This censure acquired resonance in a working-class context because gossip was particularly visible in the lives of the urban poor due to the largely public existence which poverty frequently forced upon them. Their gossip conflicted with notions of privatized domestic behaviour which were considered appropriate to a respectable way of life. However, attacks upon gossip among working-class women condemned precisely those supportive, integrative aspects of local networks which were so vital to the functioning of neighbourhood life. In such overwhelmingly masculine environments as mining communities, 'callin'' was one of the few opportunities women had to sift and assess the minutiae of their daily lives and was the main form of female solidarity. 'Work is suspended intermittently when neighbours and friends come "callin'"', come that is, to gossip. In the time spent on it, "callin'" is the main leisure activity for women in Ashton.'[16] 'Canting' and 'callin'', with their dialect connotations of storytelling, helped give interest, substance and relief to otherwise mundane and stressful lives.

Elizabeth Roberts observed of her respondents that 'women talk of friendly, helpful or good neighbours, but they rarely talk simply of friends'.[17] Given the pressure under which women of the urban poor so frequently laboured, it is scarcely surprising that they had little time to devote to the nurturing of individual friendships and seem to have derived comfort and support from the communal friendship expressed in street conversations, which contributed to the extensive sharing networks between women that stemmed largely from lack of male support due to irregular income.[18] Roberts has argued that 'the concept of a privatised, isolated family life was much later in reaching the working class than other strata of society', and suggests that the 'public sociability, usually in the form of conversations in the street' which characterized much working-class life in the late nineteenth and early twentieth centuries, survived from earlier days when it once had a far broader social application.[19] Her conclusions draw on the work of Philippe Ariès who suggested that life for all sections of society was a public affair until the seventeenth century, when it was superseded by a more inward looking, 'privatised' family existence. In a sense, the early, benevolent connotations of gossip and later deterioration of meaning are suggestive of these changes, for the distancing effects of a withdrawal into more introspective domestic life undermined feelings of commonality, and helped reinforce gossip's reputation as an idle and feckless activity frequently associated with socially irresponsible working-class women.[20]

Such withdrawal from a general, public sociability to a more gender specific familiarity was in keeping with the compartmentalization of industrial life which tended to segregate male from female roles, although it is difficult and misleading to generalize about apparent lack of friendship between working-class women. (Margaret Loane, for example, felt that 'Friendship between poor women is often both strong and lasting ... In many instances friendship takes forms as ungrudging and self-devoted as it does with the closest blood relationship'.)[21] As has been suggested in earlier chapters, 'domestic' and 'public' distinctions can be similarly unhelpful in this context, since many women of the urban poor did lead 'public' lives, although not necessarily in terms which were recognized or acceptable to male society. Their 'public' life was a sociable experience which if constrained and localized to possibly a yard or a few streets, nevertheless sustained a verbal 'grapevine' which often extended the mental parameters of the area which people felt they 'knew'. Gossip derived its power in 'traditional' working-class communities from the close-knit nature of local kin and neighbourly relationships. Even in less settled localities, with a relatively high incidence of 'flitting', movement was likely to be within a fairly limited area, which ensured that the people round about remained reasonably familiar. A.S. Jasper, writing of his Hoxton childhood during the First World War, had 'never heard of a family who moved more than we did', yet on the whole remained comfortably part of the social landscape which changed around him.[22] Relations with kin and old friends meant that women often had links across a number of households in a neighbourhood, a complex web of connections whose gossip could give life to absent faces. Elizabeth Roberts has described the lack of effort put into keeping in touch with those who moved away from a neighbourhood, yet neighbourly gossip could actually ensure that a former presence remained in the memory if not in fact, sometimes feeding off literary sources.[23] The halfpenny postcard, for example, had a significant effect on communication within many working-class families in the 1900s, by enabling them to maintain easy contact at all times of the year. 'News, gossip, small services, tokens of affection' being exchanged 'with little effort and less expense'.[24]

Gossip also helped sustain the mythical aspects of family and neighbourhood, as Mogey observed in his study of St Ebbe's, a central working-class neighbourhood in Oxford, in the early 1950s: 'most families have been living in the house long enough for the neighbours to become familiar shapes in the landscape. Names and characteristics are known too, carried along the gossip chain and treasured as a way of making contact with the world beyond the front door.' Gossip could preclude the need for physical communication with those being talked about. St Ebbe's people were often critical of their neighbours, but felt the area to be a friendly place, and Mogey felt the reason for this was that many people were known vaguely by sight 'and by hearing about them through local gossip and in consequence there is less need to depend on proximity to have human contacts'. One withdrawn family, which had nothing to do with the neighbours, was nevertheless 'reasonably well informed' about what was going on locally 'thanks to the gossip of the general store ... Such a family moved to a new estate would disintegrate rapidly.'[25] These frequent and often subtle reinforcements of memory and custom did not have to depend on friendship or an intimate relationship with neighbours. They did owe much to the greater opportunities for casual conversation which were a characteristic of more 'traditional' working-class areas and which helped people sustain vivid mental maps of the areas in which they lived.[26]

A mental landscape

Oral testimony and autobiography have played a significant part in this reconstruction of the role which gossip played in the lives of working-class women. Despite difficulties in interpretation and the need to avoid over-generalization, gossip seems to be a particularly fruitful way of examining women's experience, given the personal emphasis and qualities which have been perceived as significant in all-female conversation. With the right prompting, women's observations about family, friends and neighbours can be richer and more detailed than the comments of their frequently less observant male counterparts. Oral witness, in particular, has been helpful in penetrating layers of experience otherwise defined only indirectly, giving insight into the dynamics of family relationships and into the complex and frequently contradictory perceptions of family and neighbours. The 'street matriarch', well-loved by her own family and appreciated by near neighbours for generosity at times of distress, could consequently also be regarded as a tartar and troublemaker by those not so closely bonded into her network of local relationships.

The passage of time may dull the memory to the detail and content of much day-to-day gossip, and give a misleadingly malicious slant to much that is remembered, but the fact that some respondents have such a vivid recollection of the scandal and petty misdemeanours of family and neighbours has its own validity in highlighting the power of gossip to both reflect and mould public behaviour and local myth. Even the most 'respectable' of streets held stories of scandal and mistakes which formed part of the mental landscape of longer established local inhabitants and was the backdrop against which comments and behaviour were tacitly judged.

A boy's perception of the working-class neighbourhood in which he lived was more likely to be a relief map based on a physical exploration of the environment. By contrast, the restrictions involved in a girl's socialization were likely to give her mental cartography a more speculative, behavioural, personal quality, based on an appreciation of complex social relationships and moral values. Thus, although a woman's concept of the area in which she lived may not have been as geographically extended as a man's, it could in some respects be seen as deeper and more richly textured precisely because gossip expanded the abstract ideal of neighbourhood.[27]

Women often attempted to define a different reality for themselves, even when mainly family centred and isolated from contact with those outside the domestic circle. Although the poorest inhabited a largely oral culture, the growth of literacy, more time to themselves or different expectations of how their time might be used made some women keen readers. The 'housewife' interviewed by Walter Greenwood in the 1930s spoke of all her energy being taken up with housework, but quickly corrected him when he suggested she probably no longer had much time for reading. She was an 'omniverous [sic] reader', she and her husband reading at meal times and in bed at night. She preferred books with 'meat in them', borrowing six a fortnight. Her most recent ones included a novel, a book on philosophy and another on international affairs.[28] Kit, a Yorkshire woman who proudly described herself as a socialist and atheist, moved to a prefab in South Kirby in 1947. In contrast to where she had previously lived, the people next door were more like acquantances than friends. She couldn't afford to go out much so she listened to the radio and 'read all the time', consuming among other things a range of political books and pamphlets.[29] Maria Goddard's mother was more keen on history and family sagas. She belonged to the library and used to buy books from secondhand stalls in Manchester, as did her husband, although he preferred 'mostly glory, wars and empire'. Maria's Aunt Agnes, the family 'rebel' also read a great deal, 'black magic, witches, she loved stuff like that'. Mrs Salter's favourite reading was ghost stories, travel books and historical novels. Although easily dismissed as escapist, such material testifies to an abiding interest in other peoples' lives, whose oral manifestation within the neighbourhood was gossip.[30]

Despite being frequently subject to a nostalgic reworking, this neigh-bourly dimension to the lives of many working-class women is important. Dale Spender has argued that there has been a traditional lack of locations in which women can meet together to talk.

> Because women have been without the space and the place to talk they have been deprived of access to discourse with each other (they have even been encouraged to accept that talking to each other does not count), as well as deprived of access to discourse in the presence of men.[31]

Such observations ignore an important aspect of working-class experience by taking as their standard the greater opportunities which men had to chat and socialize in institutionalized arenas such as the pub, football or union meetings. In particular, they underestimate the historical importance of gossip and neighbourliness among women of the urban poor, for whom such activities had an important collective significance. John Burnett, while recognizing the reciprocal aspect of mutual help in working-class communities, has concluded that 'what autobiographers most frequently stress is the sense of local community in working-class districts and the importance of an informal network of support composed of relatives, friends and neighbours'.[32] Gossip in this neighbourhood context was largely, although not invariably, a women's resource. This is not to underestimate the significance of the male gossip which took place in other venues or at the street corner. But men's gossip was largely marginal in the maintenance of family and neighbourly relations and did not have the same formative effect upon neighbourhood mores. It occurred at their places of work, or during leisure activities which were largely removed from the life of the street. To see such women's experience largely in terms of the 'private' domain is to ignore the central contribution which women made to the public life of neighbourhood and community. The definitions of public and private often applied to women's experience in the nineteenth and early twentieth centuries help perpetuate certain stereotypes of women's behaviour. This is particularly true for women of the urban poor, who indeed derived power from certain public spaces. They had, for example, possession of public territory in street life, although its identification with roughness often led respectable women to withdraw and deny sociability (other than within an institutional setting, the church for example, or largely domestic setting). The scenes enacted within this public sphere often seemed part of an exclusive society to outsiders. The whispers which kept children at bay when their mothers were gossiping about sex and scandal led many working-class writers and autobiographers to look back on their childhood as a world full of dark, strange secrets, while middle-class visitors frequently felt threatened by omnipresent eyes and muttered comments:[33]

> the mere passage of a stranger walking down the street will bring every one of them out on to the doorstep to look after him, often to the great discomfiture of the unwary passer by.[34]

Local residents were sure of their own place there, however, and were careful to assert their right to their own space. A Northampton man recalled his mother sunning herself on the doorstep during the 1930s:

> Mum 'd be sitting on the step, in the summertime and, er, dad'd be in the house, of course, and she, she spoke to everybody, "Ello m'duck', those were the reg'lar ones, "Ello m'duck, 'ow are you?', 'Alright'. Then all of a sudden her voice 'd change, she'd say, (putting on a posh accent), 'Hello, how are you?', that was one of the nobs from down the street. Our dad used to say, 'Old so-and-so's going by, I bet!' ... Because, you realise that people in offices were sort of, always thought themselves a bit better than those that worked in the factories.

Manual workers weren't quite so high in the hierarchy.
Q. So what did your mum think about that, when her voice changed,
was she being sarky?
A. No, no, no, she was living with them like, you see what I mean?
She was putting herself in with them, like. They wouldn't get one over
on mum. And he'd say, 'Oh, she's got 'er posh voice on again', said
dad, 'She's, must be one of the nobs from further down the street
coming by, like'.[35]

A critical part of the discomfort experienced by middle-class adventur-
ers into working-class life, particularly in the late nineteenth and early
twentieth centuries, was the fact that women's visibility in these public
locales represented a disordering of the spatial assumptions traditionally
made about them. Privacy had, since the sixteenth and seventeenth
centuries, been an important feature of respectable domestic life, yet
poverty made its attainment extremely difficult. Neighbourliness, as
sustained by the interchange of gossip, was vital to the survival of the
working-class family. The social space of the neighbourhood has been
described as 'primarily an area of communication and of reciprocal
exchange where the relative prestige and rank of families is assessed', and
it was this later aspect, in which gossip was so crucial, which made neighbouring suspect in the eyes of many working-class men.[36] While it was
accepted as a necessity when lack of resources meant little alternative aid
was available, perceptions were often less favourable among the more
affluent who could afford to stand apart. The reciprocity implicit in neighbourliness indicated that a family was unable to get by under its own
resources. It testified to a woman's apparent inability to manage, which in
turn reflected badly on a man's own reputation. In the same way that an
employed wife came to adversely affect the status of the working-class
male, so the revelations and exchanges of neighbourly gossip threatened
his 'prestige and comfort', and implied that he did not have his wife under
control.[37] Gossip with other women interfered with male needs and
demands which were predicated upon a 'particular form of domestic life'.[38]
As Margery Spring-Rice observed of working-class women in the 1930s,
the 'crown' of a woman's life was to be a wife and mother, women's voca-
tion being to service their husbands and family, not each other.[39]

So many of our men think we should not go out until the children are
grown up ... It isn't the men are unkind. It is the old idea that we
should always be at home.[40]

Neighbourhood gossip defined a space in which men played a marginal
role. Encouragement to withdraw from it was a denial of reciprocity and
evidence of a lack of trust in a domain of activity largely controlled by
women. Men who encouraged such withdrawal preferred their wives to
remain house-bound rather than linked into a network of external social

relationships whose gossip commonly articulated the money and marital struggles that men regarded as private. As a small girl in late Victorian and Edwardian Bolton, Alice Foley found 'endless pleasure' in gazing about at the crowded, untidy wares of the corner shop, 'half absorbing grown up gossip about bad husbands and hard times'.[41] In the London working-class culture described by Ellen Ross, the domestic verbal battles with their husbands in which women frequently displayed their superior skills were likely to be replayed in the public arena of the street:

> Cockney women … formulated their thoughts about husbands and marriage in regular doorstep gossip, and could count on support for their claims from their neighbors, kin and children. No expectation about 'privacy' or marital 'unity' clouded their thinking about their differences from their husbands.[42]

Clementina Black remarked, in 1915, on the growing isolation of many working-class women in both rural and urban districts for whom keeping apart from their neighbours was an important mark of respectability. To them, neighbouring and street life represented a verbal battleground in which the contradictions of domestic life were continually sifted and exposed.[43] There was little room for those unsettled by discord in human relationships. Shouting, quarrelling – conflict – were integral to the over-crowding, poverty and frustrations of life among the urban poor. This was an arena in which what were considered 'appropriate' female virtues, such as harmony and conciliation, often played little part. The comic character of the gossip epitomized the ambivalent power which women exerted in such contexts, yet the public nature of much of this discourse provided valuable psychic reinforcement, which Edwin Pugh touched on in chronicling the conversations of women in a working-class shop, where they talked, among other things, of their husbands, children, quarrels with neighbours and relations. A 'favourite' conversational theme among these women concerned their own 'sharpness and intelligence'. Such self-congratulation asserted an identity which was otherwise in perpetual conflict with the burdens of domestic life, and is a salutary reminder of the important part which 'women's talk' played in reinforcing self-esteem and confidence among women of the urban poor.[44]

Gossip's controlling aspects could be extremely oppressive when used to reinforce stereotypical expectations of female behaviour, yet it was also an important weapon and source of strength. Its use as an analytical tool not only allows us to penetrate the informal strategies which working-class women were so often forced to employ but also suggests the intricate connections and observations which made working-class life so diverse and complex. It lets us consider aspects of women's lives which otherwise remain frustratingly elusive, leaving a misleading sense of emptiness and impotence, and lifts them from the realm of victim to that of agent. This book is but a small contribution to a vast field. If I have concentrated on the gossip of the 'women of the washtub' at the expense of women's other experiences and employment, it is not because I believe this is more important. Rather, it is in the hope of showing that even the unseen and ignored have a voice, if only we know how to listen.

Notes

1. Rowbotham 1983, 216.
2. For a more contemporary account of the differences in behaviour between retired men and women in this area, see Wimbush and Talbot 1988, 83.
3. See, for example, Lance Percival's 'Gossip Calypso'; 'Gossip calypso, gossip calypso, Hear all about it, yakkety yak, Every woman up at the window, Giving out the gossip and getting it back'. Thanks to Joan, Jenny, Margaret and Joyce, The Library, Tameside College of Technology, Ashton.
4. Jones 1980, 196.
5. Miscellaneous tapes, May Thompson.
6. Mellor 1982, 24–25. Norman Evans, 1901–1962.
7. Clark, Heinemann, Margolies and Snee 1979, 174; Greenwood 1933: 1969, 15.
8. Heron 1985, 7; Radford 1986, 144.
9. Gorer 1955, cited in Klein 1965: 1970, 130–31; Gittins 1982, 179.
10. See Dyer 1981, 2.
11. '...it may be that one of the most important and hard-fought functions of British soaps in the eighties has been to keep the ideal of the community as a utopian possibility at a time when the tide in political thought was firmly running the other way'. Geraghty 1991. 122.
12. Geraghty 1991, 77–79, 97, 125, 137.
13. Geraghty 1991, 81–83, 122.
14. Geraghty 1991, 41, 42, 101–02.
15 . Northampton tapes, Mrs Gee.
16. Dennis, Henriques and Slaughter 1956, 170, 205–06.
17. E. Roberts 1984: 1986, 188–89.
18. For an examination of these networks see Ross 1983, 4–27.
19. Roberts 1984: 1986, 189. She attributes this late development to 'financial, social and moral reasons'.
20. Ariès 1962: 1973, 405, 407.
21. Loane 1910, 201–02.
22. Jasper 1969, 98, 104.
23. E. Roberts 1984: 1986, 188.
24. Vincent 1989: 1993, 46, 49, 51–52, 276.
25. Mogey 1956, 84, 86, 93.
26. In a social survey of Middlesbrough in the early 1950s, 30 per cent of working-class households did not wish to move to new accommodation. Of these 70 per cent 'gave as their reason the fact that they liked their house', explaining their reluctance to move in terms of employment and the fact that 'they were born there and were used to it'. Cited in Bourke 1994, 159.
27. Vincent 1989: 1993, 57.
28. Greenwood 1939, 128.
29. Hubbard 1985, 62–63.

30. Miscellaneous interviews, Maria Goddard; Northampton interviews, Mrs Salter.
31. Spender 1980: 1985, 107.
32. Burnett 1982, 227.
33. Working-class people could feel similarly intimidated by the moral judgments levelled at them when they ventured out of their own neighbourhoods. In the 1950s, for example, it was reported that a working-class informant was reluctant to go for a walk with his family on a middle-class housing estate because 'they look at you and say, Oh look at all those children!' Lewis 1984: 1986, 15, quoting from B. Harrison, 'Underneath the Victorians', *Victorian Studies*, X, (March 1967), 258.
34. Bell 1907: 1985, 236.
35. Northampton tapes, Mr Billingham.
36. Ardener 1993, 82.
37. Ardener 1993, 17.
38. Dyhouse 1981, 6.
39. Spring-Rice 1939: 1981, 95.
40. Spring-Rice, 1939: 1981, 94.
41. Foley 1973: 1990, 19.
42. Ross 1993, 90.
43. Black 1915: 1983, 238, 247.
44. E. Pugh, 'A Small Talk Exchange', in Keating 1971, 106. Margaret Loane made a similar (if patronizing) observation when she remarked that 'Open self-praise forms an amusingly large part of the conversation of many of the best members of the working-classes.' Loane 1905, 88–89.

Bibliography

Abrahams, R.D. (1970), 'A performance-centred approach to gossip', *Man*, 5.

Almirol, E.B. (1981), 'Chasing the elusive butterfly; gossip and the pursuit of reputation', *Ethnicity*, 8.

Ardener, S. (ed.), (1993), *Women and Space: Ground Rules and Social Maps*, Oxford: Berg.

Ariès, P. (1962: 1973), *Centuries of Childhood: A Social History of Family Life*, London: Peregrine Books.

Baker, A.E. (1854), *Glossary of Northamptonshire Words and Phrases*, Northampton: Abel and Sons and Mark Dorman.

Barnes, R. (1976), *Coronation Cups and Jam Jars: A Portrait of an East End Family Through Three Generations*, London: Centreprise.

Beales, H.L. and Lambert, R.S. (eds), (1934: 1973), *Memoirs of the Unemployed*, Wakefield: EP Publishing.

Beckwith, L. (1982), *About My Father's Business*, London: Arrow Books.

Bell, F. (1907: 1985), *At the Works: A Study of a Manufacturing Town*, London: Virago.

Benson, J. (1989), *The Working Class in Britain, 1850–1939*, London and New York: Longman.

Bentley, M. (1985), *Born 1896: Childhood in Clayton and Working in Manchester and Cheshire*, Swinton, Manchester: Neil Richardson.

Bertenshaw, M. (1980), *Sunrise to Sunset*, Patricroft, Manchester: Pan Visuals.

Black, C. (1915: 1983), *Married Women's Work*, London: Virago.

Blair, A. (1985), *Tea at Miss Cranston's. A Century of Glasgow Memories*, London: Shepheard-Walwyn.

Bleek, W. (1976), 'Witchcraft, gossip and death: a social drama', *Man*, 11, December.

Booth, C. (ed.) (1892), *Life and Labour of the People in London*, I, VIII, London: Macmillan.

Bott, E. (1957: 1968), *Family and Social Network*, London: Tavistock.

Bourke, J. (1994), *Working-Class Cultures in Britain, 1890–1960: Gender, Class and Ethnicity*, London and New York: Routledge.

Boyer, A. (1700: 1971), *The Royal Dictionary Abridged*, Menston: Scolar Press.

Broad, R. and Fleming, S. (eds), (1981), *Nella Last's War: A Mother's Diary, 1939–45*, London: Sphere Books.

Broady. M. (1956), 'The organisation of coronation street parties', *Sociological Review*, New Series IV, December.

Buchanan, J. (1757: 1967), *Lingua Britannicae, Vera Pronunciatio*, Menston: Scolar Press.

Buckley, A. (1983), 'Neighbourliness – myth and history', *Oral History Journal*, 11, (1).

Burnett, J. (1982), *Destiny Obscure: Autobiographies of Childhood, Education and the Family from the 1820s to the 1920s*, Harmondsworth: Penguin.

Burnett, J., Vincent, J. and Mayall, D. (eds), (1984), *The Autobiography of the Working Class – An Annotated Critical Bibliography*, Brighton, Sussex: Harvester Press

Centerprise (1979), *The Island: The Life and Death of an East London Community, 1870-1970*, London: Centerprise Trust.

Chamberlain, M. (1975: 1977), *Fenwomen: A Portrait Of Women in an English Village*, London: Virago.

Chamberlain, M. (1981), *Old Wives' Tales, Their History, Remedies and Spells*, London: Virago.

Chamberlain, M. (1989), *Growing Up in Lambeth*, London: Virago.

Champion, S.D. (1938), *Racial Proverbs: A Selection of the World's Proverbs Arranged Linguistically*, London: George Routledge and Sons.

Chew, D.N. (1982), *Ada Nield Chew: The Life and Writings of a Working Woman*, London: Virago.

Chinn, C. (1988), *They Worked All Their Lives: Women of the Urban Poor in England, 1880–1939*, Manchester: Manchester University Press.

Clark, J., Heinemann, M., Margolies, D. and Snee, C. (1979), *Culture and Crisis in Britain in the Thirties*, London: Lawrence and Wishart.

Coates, J. (1986), Women, Men and Language, London: Longman

Coates, J. and Cameron, D. (1988), *Women in Their Speech Communities*, London: Longman.

Constantine, S. (1981), 'Amateur gardening and popular recreation in the nineteenth and twentieth centuries', *Journal of Social History*, 14, (3), Spring.

Conway, M. (1983), *Half Timer: A Stockport Mill Boy Remembers*, Stockport: Stockport Metropolitan Borough Recreation and Culture Division.

Crook, R. (1982), '"Tidy women": women in the Rhondda between the wars', *Oral History*, 10, (2), Autumn.

Crystal, D. (1987), *Cambridge Encyclopedia of Language*, Cambridge: Cambridge University Press.

Davidoff, L. (1973: 1986), *The Best Circles, Society Etiquette and the Season*, London: The Cresset Library

Davidoff, L. and Hall, C. (1987), *Family Fortunes: Men and Women of the English Middle Class, 1790–1850*, London: Hutchinson.

Davies, A. (1992), *Leisure, Gender and Poverty: Working Class Culture in Salford and Manchester, 1900–39*, Buckingham and Philadelphia: Open University Press.

Davies, A. and Fielding, S. (eds), (1992), *Cultures and Communities in Manchester and Salford, 1880–1939*, Manchester: Manchester University Press.

Davies, C. (1988), 'The health visitor as Mother's friend', in *Social History of Medicine*, **I**, (1).

Davies, C.S. (1963), *North Country Bred. A Working Class Family Chronicle*, London: Routledge and Kegan Paul.

Davies, F. (1985), *My Father's Eyes: Episodes in the Life of a Hulme Man*, Swinton, Manchester: Neil Richardson.

Davies, M.L. (ed.), (1915: 1978), *Maternity: Letters from Working Women*, London: Virago.

Davies, M.L. (ed.), (1931: 1984), *Life as We Have Known It, By Co-Operative Working Women*, London: Virago.

Davin, A. (1978), 'Imperialism and Motherhood', *History Workshop*, 5, Spring.

Dayus, K. (1982: 1987), *Her People*, London: Virago.

Dayus, K. (1985: 1986), *Where There's Life*, London: Virago.

Dayus, K. (1991), *Best of Times*, London: Virago.

Demos, J. (1982), *Entertaining Satan: Witchcraft and the Culture of Early New England*, New York: Oxford University Press.

Dennis, N., Henriques, F. and Slaughter, C. (1956), *Coal Is Our Life: An Analysis of a Yorkshire Mining Community*, London: Eyre and Spottiswoode.

Dixon, C. (1989), *Recollections of Inter-War Northampton* (unpublished manuscript).

Donnelly, P. (1950), *The Yellow Rock*, London: Eyre and Spottiswoode.

Donnison, J. (1977: 1988), *Midwives and Medical Men. A History of Inter-Professional Rivalries and Women's Rights*, London: Heinemann.

Dulumeau, J. (1978), *La Peur en Occident*, Paris: Pluriel.

Dunbar, R. (1992), 'Why gossip is good for you', *New Scientist*, 21 November.

Dyer, R. (ed.), (1981), *Coronation Street*, London: British Film Institute.

Dyhouse, C. (1981), *Girls Growing Up in Late Victorian and Edwardian England*, London: Routledge and Kegan Paul.

Ezard, E. (1979), *Battersea Boy*, London: William Kimber.

Farrell, T., Farrell, J. and Tomlin, D. (The Bow Group), (1983), 'A glancing view of childhood: Bow Bridge Island Council Estate 1947–1962', *Oral History Journal*, **11**.

Fine, G.A. (1977), 'Social components of children's gossip', *Journal of Communication*, **27**, (1), Winter.

Fishman, W.J. (1988), *East End 1888*, London: Duckworth.

Flinn, M.W. and Smout, T.C. (1974), *Essays in Social History*, Oxford: Clarendon Press.

Foley, A. (1973: 1990), *A Bolton Childhood*, Bolton: Bolton Libraries and Arts/Workers' Educational Association Bolton Branch.

Forrester, H. (1974: 1981), *Twopence to Cross the Mersey*, Glasgow: Fontana/Collins.

Furniss, T. (1979), *The Walls of Jericho: Slum Life in Sheffield Between the Wars*, Sheffield: Rebel Press.

Gelles, E.B. (1989), 'Gossip: An Eighteenth-Century Case', *Journal of Social History*, **22**, (4).

Geraghty, C. (1991), *Women and Soap Opera: A Study of Prime Time Soaps*, Cambridge: Polity Press.

Gilligan, C. (1982), *In a Different Voice: Psychological Theory and Women's Development*, Cambridge, MA: Harvard University Press.

Gillis, J.R. (1985), *For Better, For Worse: British Marriages 1600 to the Present*, New York and Oxford: Oxford University Press.

Gittins, D. (1977), 'Women's work and family size between the wars', *Oral History*, **5**, (2).

Gittins, D. (1982), *Fair Sex: Family Size and Structure, 1900–39*, London: Hutchinson University Library.

Glasgow Women's Studies Group (1983), *Uncharted Lives. Extracts from Scottish Women's Experiences, 1850–1982*, Glasgow: Glasgow Women's Studies Group.

Glastonbury, M. (1979), 'The best kept secret – How working class women live and what they know', *Women's Studies International Quarterly*, **2**, (2)

Gluckman, M. (1963), 'Gossip and scandal', *Current Anthropology*, **4**.

Gorer, G. (1955), *Exploring English Character*, London: The Cresset Press.

Gosling, R. (1980), *Personal Copy: A Memoir of the Sixties*, London: Faber and Faber.

Graddol, D. and Swann, J. (1989), *Gender Voices*, Oxford: Blackwell.

Greenwood, W. (1933: 1969), *Love on the Dole*, London: Penguin Modern Classics.

Greenwood, W. (1939), *How the Other Man Lives*, London: Labour Book Service.

Greenwood, W. (1967), *There was a Time*, London: Jonathan Cape Ltd.

Grimes, D.A. (1991), *Like Dew Before the Sun: Life and Language in Northamptonshire*, Northampton: published privately by Mrs Dorothy A. Grimes, 27 Winchester Road, Delapre, Northampton, NN4 9AZ.

Hall, C. (1977), 'Married women at home in the 1920s and 1930s', *Oral History*, 5 (2).

Handelman, D. (1973), 'Gossip in encounters: The transmission of information in a bounded social setting', *Man*, 8.

Harding, S. (1975), 'Women and Words in a Spanish Village' in Reiter, R. (ed.), *Toward an Anthropology of Women*, New York: Monthly Review Press.

Harris, M. (undated), *War Memories of London and Manchester, 1941*, unpublished.

Harrison, B. (1971), *Drink and the Victorians: The Temperance Question in England, 1815–1972*, London: Faber.

Hart, N. (1989), 'Gender and the rise and fall of class politics', *New Left Review*, **175**, May/June.

Haviland, J.B. (1977), 'Gossip as competition in Zinacantan', *Journal of Communication*, **27** (1), Winter.

Haworth, D. (1986), *Figures in a Bygone Landscape: A Lancashire Childhood*, London: Methuen Paperback.

Haythorne, E. (1986), *In Our Backs*, Pontefract: Yorkshire Art Circus.

Hazlitt, W.C. (MGMVII), *English Proverbs and Proverbial Phrases*, London: Reeves and Turner.

Heaton, R. (1982), *Salford, My Home Town*, Swinton, Manchester: Neil Richardson.

Heron, L. (ed.), (1985), *Truth, Dare or Promise: Girls Growing Up in the Fifties*, London: Virago.

Hinson, E. (1984), *Mary Ann's Girl: Memories of Newbridge Lane*, Stockport: Metropolitan Borough of Stockport, Recreation and Culture Division.

Hobsbawm, E.J. (1964), 'The Nineteenth Century London Labour Market', *London: Aspects of Change*, London: Centre for Urban Studies.

Hodges, M.W. and Smith, C.S. (1954) 'The Sheffield Estate', in *Neighbourhood and Community: An Enquiry into Social Relationships on Housing Estates in Liverpool and Sheffield*, Liverpool: The University Press of Liverpool.

Hoggart, R. (1958: 1962), *The Uses of Literacy*, Harmondsworth: Penguin.

Hooley, J. (1981), *A Hillgate Childhood – Myself When Young*, Stockport: Age Concern.

Hornsey, J. (1824), *English Exercises Orthographical and Grammatical*, York.

Hubbard, J. (ed.), (1985), *We Thought It Was Heaven Tomorrow: Local Voices from Pontefract, Castelford, Ledston Luck, Meanwood and Thorner, 1945–55*, Pontefract, Yorkshire: Yorkshire Arts Circus.

Hudson, P. and Lee, W.R. (eds), (1990), *Women's Work and the Family Economy in Historical Perspective*, Manchester: Manchester University Press.

Hughes, A. and Hunt, K. (1992), 'A Culture Transformed? Women's Lives in Wythenshawe in the 1930s', in Davies, A. and Fielding, S. (eds), *Workers' Worlds: Cultures and Communities in Manchester and Salford, 1880–1939*, Manchester and New York: Manchester University Press.

Jackson, B. (1968: 1972), *Working Class Community*, Harmondsworth: Penguin.

Jackson, J. (1990), *Under the Smoke: Salford Memories, 1922–41*, Swinton, Manchester: Neil Richardson.

Jaegar, C. (ed.), (1968), *Annie: Annie Jaegar Tells Her Own Story*.

Jasper, A.S. (1969), *A Hoxton Childhood*, London: Centerprise Publications.

Johnson, S. (1755), *A Dictionary of the English Language*, London: W. Strachan.

Jones, D. (1980), 'Gossip: Notes on women's oral culture', *Women's Studies International Quarterly*, 3, (2/3)

Jones, J. (1985), *Labor of Love, Labor of Sorrow: Black Women, Work and the Family, from Slavery to the Present*, New York: Vintage Books.

Joyce, P. (1991: 1994), *Visions of the People: Industrial England and the Question of Class, 1848–1914*, Cambridge: Cambridge University Press.

Kapferer, Jean-Noel (1987), *Rumeurs, Le Plus Vieux Media du Monde*, Paris: Editions du Seuil.

Kay, A. (1993), *Wythenshawe Circa 1932–1955: The Making of a Community?*, University of Manchester, PhD thesis, Faculty of Arts.

Kay, J. (1990), *North Manchester Remembered, 1914–1950: More Chronicles of a Harpurhey Lad*, Swinton, Manchester: Neil Richardson.

Keating, P.J. (ed.), (1971), *Working Class Stories of the 1890s*, London: Routledge and Kegan Paul.

Kershaw, H.V. (1981), *The Street Where I Live*, London: Granada.

Klein, J. (1965: 1970), *Samples from English Culture*, London: Routledge and Kegan Paul.

Kramerae, A.C. and Treichler, P.A. (1985), *A Feminist Dictionary*, London: Pandora Press.

Kuper, L. (ed.), (1953), *Living in Towns*, London: The Cresset Press.

Labov, W., Cohen, P., Robins, C. and Lewis, J. (1968), *A Study of the Non-Standard English of Negro and Puerto Rican Speakers in New York City*: US Office of Education Co-operative Research Project 3288–1.

Ladurie, E. Le Roy, (1978; 1980), *Montaillou*, Harmondsworth: Penguin.

Lakoff, R. (1975), *Language and Women's Place*, New York: Harper and Row.

Landes, D.S. (1983), *Revolution in Time*, Cambridge, MA: Harvard University Press.

Law, J. (pseudonym of Margaret Harkness), (1899), *In Darkest London: Captain Lobo, Salvation Army*.

Lees, L.H. (1979), *Exiles of Erin*, Manchester: Manchester University Press.

Levin, J. and Arluke, A. (1985), 'An exploratory analysis of sex differences in gossip', *Sex Roles*, **12**.

Lewis, J. (1980), 'Women Between the Wars', in Gloversmith, F. *Class, Culture and Social Change: A New View of the 1930s*, Sussex: The Harvester Press, New Jersey: Humanities Press.

Lewis, J. (1984: 1986), *Women in England, 1870–1950: Sexual Divisions and Social Change*, Sussex: Wheatsheaf Books, Bloomington, IN: Indiana University Press.

Linkman, A. and Warhurst, C. (1982), *Family Albums*, Manchester: Manchester Studies, Manchester Polytechnic.

Linton, A. (1982), *Not Expecting Miracles*, London: Centerprise.

Loane, M.E. (1905), *The Queen's Poor*, London: Edward Arnold.

Loane, M.E. (1907), *The Next Street But One*, London: Edward Arnold.

Loane, M.E. (1908), *From Their Point of View*, London: Edward Arnold.

Loane, M.E. (1909), *An Englishman's Castle*, London: Edward Arnold.

Loane, M.E. (1910?), *Neighbours and Friends*, London: Edward Arnold.

Macintyre, S. (1980), *Little Moscows: Communism and Working Class Militancy in Inter-War Britain*, London: Croom Helm.

McCrindle, J. and Rowbotham, S. (eds.), (1977: 1979), *Dutiful Daughters*, Harmondsworth: Penguin.

McCullough, L. (1985), *The Pit Village and the Store: The Portrait of a Mining Past*, London: Pluto Press.

McKelvie, D. (1965), 'Proverbial elements in the oral tradition of an English industrial region', *Journal of the Folklore Institute*, **2**.

McKelvie, D. (1963), *Some Aspects of Oral, Social and Material Tradition in an Industrial Urban Area*, PhD thesis, Leeds University.

McKibbin, R. (1990: 1991), *The Ideologies of Class: Social Relations in Britain, 1880–1950*, Oxford: Oxford University Press.

Madoc-Jones, B. (1977: 1979), 'Patterns of Attendance and their Social Significance: Mitcham National School, 1830–39', in McCann, P., (1977) *Popular Education and Socialisation in the Nineteenth Century*, London: Methuen.

Malvery, O.C. (1907), *The Soul Market*, London: Hutchinson and Co.

Martin, A. (1911), *The Married Working Woman*, London: National Untion of Women's Suffrage Societies.

Mass Observation (1943: 1987), *The Pub and the People* (New introduction by Godfrey Smith), London: The Cresset Library.

Mellor, G.J. (1982), *Are You Putting It About That I'm Barmy? They Made Us Laugh: A Compendium of Comedians Whose Memories Remain Alive*, Littleborough, Lancashire: George Kelsall.

Mitchell, G. (ed.), (1968: 1977), *The Hard Way Up: The Autobiography of Hannah Mitchell, Suffragette and Rebel*, London: Virago.

Mitchell, G.D. and Lupton, T. (1954) 'The Liverpool Estate', in *Neighbourhood and Community: An Enquiry into Social Relationships on Housing Estates in Liverpool and Sheffield*, Liverpool: The University Press of Liverpool.

Mitchell, W.R. (1991), *By Gum, Life were Sparse! Memories of Northern Mill Towns*, London: Warner Books.

Mogey, J.M. (1956), *Family and Neighbourhood: Two Studies in Oxford*, Oxford: Oxford University Press.

Mowat, C.L. (1955: 1978), *Britain Between the Wars, 1918–40*, London: Methuen.

Murray, J.A.H. (1901), *A New English Dictionary on Historical Principles (OED)*, Oxford: Clarendon Press.

Murray, V. (ed.), (1986), *Where Have All the Cowslips Gone?*, London: Futura.

Northampton Arts Development (1987), *In Living Memory: Life in 'The Boroughs'*, Northampton.

Oakley, A. (1972), *Sex, Gender and Society*, Sun Books: Melbourne.

Oakley, A. (1974), *The Sociology of Housework*, Martin Robertson: Oxford.

Obelkevich, J. (1987), 'Proverbs and Social History', in Burke, P. and Porter, R. (eds), *The Social History of Language*, Cambridge: Cambridge University Press.

Ong, W.J. (1982), *Orality and Literacy: The Technologizing of the Word*, London and New York: Methuen.

Orton, H. (1962), *Introduction to the Survey of English Dialects*, Leeds: E.J. Arnold.

Orwell, G. (1937: 1974), *The Road to Wigan Pier*, Harmondsworth: Penguin.

Paine, R. (1967), 'What is gossip about? An alternative hypothesis?', *Man*, 2

Painting, N. (1975: 1976), *Forever Ambridge: Twenty-Five Years of the Archers*, London: Sphere.

Paterson, A. (1911), *Across the Bridges*, London: Edward Arnold.

Pearson, J. (1988), *Why Waste it on a Girl? Growing up in Methley and Castelford*, Castelford: Yorkshire Arts Circus.

Pember Reeves, M. (1913: 1979), *Round About a Pound a Week*, London: Virago.

Pettigrew, E. (1989), *Time to Remember: Growing Up in Liverpool from 1912 Onwards*, Liverpool: Toulouse Press.

Pickett, K.G. and Boulton, D.K. (1974), *Migration and Social Adjustment: Kirkby and Maghull*, Liverpool: Liverpool University Press.

Pollock, L. (1990), 'Embarking on a Rough Passage: the Experience of Pregnancy in Early-Modern Society', in Fildes, V. (ed.), *Women as Mothers in Pre-Industrial England*, London and New York: Routledge.

Prochaska, F.K. (1980), *Women and Philanthropy in Nineteenth Century England*, Oxford: Clarendon Press.

Radford, J. (1986), *The Progress of Romance: The Politics of Popular Fiction*, London and New York: Routledge and Kegan Paul.

Rendall, J. (1990), *Women in an Industrialising Society: England, 1750–1880*, Oxford: Basil Blackwell.

Retail Credit Drapers' Training Guide (undated), Manchester: J. Stewart and Sons Ltd.

Roberts, E. (1984: 1986), *A Woman's Place: An Oral History of Working Class Women, 1890–1940*, Oxford, Basil Blackwell.

Roberts, E. (1993), 'Neighbours: North-West England, 1940–1970', *Oral History*, **21** (2).

Roberts, M. (1985), '"Words they are Women and Deeds they are Men": Images of Work and Gender in Early Modern England', in Charles, L. and Duffin, L. (eds), *Women and Work in Pre-Industrial England*, London: Croom Helm.

Roberts, R. (1970: 1978), *A Ragged Schooling: Growing Up in the Classic Slum*, Glasgow: Fontana/Collins.

Roberts, R. (1971: 1974), *The Classic Slum: Salford Life in the First Quarter of the Century*, Harmondsworth: Penguin.

Robinson, J. (1975), *The Life and Times of Francie Nichol of South Shields*, London: George Allen and Unwin.

Rodaway, A. (1960: 1985) *A London Childhood*, London: Virago.

Room, A. (1986), *Dictionary of Changes in Meaning*, Colchester: NTC Publishing Group.

Rose, L. (1986), *Massacre of the Innocents: Infanticide in Great Britain, 1800–1939*, London, Boston: Routledge and Kegan Paul.

Ross, E. (1982), ' "Fierce Questions and Taunts": Married Life in Working Class London, 1870–1914', *Feminist Studies*, **8** (2).

Ross, E. (1983), 'Survival Networks: Women's neighbourhood sharing in London before World War One', *History Workshop*, **15**.

Ross, E. (1985), '"Not the Sort that Would Sit on the Doorstep": Respectability in Pre-World War I London Neighborhoods', *International Labor and Working Class History*, **27**, Spring.

Ross, E. (1993), *Love and Toil: Motherhood in Outcast London, 1870–1918*, New York: Oxford University Press.

Rowbotham, S. (1983), *Dreams and Dilemmas*, London: Virago.

Rowntree, B.S. and Lavers, G.R. (1951), *English Life and Leisure: A Social Study*, London: Longmans.

Saint Teresa of Avila (*c.* 1562: 1942), *The Way of Perfection*, Trans. by a Discalced Carmelite.

Samuel, R. and Thompson, P. (eds), (1990), *The Myths We Live By*, London and New York: Routledge.

Sant, M.J. (1985), *To Be Continued … Or Can I Have My Pictures Money, Mam?* *Childhood Memories of Salford*, Swinton, Manchester: Neil Richardson.

Schwarz Cowan, R. (1983), *More Work for Mother: The Ironies of Household Technology from the Open Hearth to the Microwave*, New York: Basic.

Seabrook, J. (1992), 'Silent shame of my mother', *The Independent on Sunday*, 20 September.

Seymour, J. (1992), '"No time to call my own": Women's time as a household resource', *Women's Studies International Forum*, **15** (2).

Shorter, E. (1975: 1977), *The Making of the Modern Family*, Glasgow: Fontana/Collins.

Slater, L. (1984), *Think On! Said Mam. A Childhood in Bradford, Manchester, 1911–19*, Swinton, Manchester: Neil Richardson.

Slawson, J. (1986), *Hopwood, Heywood and Me*, Swinton, Manchester: Neil Richardson.

Southgate, W. (1982), *That's The Way It Was: A Working Class Autobiography 1890–1950*, London: New Clarion Press.

Spacks, P.M. (1985: 1986), *Gossip*, Chicago and London: The University of Chicago Press.

Spender, D. (1980: 1985), *Man Made Language*, London and New York: Routledge and Kegan Paul.

Spender, D. (1986: 1987), *Mothers of the Novel*, London: Pandora.

Spring-Rice, M. (1939: 1981), *Working Class Wives*, London: Virago.

Stacey, M. (1960), *Tradition and Change: A Study of Banbury*, Oxford: Oxford University Press.

Steedman, C. (1985), 'Landscape for a Good Woman', in Heron, L. (ed.), *Truth, Dare or Promise: Girls Growing Up in the Fifties*, London: Virago.

Storey, J. (1990: 1992), *Joyce's War, 1939–45*, London: Virago.

Stride, L. (undated), *Memoirs of a Street Urchin*, Bath: Bath University Press.

Swindells, J. and Jardine, L. (1990), *What's Left? Women and Culture and the Labour Movement*, London and New York: Routledge.

Tebbutt, M. (1983), *Making Ends Meet: Pawnbroking and Working Class Credit*, Leicester: Leicester University Press.

The Century Dictionary. An Encyclopedic Lexicon of the English Language, (1889: 1899), London: W.D. Whitney.

Tildsley, D. (1985), *Remembrance: Recollections of a Wartime Childhood in Swinton*, Swinton, Manchester: Neil Richardson.

Thiselton-Dyer, T.F. (1905: 1990), *Folk-lore of Women*, Dumfriesshire: Tynron Press.

Thompson, E.P. (1974), 'Time, Work-Discipline, and Industrial Capitalism', in Flinn, M.W. and Smout, T.C., *Essays in Social History*, Oxford: Clarendon Press.

Thompson, F. (1945: 1982), *Lark Rise to Candleford*, Harmondsworth: Penguin.

Thorne, B. and Henley, N. (eds), (1975), *Language and Sex: Difference and Dominance*, Newbury, MA: Rowley House.

Turner, M. (1988), *The Wash House*, unpublished manuscript.

Vicinus, M. (1985), *Independent Women: Work and Community for Single Women, 1850–1920*, London: Virago.

Vincent, D. (1989: 1993), *Literacy and Popular Culture: England, 1750–1914*, Cambridge: Cambridge University Press.

Vincent, D. (1991), *Poor Citizens: The State and the Poor in Twentieth Century Britain*, London and New York: Longman.

Wakefield, T. (1980: 1988), *Forties Child: An Early Autobiography*, London: Routledge and Kegan Paul.

Walton, J.K. (1992), *Fish and Chips and the British Working Class, 1870–1940*, Leicester: Leicester University Press.

Warner, M. (1993), 'Provocations: Marina Warner on gossip', *The Independent Magazine*, 1 May.

Watkin, H. (1985), *From Hulme All Blessings Flow: A Collection of Manchester Memories*, Swinton, Manchester: Neil Richardson.

Westwood, S. (1984), *All Day Every Day: Factory and Family in the Making of Women's Lives*, London and Sydney: Pluto Press.

White, D.G. (1985), *Ar'n't I a Woman?: Female Slaves in the Plantation South*, New York and London: W.W. Norton.

White, J. (1986), *The Worst Street in North London: Campbell Bunk, Islington, Between the Wars*, London: Routledge and Kegan Paul.

White, W. (1890), *Life in a Court: How to Stop Neighbours' Quarrels*, Birmingham: White and Pike, Moor Street Printing Works.

Widdowson, J. in Rogers, S. (ed.), (1976), *They Don't Speak Our Language: Essays on the Language World of Children and Adolescents*, London: Edward Arnold.

Williamson, B. (1982), *Class, Culture and Community: A Biographical Study of Social Change in Mining*, London: Routledge and Kegan Paul.

Willmott, P. and Young, M. (1960: 1976), *Family and Class in a London Suburb*, London: New English Library.

Willughby, P. (1863: 1972), *Observations in Midwifery*. Ed. from the original manuscript by Henry Blenkinsop, with a new introduction by John L. Thornton, Wakefield: SR Publishers.

Wilson, A. (1990), 'The ceremony of Childbirth and its Interpretation', in Fildes, V. (ed.), *Women as Mothers in Pre-Industrial England*, London and New York: Routledge.

Wilson, P.J. (1974), 'Filcher of good names: An enquiry into anthropology and gossip', *Man*, 9.

Wimbush, E. (1988), 'Mothers Meeting', in Wimbush, E. and Talbot, M. (eds), *Relative Freedoms: Women and Leisure*, Milton Keynes: Open University Press.

Woodward, K. (1928: 1983), *Jipping Street*, London: Virago.

Wright, E.M. (1913), *Rustic Speech and Folklore*, Oxford: Oxford University Press.

Wright, J. (1900), *The English Dialect Dictionary*, London: Henry Frowde.

Yass, M. (1983), *This is Your War: Home Front Propaganda in the Second World War*, London: HMSO.

Yerkovich, S. (1977), 'Gossiping as a way of speaking', *Journal of Communication*, **27** (1), Winter.

Young, M. and Wilmott, P. (1957: 1979), *Family and Kinship in East London*, London: Penguin.

Zmroczek, C. (1992), 'Dirty linen: Women, Class, and Washing Machines, 1920s–1960s', *Women's Studies International Forum*, **15** (2).

Manchester Studies Tape Collection

12   Woman, born 1904. Lived in Victoria Park, Salford.
36   Woman, born 1915. Lived in Macclesfield, Mossley, Timperley and Sale.
39   Woman, born 1903. Lived in Preston, Swinton, Didsbury and Bury.
42   Woman, born 1893 in Bredbury, near Stockport.
163   Edited transcript. Mr W. Cahill?
247   Man, born 1903 in Nelson.
251   Woman, born 1913.
493   Woman, born 1902 in Salford.
506/2 Woman, born 1913 in Ordsall.
515   Man, born 1902, Ordsall.
541   Man. Worked in a pawnbroker's shop, Salford, during 1930s.
544   Woman, born in Salford.
558   Woman, born 1914 in Ordsall.
582   Woman, born 1912. Lived in Liverpool, Warrington, Nottingham and Manchester.
604   Man, born 1913, in Hillgate, Stockport.
628   Woman born in Colne.
665   Woman, born, 1896, Burnley.
795   Man, worked in pawnbroker's shop during 1930s and 1940s.
803   Woman, born 1911, in Sale.
964   Woman. Worked as a midwife in Birmingham during the 1930s.

Ordsall Local History Group Tapes

AB   Woman, born 1914, Salford.
AM   Woman, born 1917, Salford.
AMD   Woman, born 1914, Salford.
DM   Woman, born 1907, Salford.
EB   Woman, born 1916, Salford.
EO   Woman, born 1918, Salford.
FW   Woman, born 1904, Salford.
IC   Woman, born 1899, Ordsall.
L   Woman, born 1914, Broughton.
M   Woman, born 1914, Harefield.

Oral History Archive, Lancaster University

Mr B   Born 1927, Preston.
Mr B7   Born 1904, Preston.
Mr CIP   Born 1884, Preston.
Mrs C2P   Born 1899.
Mr FIP   Born 1906, near Whitehaven, Cumberland.
Mr GIP   Born 1903, Preston.
Mrs H8P   Born 1903, Preston.

Bolton Oral History Project

18   Man, born 1908, Bolton; Woman, born 1904, Bolton.
23a/b   Woman, born 1898, Prestolee.
26   Woman, born 1899, Halliwell.
28a/b   Woman, born 1916, Deane, Bolton.
32a/b   Man, born 1904, Bolton; Woman, born 1906, Bolton.
35   Woman, born 1919, Bolton.
40   Woman, born 1917, Scotland. Moved to Bolton on marriage in 1943.
43   Man, born 1904, Daubhill, Bolton.
48   Woman, born 1907, Bolton.
51a   Man, born 1908, Bolton.
55a/d   Man, born 1912, Astley Bridge, Bolton.

Northampton interviews

Mrs Atkins   Born 1919, Northampton. Father a farm labourer.

Mr Billingham	Born 1918, Northampton. Father a warehouseman.
Sally Chambers	Born 1950, Northampton. Father worked in engineering factory.
Mr Edmund	Born Northampton 1916. Father a market gardener.
Celia Dixon	Born 1922, Northampton. Father gardener/nurseryman (nine tapes, a–i).
Mrs Flower	Born 1916, Northampton. Father a painter and decorator.
Mrs Gee	Born 1921, Northampton. Father a gardener.
Mrs Grant	Born 1921, Northampton. Father a steel erector.
Mrs Hampson	Born 1923, Northampton. Unwaged. 2 children. Husband a toolmaker.
Mrs Harper	Born 1924. Unwaged. 2 children. Husband a welder.
Mrs Hill	Born 1923, Northampton. Father a clerical worker.
Mrs West	Born 1923, Northampton. Father a warehouseman.
Mrs King	Born 1925, Northampton. Father a factory worker.
Mrs Knott	Born 1923, Northampton. Unwaged. 2 children. Husband a printer.
Mrs Mitford	Born 1930, Northampton. Unwaged. 2 children. Husband a self-employed plasterer.
Mrs Perkins	Born 1920, Northampton. Father a skilled factory worker.
Mrs Roberts	Born 1927, Northampton. Father a gardener/nurseryman.
Mrs Salter	Born 1924, Northampton. Unwaged. 2 children. Husband a salesman.
Mrs Thorpe	Born 1922, Northampton. Unwaged. 2 children. Husband a salesman.
Mr Timson	Born 1928, Northampton. Father a bricklayer.
Mrs Waddell	Born 1924, Northampton. Unwaged. 2 children. Husband an office worker.
Mrs York	Born 1924, Northampton. Father a factory worker.

Miscellaneous interviews

Miss Badby	Born early 1920s, Manchester.
Joan Green	Date of birth n/a. Born Ashton-u-Lyne, Lancashire.
Maria Goddard	Born 1920, Chorlton-on-Medlock, Manchester.
Mrs Palmerston	Born 1917, New Mills, Derbyshire.
May Thompson	Born 1921, Manchester. Father's occupation not available.

Tameside Local Studies Library

Dennis Blake Lobb. Born 1921, Hyde, Cheshire.

Index

textile workers 85
Thew, Linda McCullough 69
Thompson, Flora 8,
Thiselton-Dyer 8, 24, 28
Thomas, Dylan 51
Throckley 20
Tildsley, Dorothy 119
Toynbee Hall 35
Turner, Mary 59

unemployment 115, 117, 120
United States 17, 46, 47, 70
    California 9, 55
    Americans 79, 120
upper class 26, 34, 35, 47, 71

Wakefield, Tom 53, 57, 61, 79, 113
Wales 39
    Ceiriog Valley 27
    Rhondda 120
Walmsley, Vincent 68
Warrington 115
wash house 59, 62, 67, 75, 142
Watkins, Harry 94, 117, 143
Webb, Beatrice 38
West, Mrs 56, 57, 106
Westmorland, Tebay 90
White, Jerry 37, 49, 69, 149, 151

Whitall, Flo 42, 53
widows 32, 54, 74, 78, 107–8, 123,
    124–5, 131–2
widowers 122, 131
Widdowson, John 47
Williamson, Bill 58, 79, 144
Willughby, Percivall 28
witches 27, 86, 180
Women's Co-Operative Guild 41
Woodward, Kathleen 11, 111, 112, 113
Woolf, Virginia 41
World War One 4, 79, 90, 124, 125,
    143, 149, 178
World War Two 3, 4, 29, 83, 105, 115,
    119–20

Wright, Elizabeth 20
Wright, Joseph 20

Yerkovich, Sally 12
York, Mrs 104
Yorkshire 24, 50, 61–2, 76, 151, 177,
    180
Young, Michael and Willmott, Peter
    156, 161

Zweig, Ferdynand 117